IMAGES
of America

BRENTWOOD

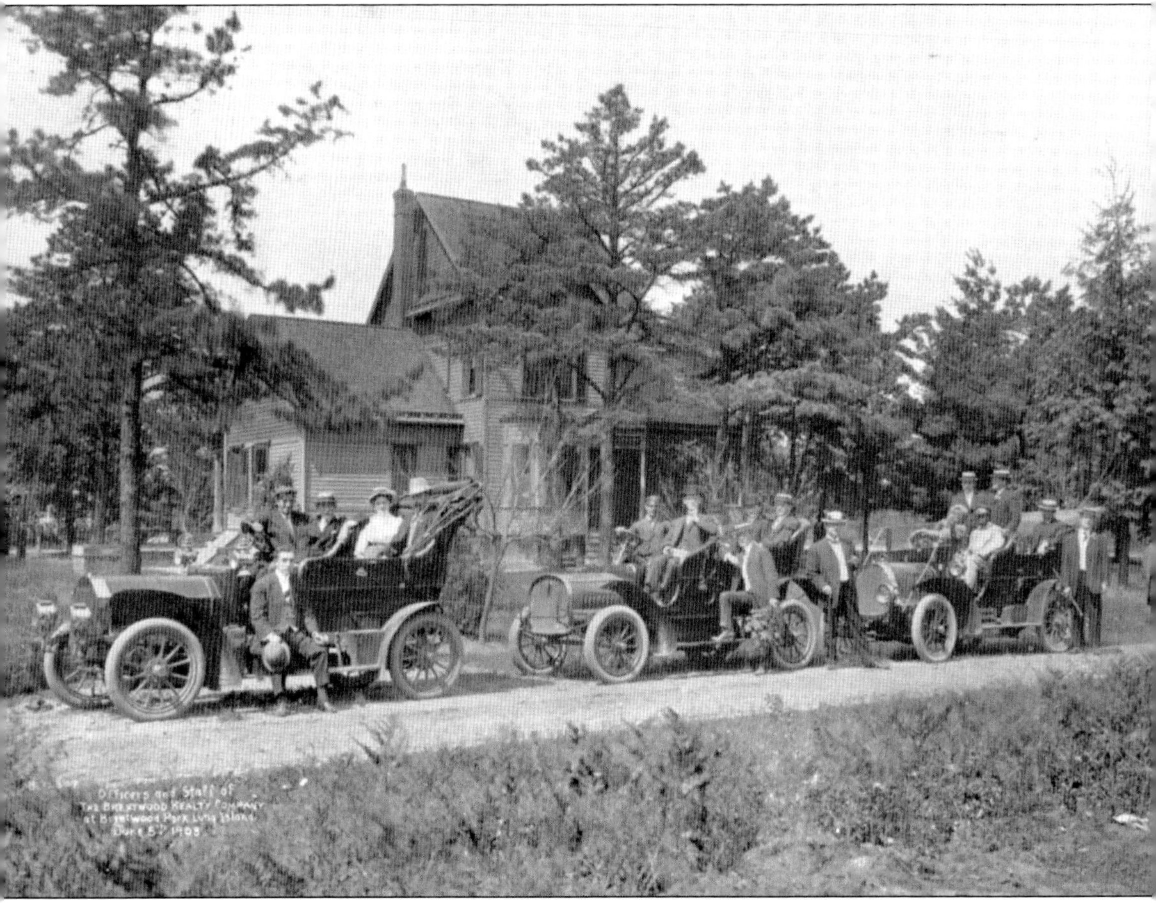

Officers and staff of the Brentwood Reality Company pose in front of their office in 1908. The Brentwood Reality Company was fundamental in building Brentwood, in particular northern Brentwood, into a large residential community, enticing many to move here and build new lives for themselves. (Courtesy of the Brentwood Public Library.)

ON THE COVER: Nestled in the pines of Brentwood, students gather around Building No 2, known as the second schoolhouse. The two-room school began its career in 1907 and would eventually be expanded to house four classrooms. Building No. 2 became for a time the center of the community, and it temporarily housed the library. Today, part of Building No. 2 remains as the Local History Room for the Brentwood Public Library. (Courtesy of the James Fordyce Collection.)

IMAGES
of America

BRENTWOOD

Jason Adam Klosowicz

ARCADIA
PUBLISHING

ISBN 978-1-4671-2082-1

Published by Arcadia Publishing
Charleston, South Carolina

Printed in the United States of America

Library of Congress Control Number: 2013943172

For all general information, please contact Arcadia Publishing:
Telephone 843-853-2070
Fax 843-853-0044
E-mail sales@arcadiapublishing.com
For customer service and orders:
Toll-Free 1-888-313-2665

Visit us on the Internet at www.arcadiapublishing.com

To my mom for all of her love, support, and sacrifices throughout the years.

Contents

ACKNOWLEDGMENTS

This book would not have been possible had it not been for the support of many individuals who found this publication as important to the identity of their community, and supplied the much-needed images, a rarity in Brentwood, and the information. Much credit is due to John Sherin, a member of the Retirees of Brentwood Schools and the Brentwood Historical Society, for his support and helping me to launch this endeavor. I owe much to Tom Tarantowicz, director of the Brentwood Public Library, for the library's support and access to the collections, and to Mary Ann Koferi, who runs the local history room. I would like to thank archivist Virginia Dowd for her patience and time from the Sisters of St. Joseph and to Ray DiMaria from the Bay Shore Historical Society and James Fordyce, who allowed me access to their collections. Thank you to Joe Bond, superintendent of the Brentwood School District, for his permission to include the district as well as support from Dr. Joel Ratner and the production staff. To Sara Kalvin and Al Cibelli, I want to extend a special thank you for the use of materials from Pilgrim Psychiatric Center. Many thanks to Cindy Miller at the Central Islip Library for helping to locate their local collection. Much aid was given by Ed Johntry and Marty Himes at the Suffolk County Police Museum. I am indebted to Prof. Ray Welch for his collection and knowledge of the Ross family. Additional thanks must be given to the many individuals who supported this project and helped to supply images and information. These people are Michael J. Grant Jr., Billy Schwarz, Alan Loeffler, Jeanne L. Taylor, Millie Kresse, Catherine Ball of Smithtown Public Library, Belinda Alvarez-Groneman, Nancy Vidal, Ricardo Montano, Joseph Sawtelle, Francesca Erale, Howard Kroplick, Al Velocci, Vince Trapani and Michael Aliffi at USA Industries, Santiago Reyes, Roland Jimenez, American Legion Post 1006, and Brentwood Legion Ambulance. Finally, a very special thank you to my love, Jennifer, for all of her hard work and help in this project. Without her, this never would have been finished.

Introduction

It all started as a dream to radically change the fabric of American towns; to suspend formal government, laws, and other institutions and dispense with religion and live under the principles of equitable commerce, individual sovereignty, positivism, and free love. With these ideas in mind, the anarchists Josiah Warren and Stephen Pearl Andrews, with a cadre of loyal followers, set out for the desolate Pine Barrens of Long Island in 1852. The little utopian colony of Modern Times, a mile east of the rail depot at Thompson's Station, which was established in 1842, was part of the Model Community Movement and attracted a variety of authors, philosophers, bohemians, and free thinkers. At Modern Times, Andrews would test his theories on Communism; Mary Grove Nichols would fight for women's rights and equality both in and out of the bedroom; and Warren would establish his barter based system of labor. Octagonal structures were a passing architectural trend in antebellum America, and the settlers of Modern Times built two such structures in their colony, the only community in the world to have two octagonal-shaped buildings. The Economic Panic of 1857, the eruption of the Civil War, and an overabundance of philosophical ideologies ended the utopian experiment. As the bloodshed and carnage raged on in the South, Modern Times, Thompson's Station, and the local vicinity, which included parts of North Islip, would be consolidated into Brentwood in 1864.

With the majority of Long Island's villages and residents hugging the shoreline, the community of Brentwood remained a quiet, out of the way place with a sorted and shady past in the island's interior. The island's hinterland was long thought to be uncultivable, but Brentwood orchards produced a variety of fruits and other local produce, along with cheap land that attracted a growing population of farmers and planters. Health related reasons put Brentwood back on the map in the late 19th and early 20th centuries. The scent of the fresh pine air, mixed with that of the nearby seashore, was thought to have curative properties for both mind and body. In an era plagued by tuberculosis, hotels sprung up across Brentwood, and the community became a destination spot for people looking to "breathe the air." The Ross Sanitarium opened as a health resort for people looking to convalesce from whatever ailed them, and Brooklyn and New York City's wealthy and elite built lavish summer homes and mansions in Brentwood for weekend and holiday retreats and vacations to breathe the clean healthy air.

Stores and businesses grew to support the hotels, and more people moved to Brentwood looking for work. The Sisters of St. Joseph built a convent and academy in the pines at Brentwood, and soon turned the facility into a premier educational institution. At the same time, the small Brentwood School District, being inundated with new students each year, was forced to expand. This brought more jobs into the community, which meant more families with children entering the school system resulting in more steady expansion, and thus the cycle continued.

The State of New York, in an attempt to end overcrowding permanently at its numerous psychiatric hospitals, designed a mammoth institution. Cheap open land in Brentwood, with a small community nearby, facilitated the construction of Pilgrim State Hospital in western Brentwood.

The hospital opened its doors in 1931 and almost overnight the community of Brentwood grew. Although the primary staff resided on the hospitals grounds, support staff moved into the Brentwood community. Visitors and staff needed a place to shop, and the community's growth mirrored that of the hospital's growth. When it quickly became apparent that one monstrous facility was not going to end the state's plight of overcrowding, a second massive hospital that would rival Pilgrim's size was planned a mile south of the Pilgrim facility in the area known as Edgewood, a tract of land that spanned both Deer Park and Brentwood. Construction began in 1938, but World War II intervened, and the federal government took control of the Edgewood State Hospital still under construction and the "80s complex" of buildings at the rear of Pilgrim State Hospital and named it all Mason General Army Hospital. Through the war years, soldiers suffering from battle fatigue were treated before being returned to civilian life. After the war, the state regained control of their property but saw no need to expand the Edgewood facility. The result was that the hospital was never fully finished, and the small collection of buildings called Edgewood State Hospital became a subunit of Pilgrim State Hospital. While Pilgrim continued to treat the mentally ill, Edgewood specifically treated the mentally ill suffering from tuberculosis, and again, the idea of clean air played a part.

The state hospitals became the number one employer in the area, and thousands moved to Brentwood and the surrounding communities because of job opportunities at Pilgrim, Edgewood, or Central Islip State Hospitals. The GI Bill, local jobs, and affordable housing were the promise of suburbia. White flight brought new residents out of the city looking for a better future in the new suburban community in Brentwood, and the village kept growing, evolving into a blue-collar, working-class town.

Because of its size, Brentwood has been broken down into various sections, and within these sections, various names have been given to signify different areas in the community. These usually coincided with building or housing developments. Brentwood is broken down like a compass—north, south, east and west. Within those larger sections, smaller subsections, tracts of land, or specific areas have included: Brentwood Pines, Brentwood Park, Edgewood, Pine Aire, Regis Park, Baywood, Laurel Park, Loretta Park, Brentwood Manor, Pine Park, Victory Farms, Secatogue Hollow, North Bay Shore, Brightwaters Farm, Bayfair, Brentwood Terrace, Pilgrim Park, Oakdale Park, and Bay Shore Heights. Some of these toponyms are still in use, while others have fallen into disuse and off the map entirely.

With the demise of agriculture and the rise of suburbia, Brentwood has remained a working-class community. First the Long Island Rail Road and later the Long Island Expressway carried the residents of our community to work in the city and other areas and back to their suburban American Dream at home. Cheap and affordable land or houses have brought successive waves of immigrants to Brentwood, each recreating Brentwood in their own image. From the faddists at Modern Times, to the Irish, Germans, and Italians in the late 19th and early 20th centuries, then came Russians, Poles, and other Eastern Europeans in the post–World War I and World War II periods. The latter half of the 20th century saw a major influx of Hispanics, first the Puerto Ricans and Mexicans in the 1950s and then the Guatemalans and Hondurans in the 1960s. The Ecuadorians and Bolivians came in the 1970s, while the 1980s saw the arrival of Cubans and Dominicans. The 1990s brought the Columbians and Peruvians, while the Salvadorians have dominated the early 21st century. Additionally, Brentwood also boasts a large population of Brazilians, Caribbean, and Portuguese. Each new group of immigrants only stays for a few generations before moving on, taking their history with them. While some always remain, Brentwood has been the starter community for each new group of Americans.

One

Modern Times

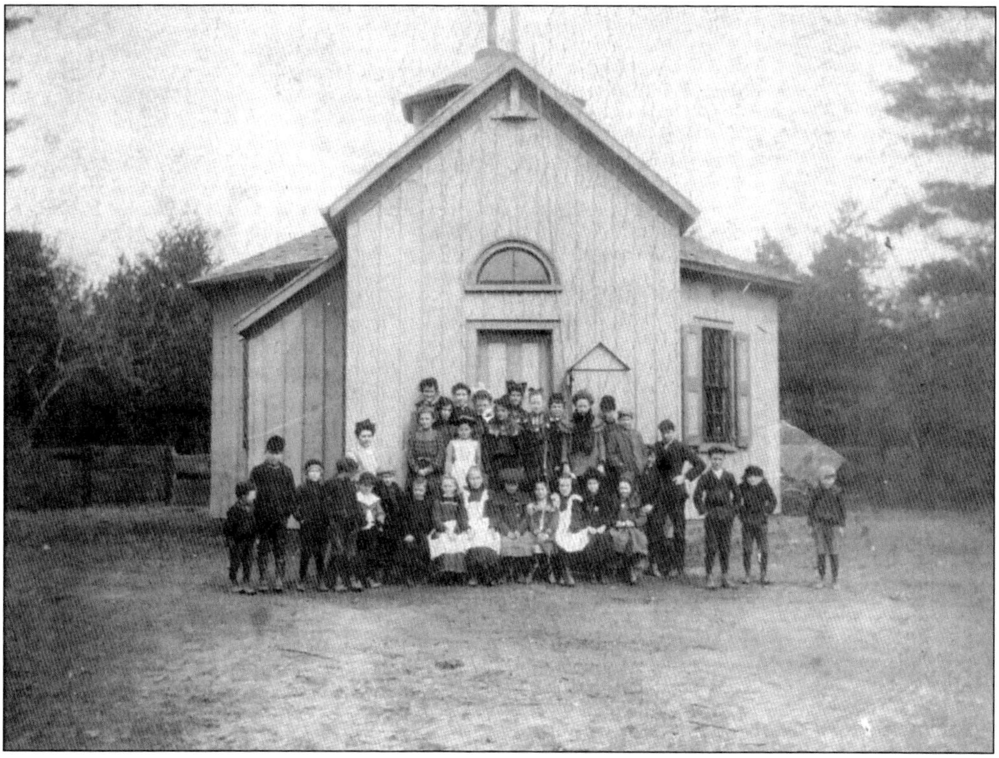

Left in private to put their beliefs into practice, the colonists built a one-room octagonal-shaped schoolhouse on the corner of Third Avenue and Fourth Street at a cost of $500. It opened in 1857 and served the community until 1907. The school became an iconic symbol of Modern Times. Shown here, the children pose with teacher Mary Swain in 1858 or 1859. (Courtesy of the Brentwood Public Library.)

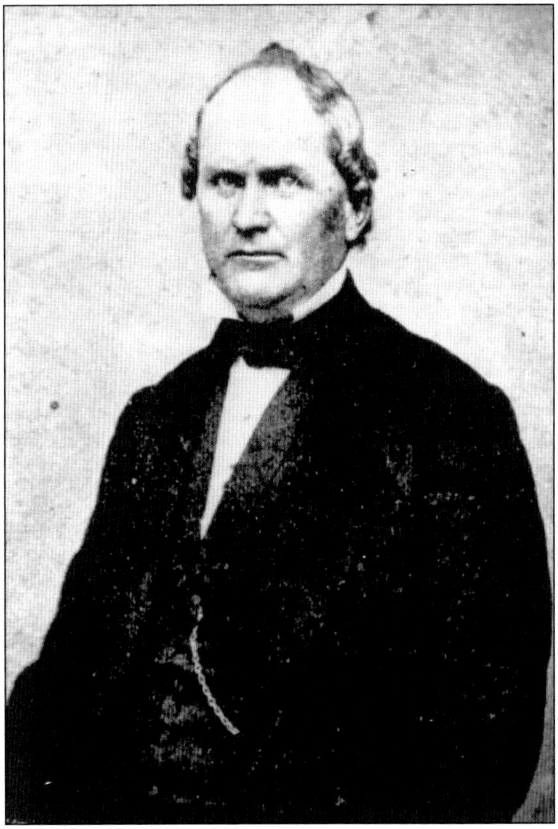

Francis Moses Ashbury Wicks (1815–1867) was an aristocrat and land baron who controlled most of the land in western Suffolk County. Ruling from his home at Thompson's Station, he was postmaster, justice of the peace, and county treasurer. He sold the land directly east of Thompson's Station to Dr. Edgar Fenn Peck, who helped establish the Modern Times settlement. He was constantly at odds with Josiah Warren. (Courtesy of the Brentwood Public Library.)

Built in 1842 and leased by the Long Island Rail Road, Thompson's Station was the first permanent settlement in the area and home to the powerful Wicks family. It served as a station for the area as well as post office, telegraph station, store, hotel, farm, and local court. For a time, it was the center of political, intellectual, and social culture in western Suffolk County. (Courtesy of the Brentwood Public Library.)

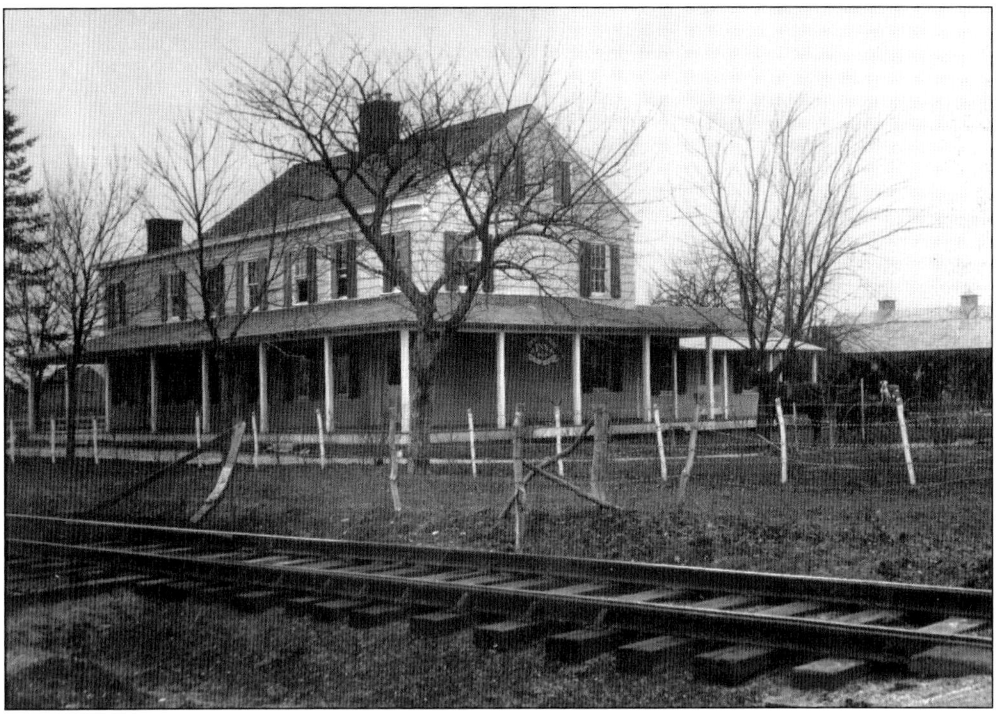

Dr. Edgar Fenn Peck, MD, (1806–1887) was a Smithtown resident who became interested in real estate and the idea of developing and cultivating Long Island's interior. He purchased 400 acres of land a mile east of Thompson's Station from Francis Moses Ashbury Wicks and sold what would become Brentwood to Josiah Warren and Stephen Pearl Andrews in 1852. Dr. Peck also sold the land for what would become Central Islip. (Courtesy of the Brentwood Public Library.)

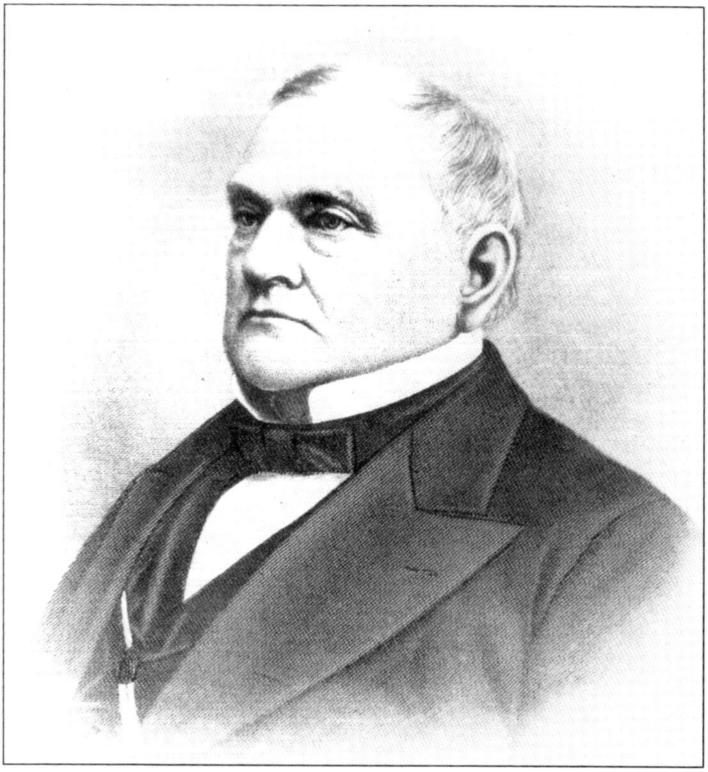

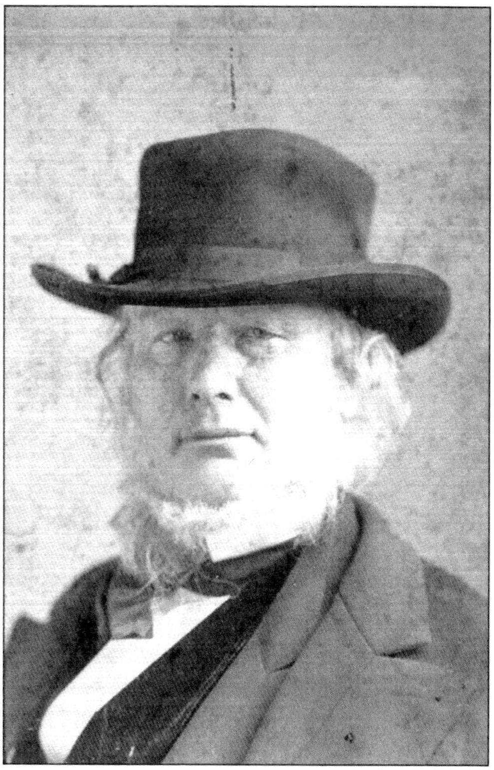

Horace Greeley (1811–1872), the eminent New York City newspaper publisher and abolitionist, was one of the primary financial backers of Warren and Andrew's Modern Times experiment. Greeley promoted Modern Times in his *New York Tribune* and published philosophical debates from the village. He even bought several lots in the village. Greeley visited Modern Times several times but never resided there. (Courtesy of Jeanne L. Taylor.)

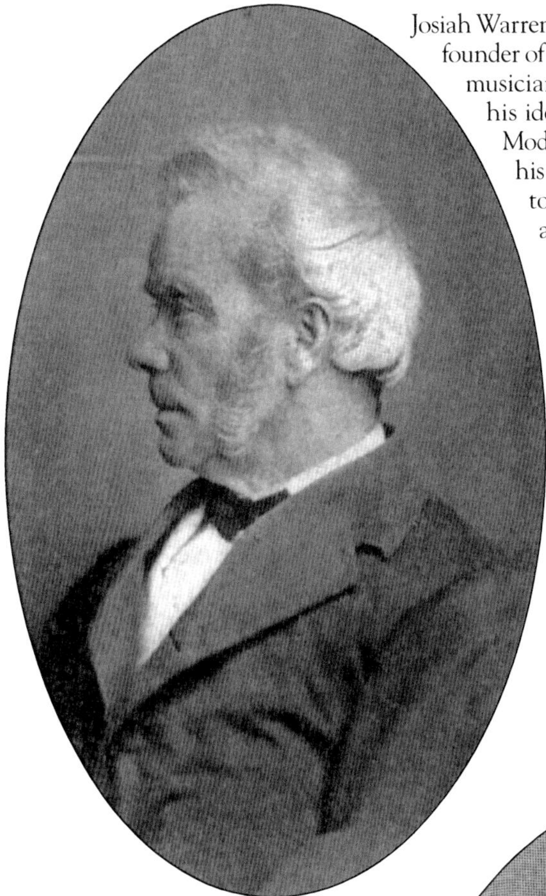

Josiah Warren (1798–1874) was the powerful and enigmatic founder of Modern Times. He was a printer and trained musician as well as a lecturer and author, preaching his ideas on equitable commerce. He established Modern Times with Stephen Pearl Andrews to test his theories. There, he built a mechanical college to teach his followers various trades. He grew apart from his followers and left the village in 1862, never to return. He died and is buried in Charlestown, Massachusetts. (Courtesy of the Brentwood Public Library.)

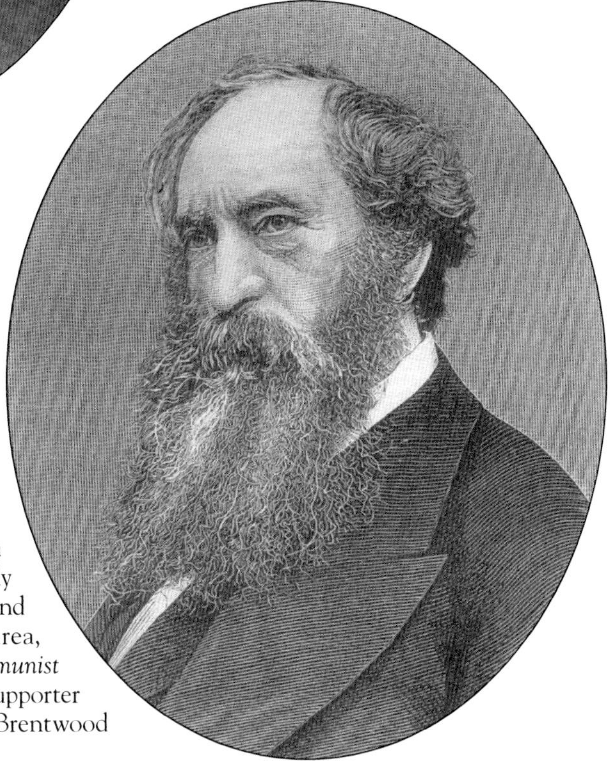

Stephen Pearl Andrews (1812–1886), the cofounder of Modern Times, was originally a lawyer and abolitionist; he was run out of Texas because of his views. Studying abroad, he began to preach about individual sovereignty. As a philosopher at Modern Times, he was interested in wage theory and universology. Never a full-time resident, he travelled regularly between his home in New York City and Modern Times. After leaving the area, Andrews translated Karl Marx's *Communist Manifesto* into English and became a supporter of female suffrage. (Courtesy of the Brentwood Public Library.)

William Upham Dame (1815–1896) arrived at Modern Times as part of the Boston group, a contingent of settlers who helped stabilize and legitimize the colony. At Modern Times and early Brentwood, Dame worked as a box builder and cabinet maker. Dame dug the first well for the community, which became a social meeting spot on the corner of Brentwood Road (then Fifth Street) and Third Avenue. He is buried in the Brentwood Cemetery. (Courtesy of the Brentwood Public Library.)

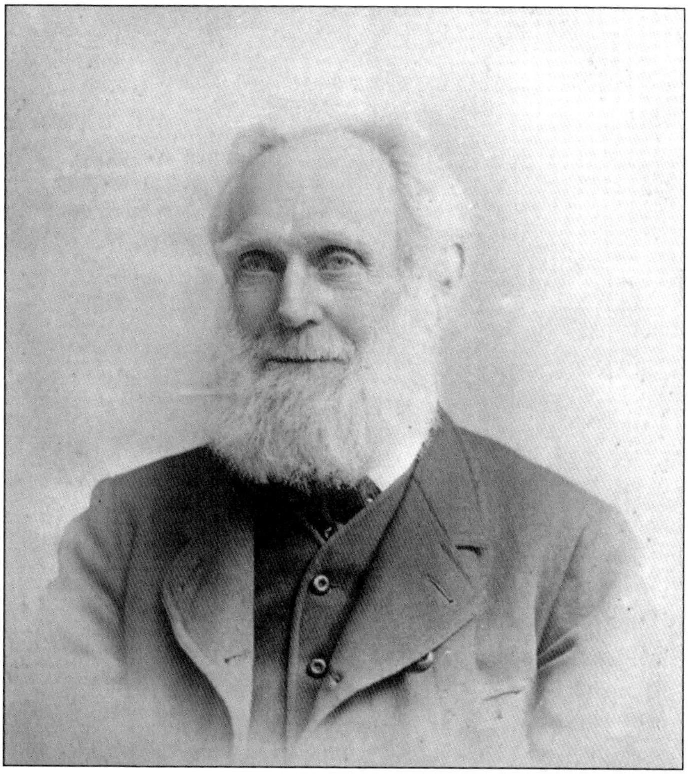

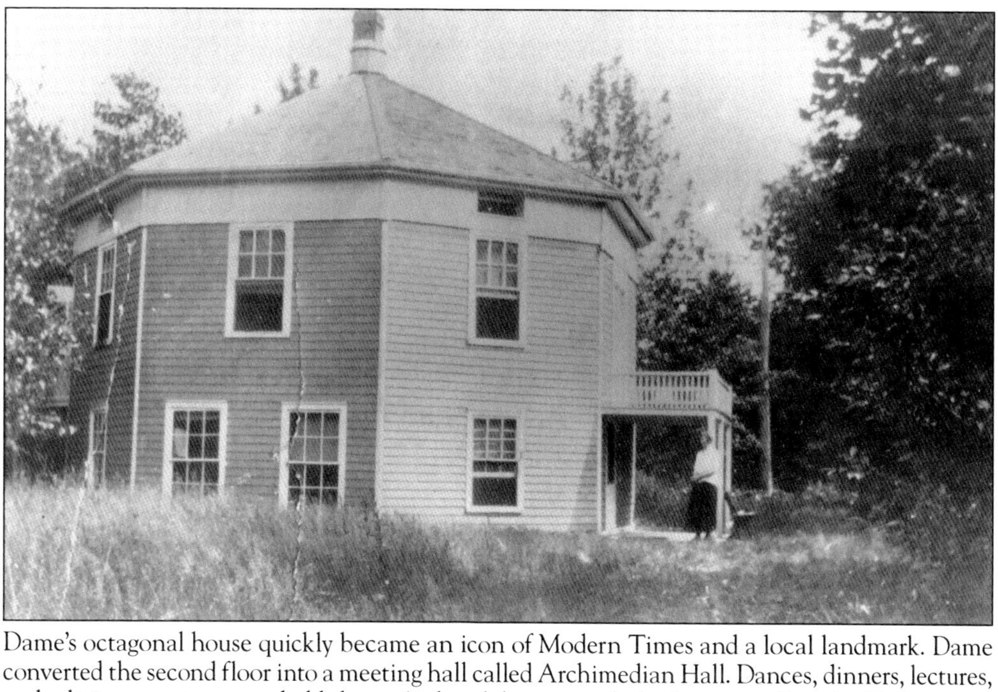

Dame's octagonal house quickly became an icon of Modern Times and a local landmark. Dame converted the second floor into a meeting hall called Archimedian Hall. Dances, dinners, lectures, and religious services were held there. A glee club met regularly there as well as the Shakespeare Reading Club. The village's first circulating library was housed in the Dame House. The building is still used as a private residence today. (Courtesy of the Brentwood Public Library.)

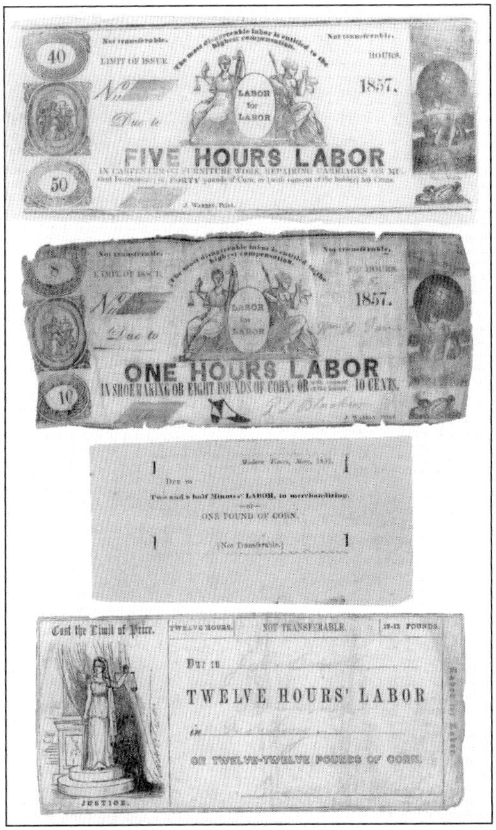

Seen here are original Modern Times labor notes, printed by Josiah Warren at Modern Times, which were used as currency in the village. Instead of legal tender, the settlers exchanged goods and services on a barter system based on labor, or its equivalent in corn. Each note promises a set amount of labor in a particular craft or trade. (Courtesy of the Richard H. Handley Collection of Long Island Americana, Smithtown Special Library District.)

William Upham Dame poses by his workshop behind his octagonal home. Dame was a skilled master carpenter and provided his services to the village. Dame worked as a box builder and cabinet maker until his death. (Courtesy of the Brentwood Public Library.)

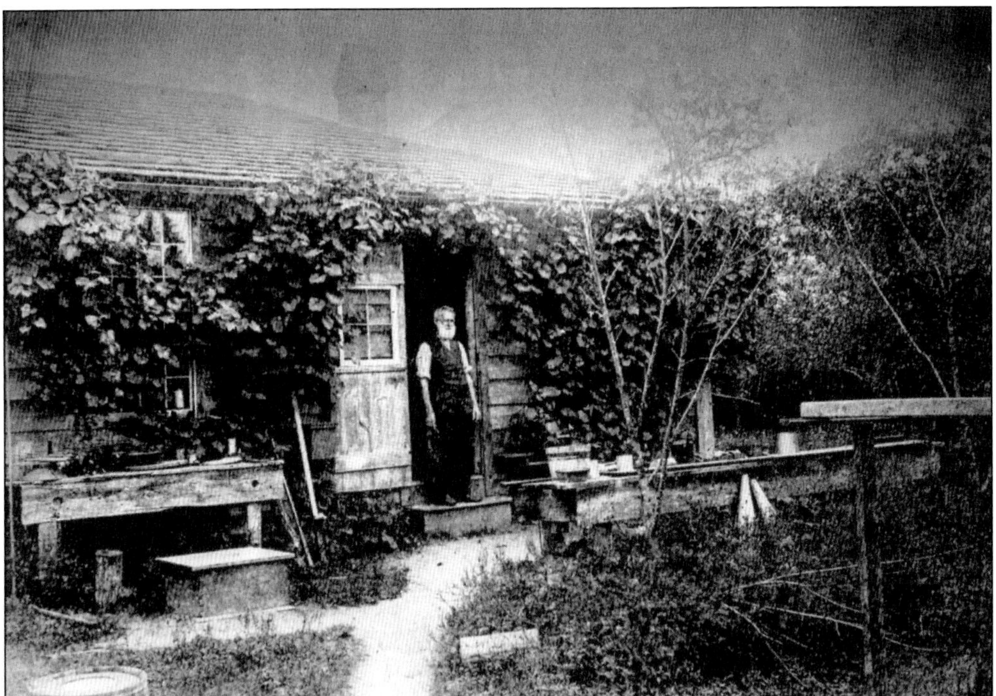

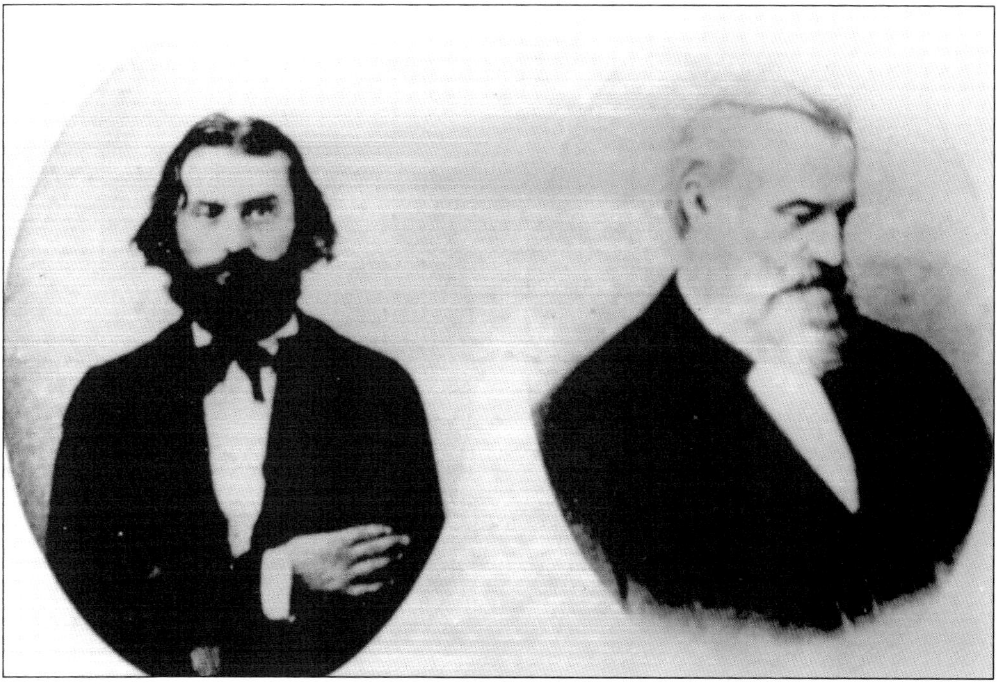

Henry Edger (1820–1888, seen above) left his home in Brentwood, England, for the United States. As a disciple of philosopher Auguste Comte, Edger became the preeminent preacher of positivism. At Modern Times, Edger worked as a nurseryman when not proselytizing. Edgar was so popular and respected in the community that the settlers chose to rename their village Brentwood, in honor of his hometown. Edger left Brentwood in 1880. (Courtesy of the Brentwood Public Library.)

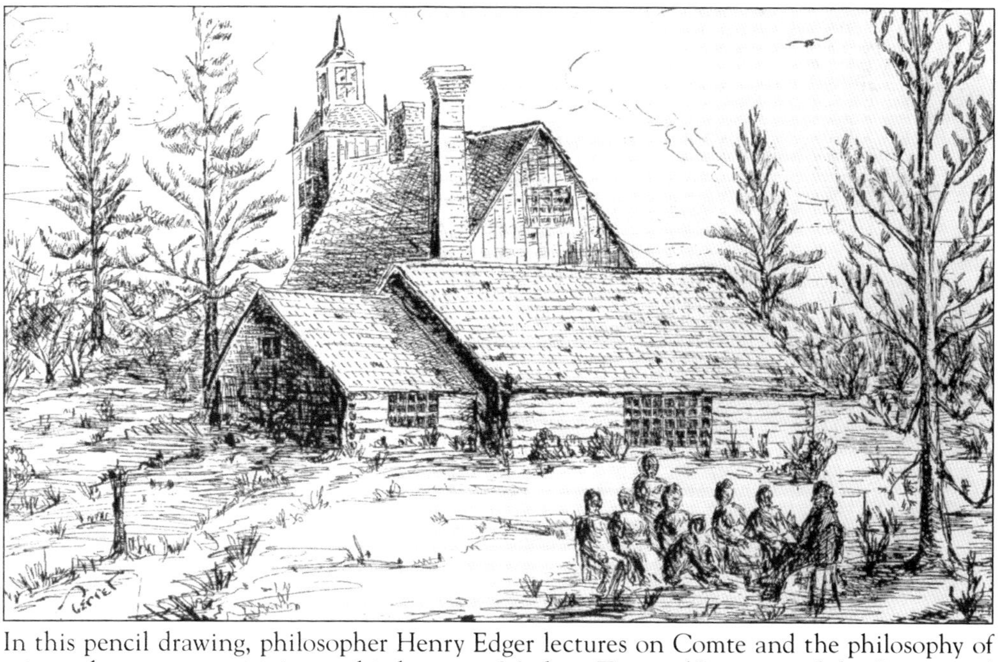

In this pencil drawing, philosopher Henry Edger lectures on Comte and the philosophy of science known as positivism at his home in Modern Times. (Courtesy of the Brentwood Public Library.)

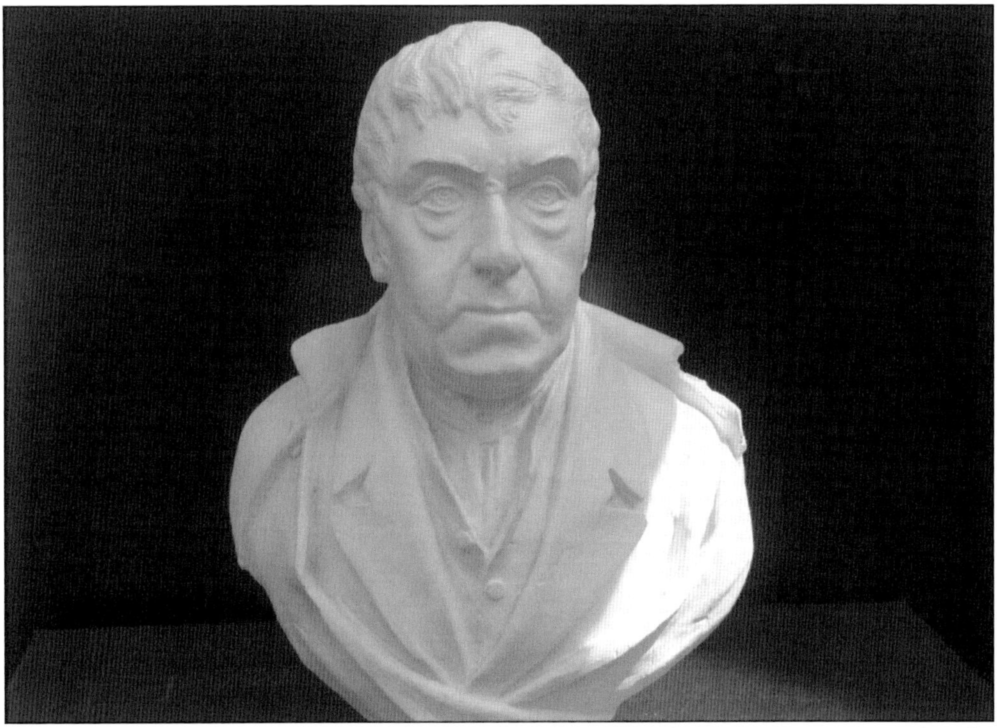

Dr. Edward Newberry, DDS, (1811–1897) emigrated from England at age 26. As an original settler at Modern Times, Dr. Newberry became Islip Town's first permanent dentist. Additionally, Dr. Newberry was a noted painter, writer, phrenologist, chemist, botanist, and zoologist. He believed eugenics would result in human perfectibility. He remained in Brentwood for the rest of his life, where he practiced his craft. He is buried in the Brentwood Cemetery. (Courtesy of the Brentwood Public Library.)

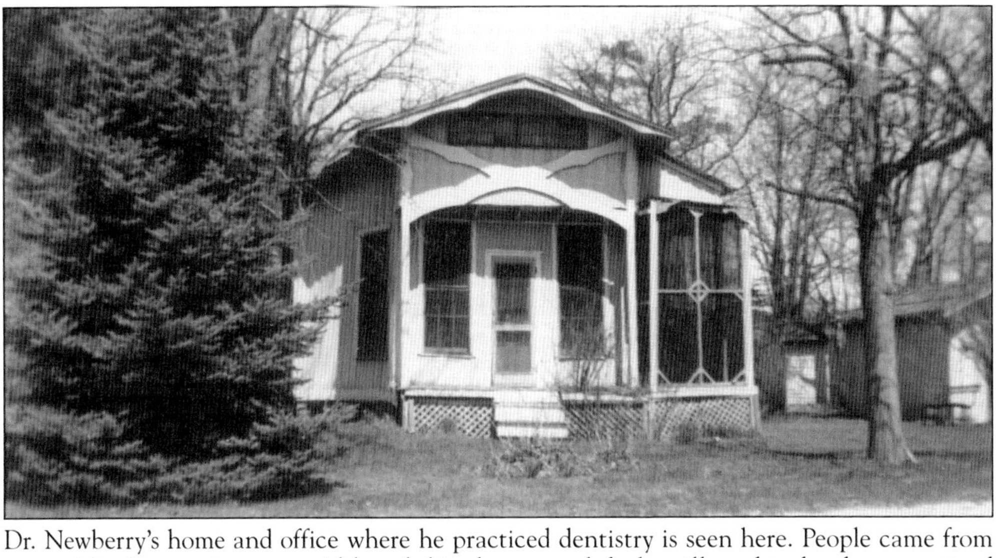

Dr. Newberry's home and office where he practiced dentistry is seen here. People came from across Islip for appointments. Although his three sons left the village, his daughter remained and married into the Shutt family, who eventually took possession of the house. (Courtesy of the Brentwood Public Library.)

Original settlers of Modern Times, including Charles Codman (center), gather together in their twilight years in the hamlet that they helped found. With their numbers thinning each passing year, the original sovereigns achieved an almost demigod status within early Brentwood. Gatherings at various locations typically included reminiscing of bygone days at Modern Times. (Courtesy of the Brentwood Public Library)

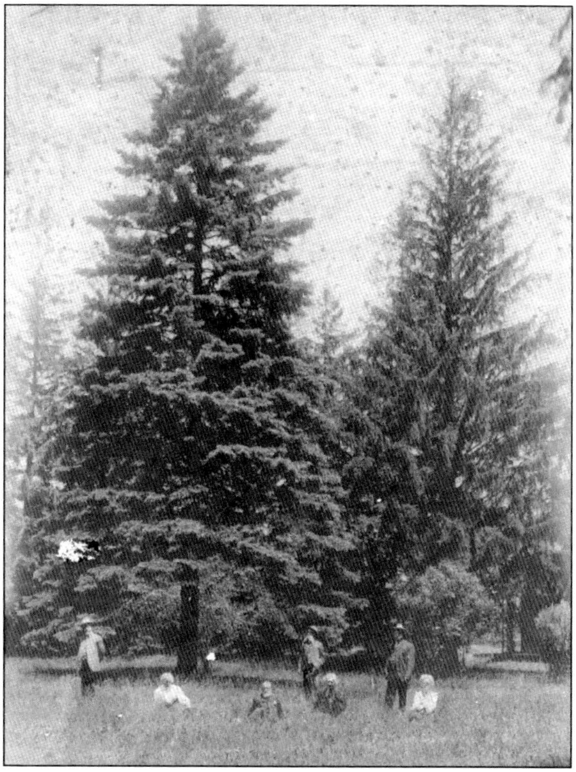

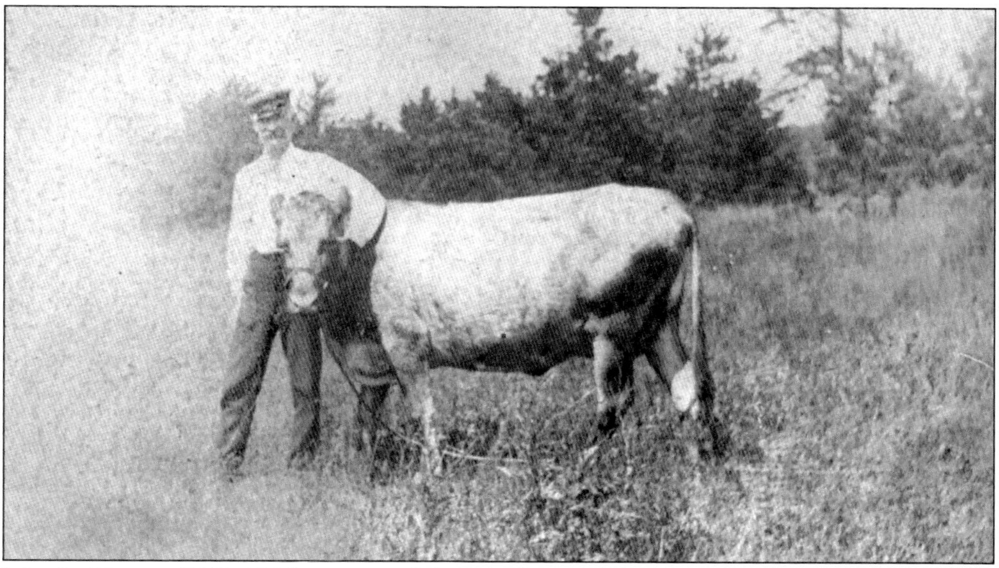

John L. Watson (1842–1910) was one of the founding members of Modern Times. He served in the Civil War with the 4th New York Infantry, enlisting five days after the fall of Fort Sumter. He returned to Brentwood where he remained for the rest of his life and worked as a school tax collector for the district. He is seen here at his farm with the family cow on August 31, 1902. Watson was a member of the Grand Army of the Republic, William Gurney Post 538 and the Brentwood Christ Episcopal Church and is buried in the Brentwood Cemetery. (Courtesy of Brentwood Public Library.)

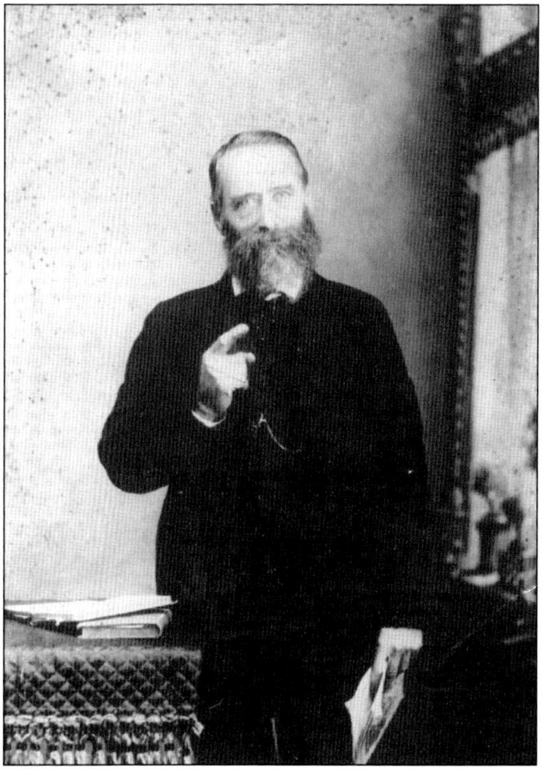

Charles A. Codman (1827–1911) joined Modern Times after its founding, quickly becoming one of the leading figures in the new community and serving on the school board. A Civil War veteran, he spent the rest of his life in Brentwood, becoming the last surviving member of the original founders. He wrote *A Brief History of Modern Times and its People*, but it was never published. He is buried in the Brentwood Cemetery. (Courtesy of the Brentwood Public Library.)

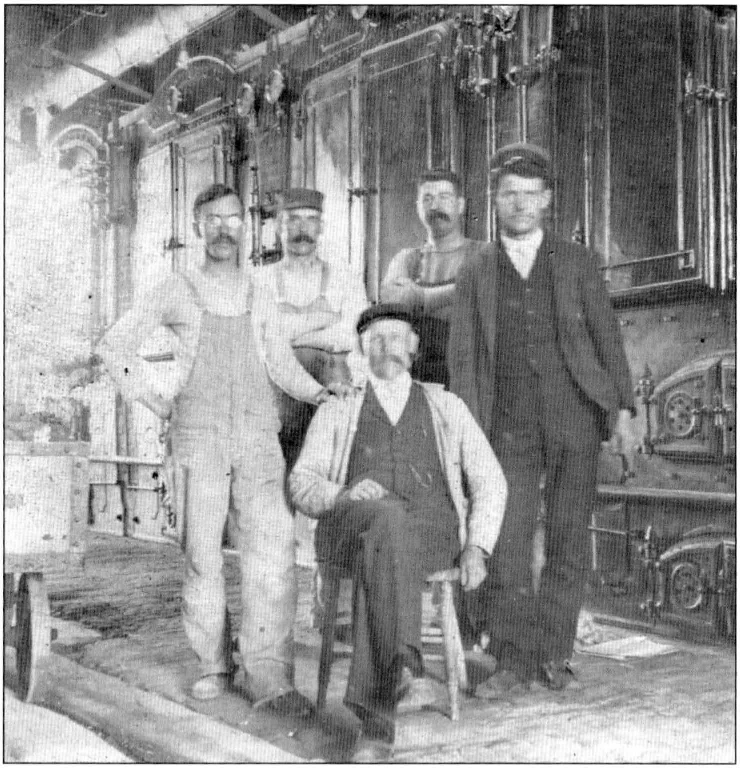

Oscar Harvey Watson (second from left), born around 1876, was the son of John L. Watson. He grew up as a child at Modern Times and early Brentwood. His brother-in-law Oliver Neil Wittberg (seated) came to Brentwood in 1890. Both men worked in the boiler room of the Austral Hotel and later the boiler room of the Manhattan State Hospital (Central Islip State Hospital), seen here around the turn of the 20th century. (Courtesy of the Brentwood Public Library.)

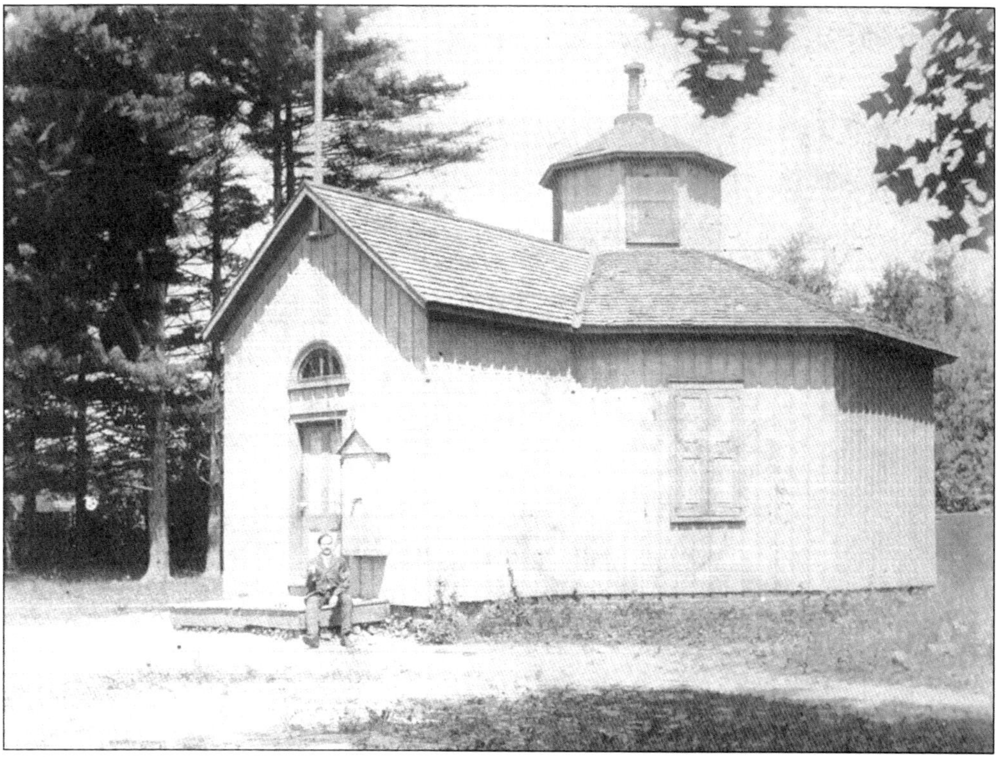

A clear side view of Modern Times's famous octagonal one-room schoolhouse is seen here in the mid-1800s. The school served the children of the community for 50 years and is the humble beginning of the Brentwood School District, one of the largest public school systems in the state of New York. (Courtesy of the Brentwood Public Library.)

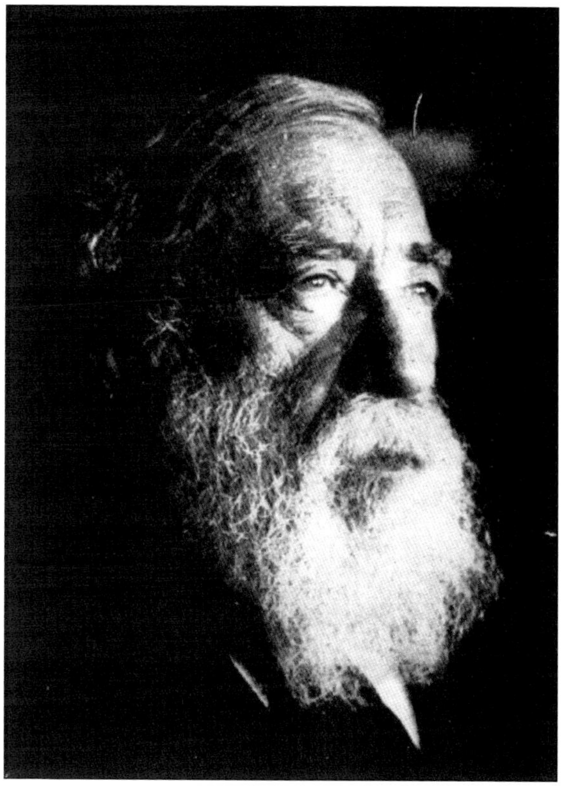

Moncure Daniel Conway (1832–1907) was a minister, author, and reformer. He visited Modern Times for one weekend in 1858 and was so taken with the community that he regularly wrote and spoke of the establishment. In response to Hawthorne's *The Blithedale Romance*, Conway wrote *Pine and Palm*, using Modern Times as the inspiration for the village of Bonheur and basing his character Maria Shelton on Mary Chilton, who was his hostess the weekend of his visit. (Courtesy of the Brentwood Public Library.)

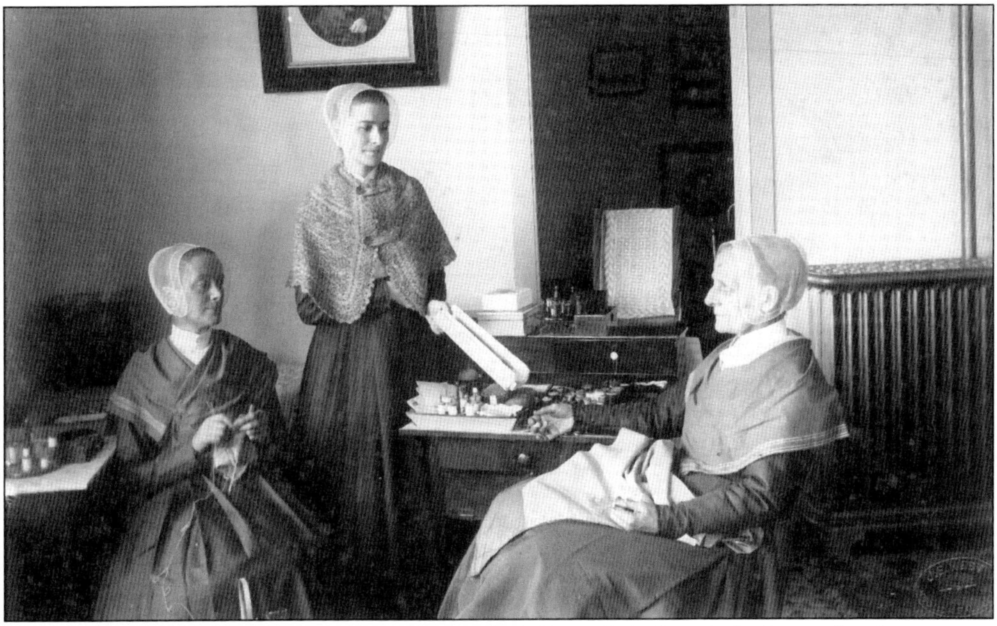

Modern Times offered a safe haven for those with different beliefs and ideals, an idea that persists in modern Brentwood. The Shakers, a Christian sect that was typically the target of persecution, found refuge at Modern Times. Here, a group of Shaker women pose during their house duties while at Modern Times. (Courtesy of the Brentwood Public Library.)

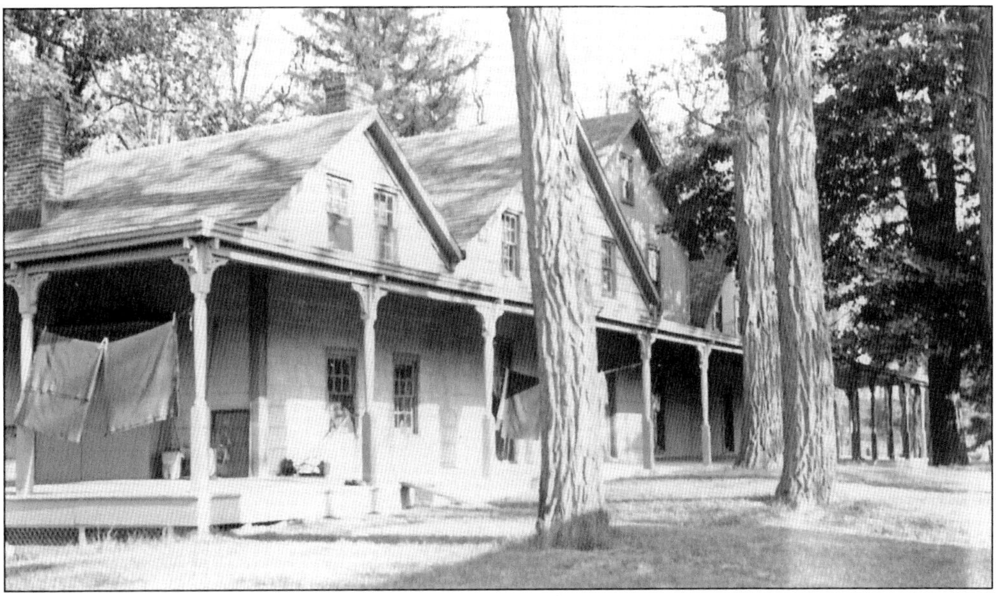

Eugene Platt, a local resident with no affiliation to Modern Times, bought a massive tract of land from Dr. Peck that stretched from Caleb's Path in the east to Wicks Road in the west in what would become North Brentwood. Construction began on the north wing of the estate house during the Modern Times era. The Platt estate later passed onto the Arbuckle brothers. (Courtesy of the Brentwood Public Library.)

Two

Becoming Brentwood

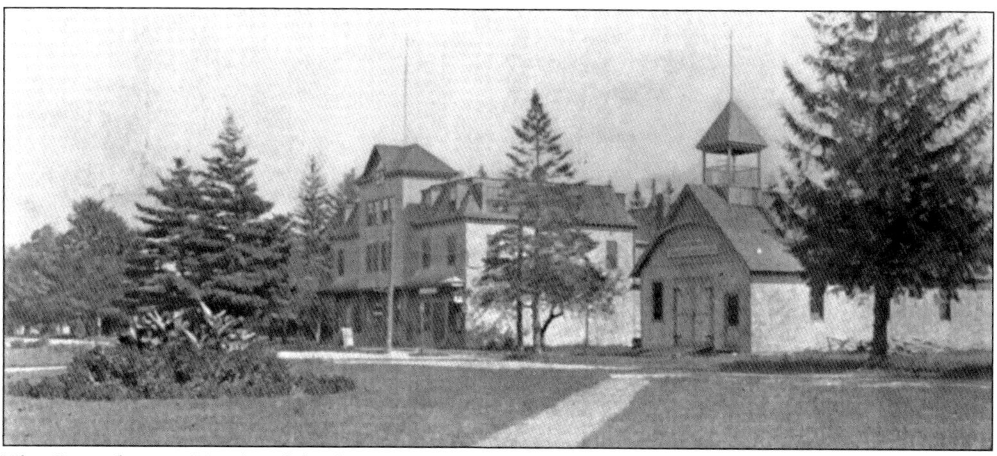

The Quanahassett Hotel and the first Brentwood Fire Department Station are shown in this postcard image of First Avenue between 1900 and 1905. The original fire station housed two horse-drawn fire carriages as well as alarm bells and siren. (Courtesy of the James Fordyce Collection.)

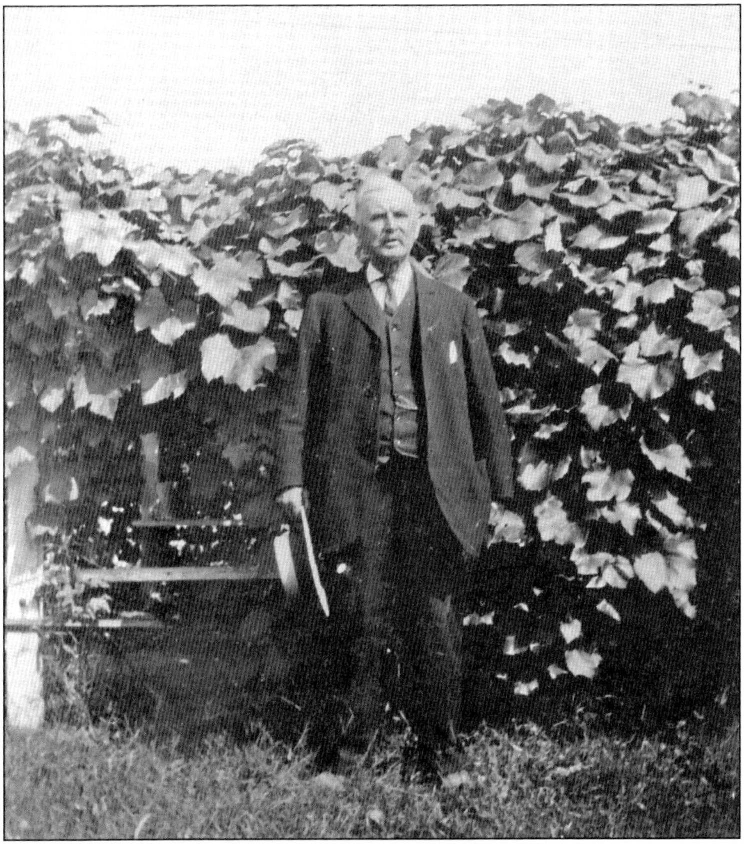

Frank E. Blacker (1848–1921), one of the original founders of Modern Times, served in the Civil War and returned to Brentwood to become one of its leading residents. He served three terms as the postmaster of Brentwood as well as working as a railroad station agent and becoming justice of the peace. He also sat on the board of education. He is buried in the Brentwood Cemetery. (Courtesy of the Brentwood Public Library.)

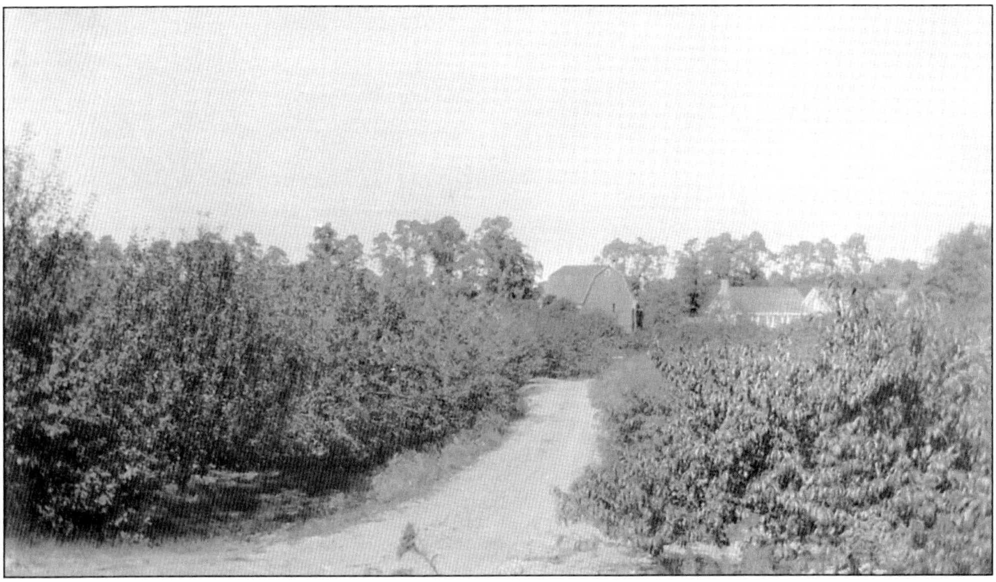

Brentwood orchards producing apples, pears, peaches, and berries became the main farming industry in the late 19th century. Edwin O. Hoyt's orchard is seen here in the mid-1880s. The farm originally belonged to Azariah Wicks and was just north of Thompson's Station in an area now called Regis Park. (Courtesy of the Brentwood Public Library.)

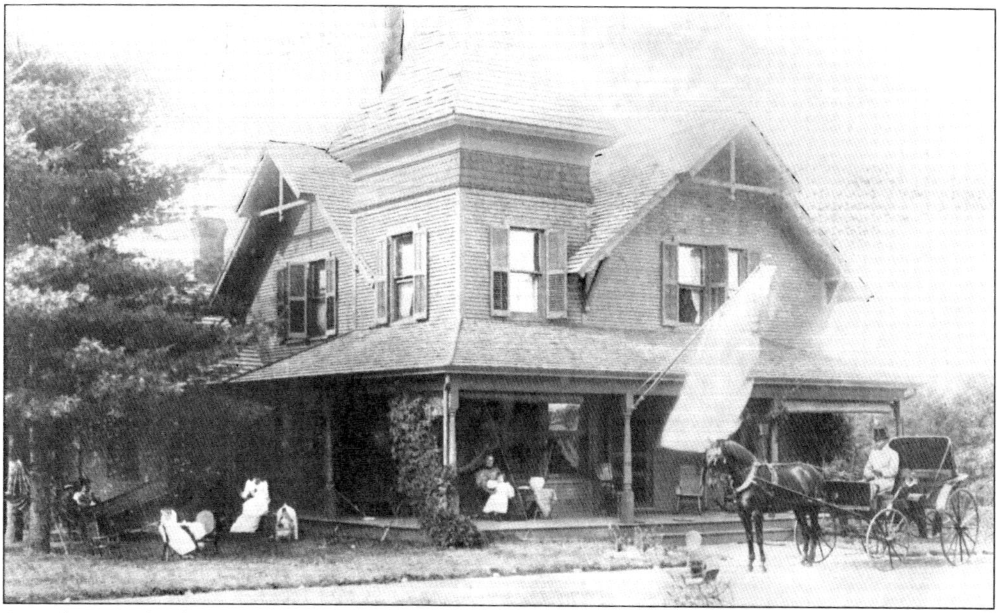

Seen here is the home of Mr. and Mrs. Anthony Hawkins Creagh in 1896. A shopping center presently occupies this site. (Courtesy of the Brentwood Public Library.)

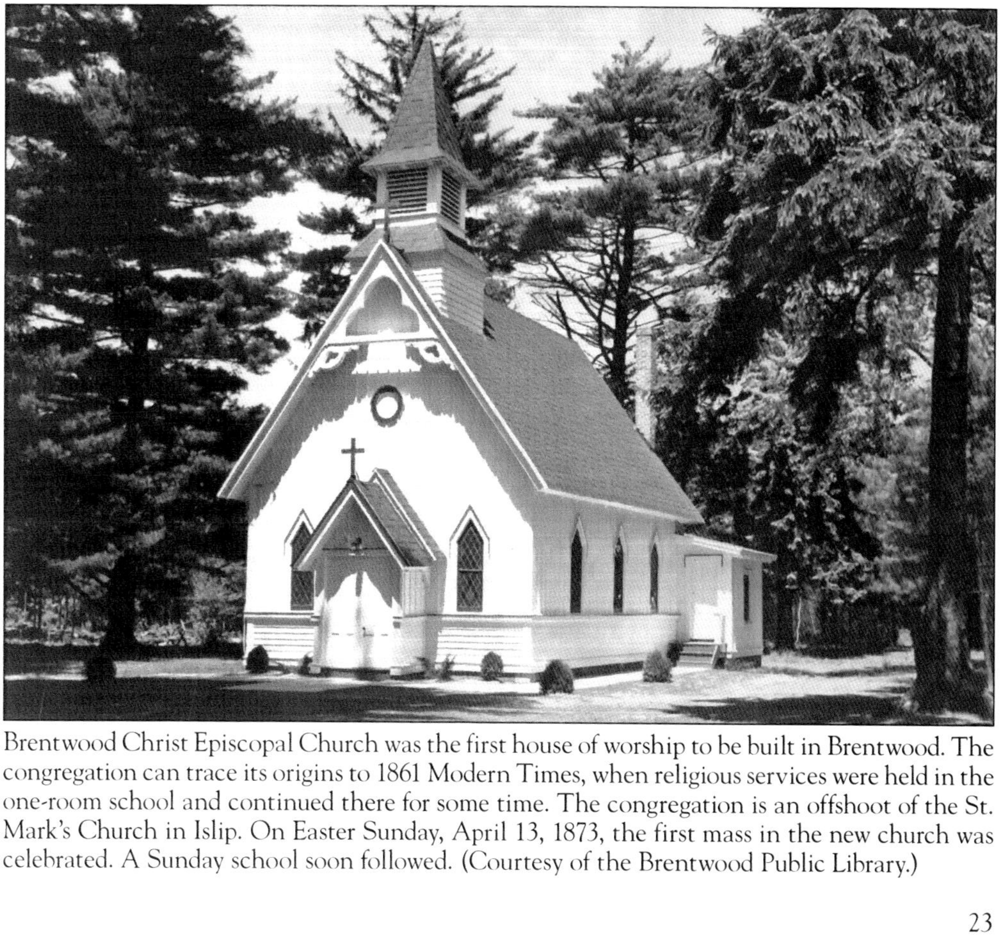

Brentwood Christ Episcopal Church was the first house of worship to be built in Brentwood. The congregation can trace its origins to 1861 Modern Times, when religious services were held in the one-room school and continued there for some time. The congregation is an offshoot of the St. Mark's Church in Islip. On Easter Sunday, April 13, 1873, the first mass in the new church was celebrated. A Sunday school soon followed. (Courtesy of the Brentwood Public Library.)

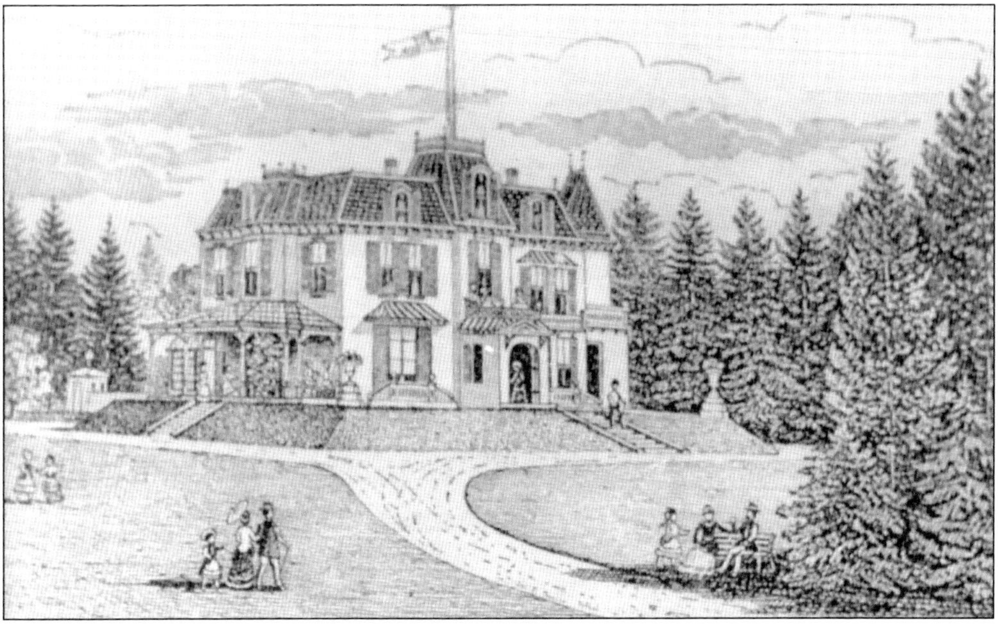

Pine Park was the name of the Pearsall estate, completed in 1870. Robert W. Pearsall, a leading capitalist, was involved in scientific agriculture and bought property in Brentwood with the intent of becoming a serious farmer. Frederick Law Olmsted was hired to design the house and grounds. Only a year after completion, Pearsall died and his widow closed the place and moved the family to Italy. (Courtesy of the Brentwood Public Library.)

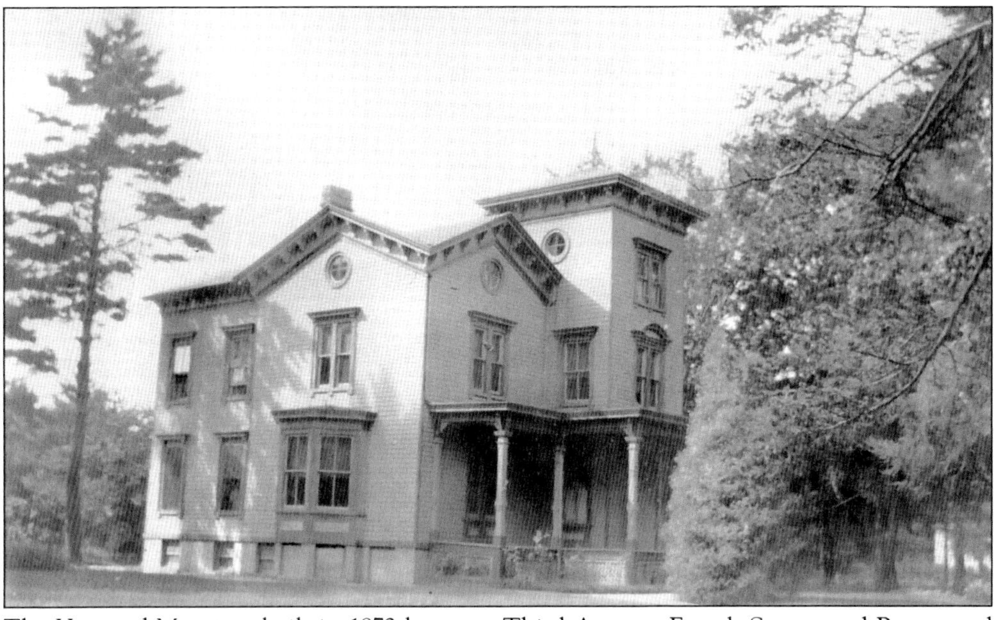

The Hayward Mansion, built in 1872 between Third Avenue, Fourth Street, and Brentwood Road (Fifth Street), was one of several large mansions constructed in the latter half of the 19th century. The Haywards were a large and prominent family within the community. The mansion was torn down in 1940. (Courtesy of the Brentwood Public Library.)

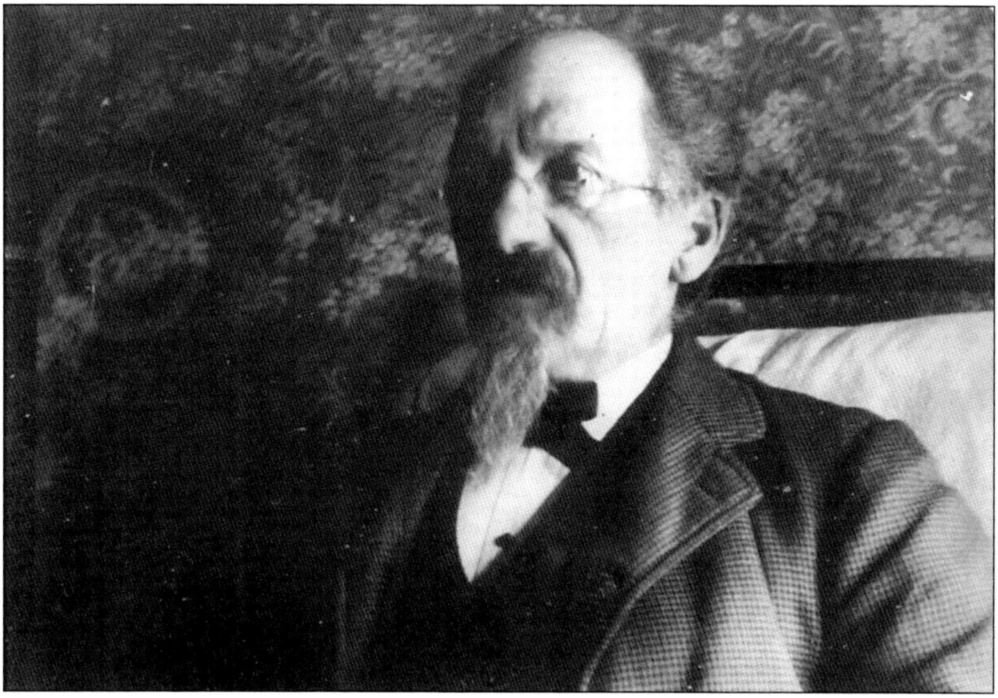

Henry Hervey Hall (1840–1907) moved to Brentwood in 1886 at the insistence of his friend Charles Codman and operated a store and nursery. He was a noted philosopher, author, lecturer, printer, and newspaper editor for the *Islip Herald*. He served on the school board and was credited with bringing learning, conservation, and an interest in civic affairs to the forefront of residents of the town through his philanthropic efforts. (Courtesy of the Brentwood Public Library.)

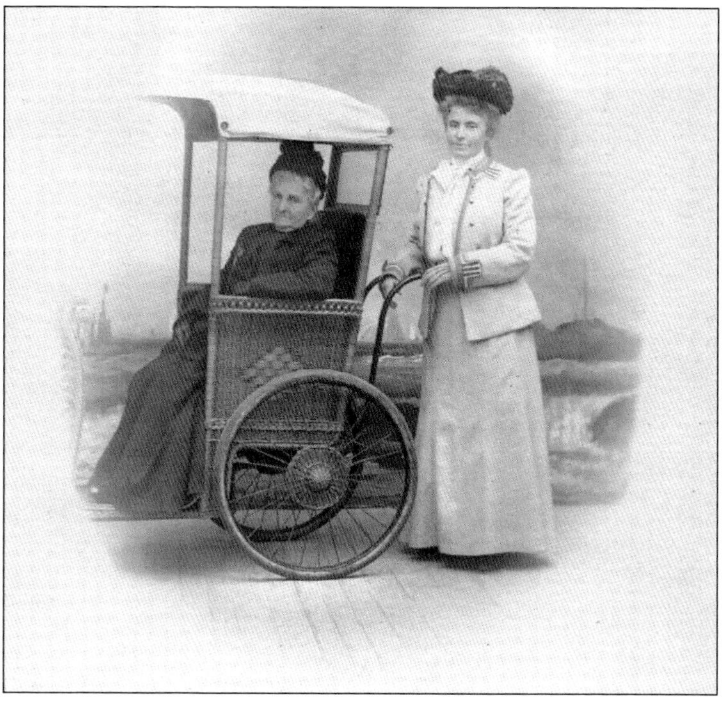

Helen Hall, who later in life suffered from medical issues and poor health, needed to be driven about town in a small cart. (Courtesy of the Brentwood Public Library.)

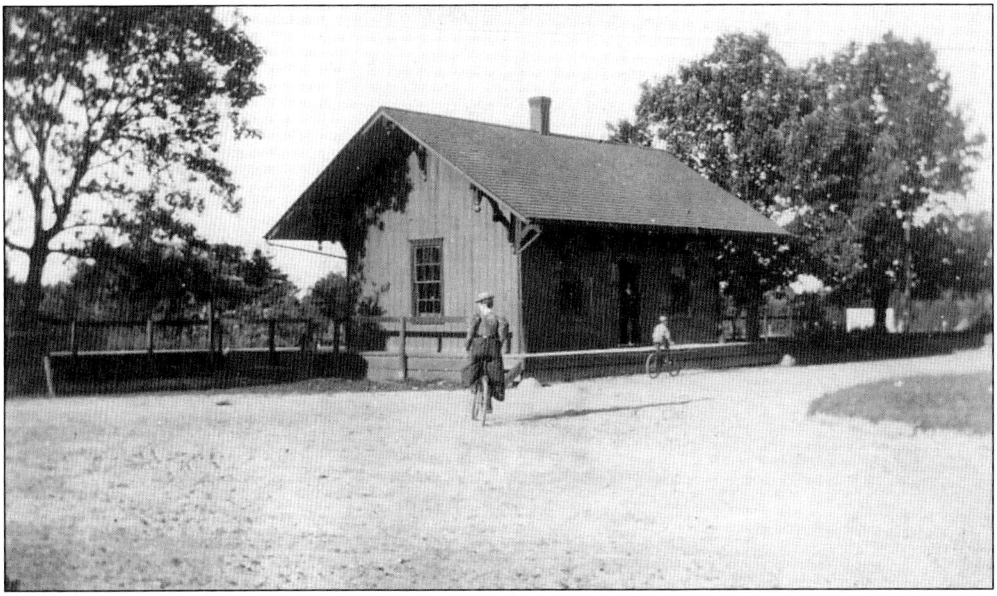

In December 1869, the Long Island Rail Road ceased using the depot at Thompson's Station and moved the station a mile east into Brentwood proper. Brentwood's first train station was a single-room rectangular building on First Avenue, seen here in the 1890s. It operated from 1869, with Frank E. Blacker as its first agent, until it burned down in 1905. (Courtesy of the Brentwood Public Library.)

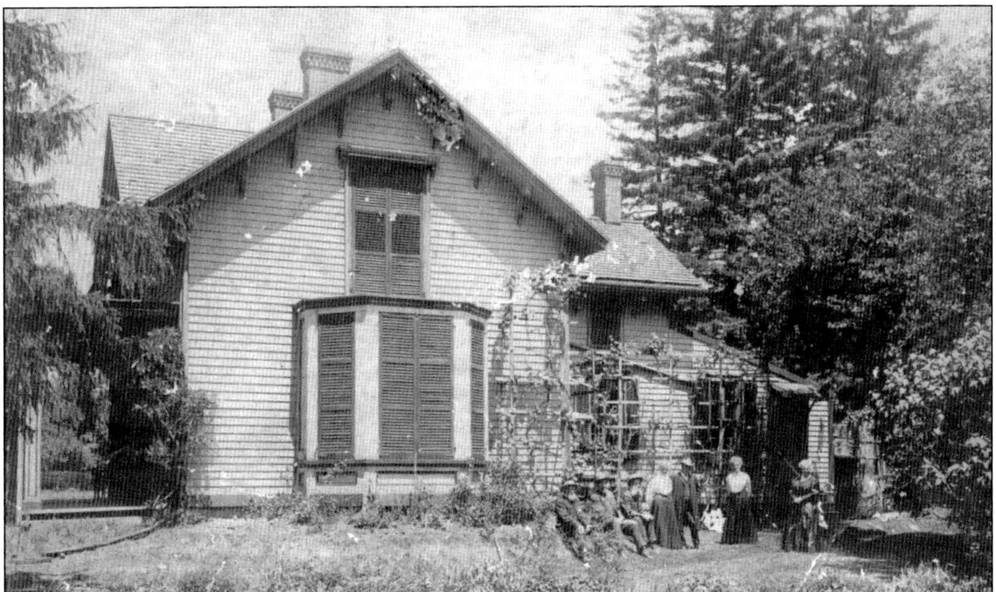

The Codman residence, also known as The Hermitage of the Red Owl, was built by Charles Codman in 1857 on the corner of Second Avenue and Brentwood Road. It was the site of a freshwater well for the community. Codman wrote his history of Brentwood here as well as many other stories, including his most famous, *The Legend of the Red Owl*. The Hermitage became the social and intellectual center for both Modern Times and early Brentwood. (Courtesy of the Brentwood Public Library.)

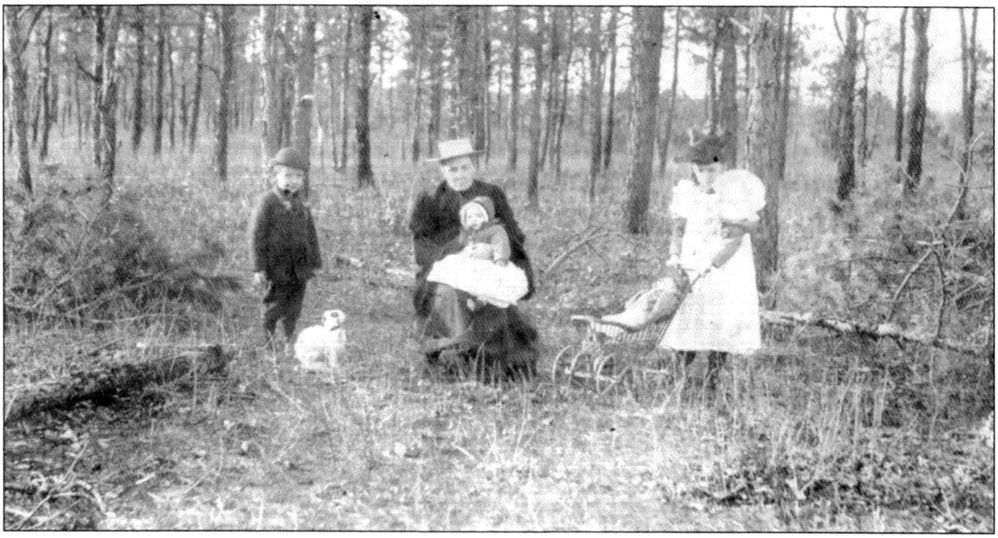

This 1896 photograph captures the conditions of what the settlers faced in the Brentwood-Central Islip area in the 19th century. The Pulling family, recent Irish immigrant arrivals, pose in the rugged landscape. Although they were Central Islip residents, baptismal records indicate that the Pullings attended St. Anne's Church in Brentwood, at least until a Catholic church was built in their own community. (Courtesy of the Sr. Anne Pulling Collection, Central Islip Library.)

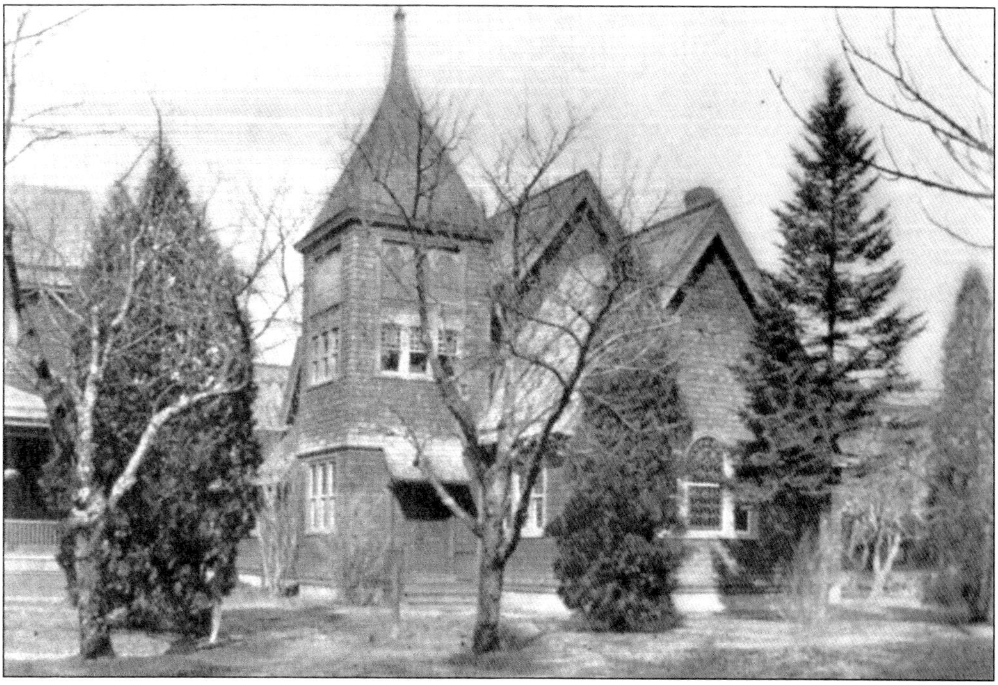

The original Brentwood Presbyterian Church was located on Brentwood Road. The congregation formed in November 1891, and the cornerstone was laid in December of that same year. The church officially opened in 1893 and remained there until a modern church was built just off Third Avenue. The building became the meeting hall of the Brentwood Free and Accepted Masons, Lodge of Antiquity No. 11 and is still in use today. This image is from 1905. (Courtesy of the James Fordyce Collection.)

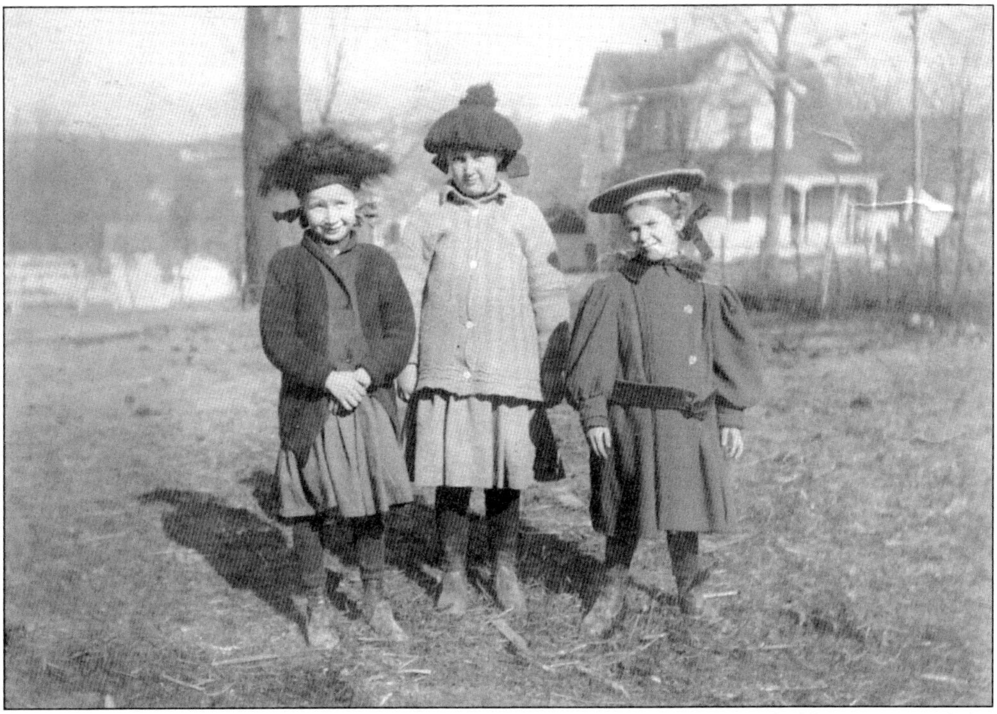

Three unidentified girls are seen here. The clothing indicates that it is probably winter, and the style points to the late 1890s. (Courtesy of the Brentwood Public Library.)

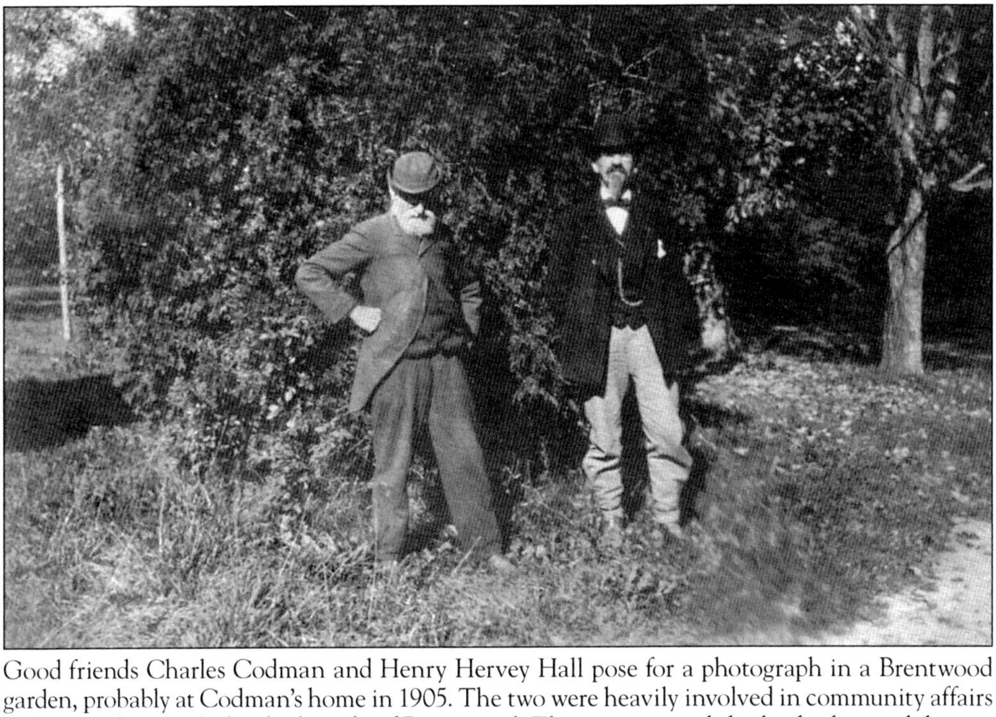

Good friends Charles Codman and Henry Hervey Hall pose for a photograph in a Brentwood garden, probably at Codman's home in 1905. The two were heavily involved in community affairs and worked tirelessly for the benefit of Brentwood. They represented the leadership and driving force behind Brentwood's early days. (Courtesy of the Brentwood Public Library.)

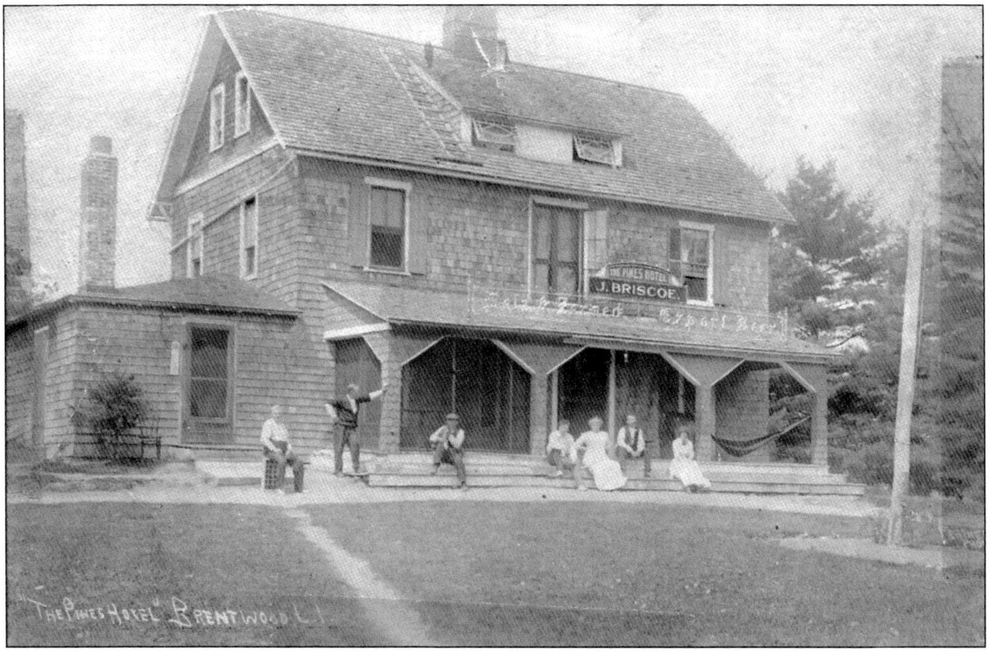

The Pines Hotel was owned and operated by J. Briscoe in the 1870s. It was a popular attraction and stood on the corner of Washington Avenue and Suffolk Avenue. The Pines Hotel eventually burned down, and the site was later occupied by a Texaco gas station. (Courtesy of the Brentwood Public Library.)

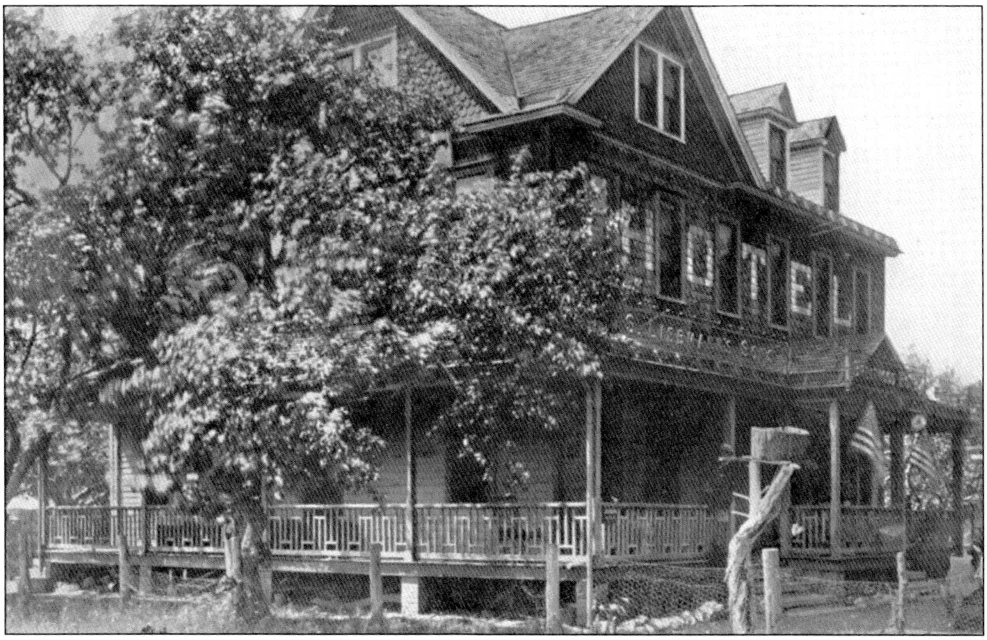

The Brentwood Hotel, seen here in 1888, was built by Charles Freund on the west side of Brentwood Road. It operated well into the mid-20th century as a hotel and later as a restaurant. It became one of the most popular and successful establishments in the community. The building still stands today. (Courtesy of the James Fordyce Collection.)

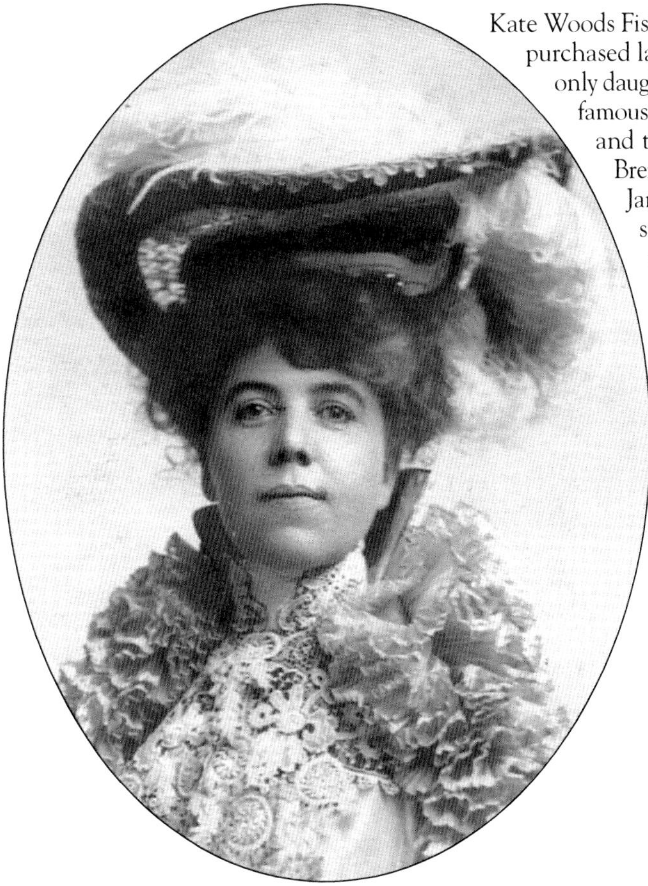

Kate Woods Fiske (1862–1947), a famous actress, purchased land in Brentwood in 1895. Kate's only daughter died in infancy. Kate married famous playwright James Kyrle McCurdy, and the two spent time in and out of Brentwood. She returned in 1936 after James died in Hollywood and lived in seclusion. As an author, she wrote under the name Katharine Wald. She is buried in the Brentwood Cemetery next to her daughter. (Courtesy of the Brentwood Public Library.)

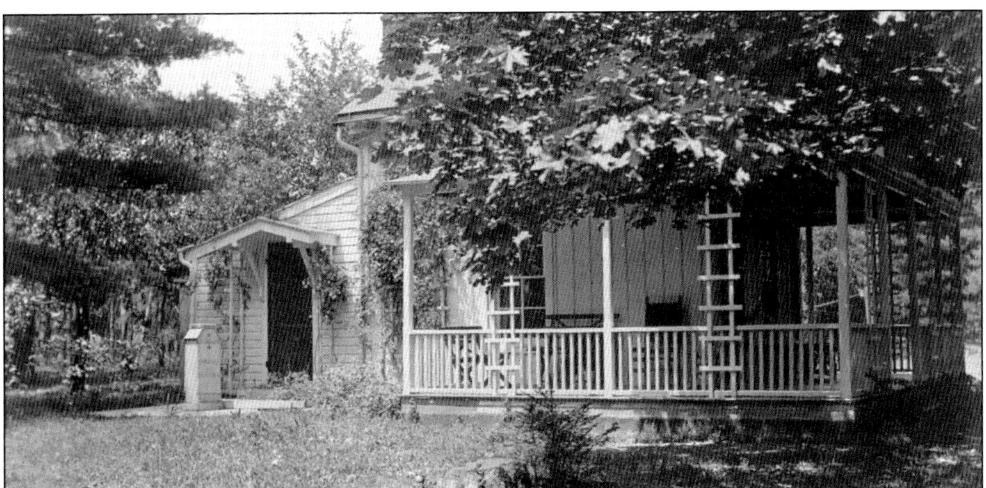

Actress and writer Kate Woods Fiske's home on the west side of Washington Avenue is seen here. It was originally used as a weekend retreat from her stage work in the city when she bought the property in 1895. Her husband, playwright James Kyrle McCurdy, wrote several plays at their Brentwood residence. Kate retired there in complete seclusion in 1935 following her husband's death. She passed away there in 1947. (Courtesy of the Brentwood Public Library.)

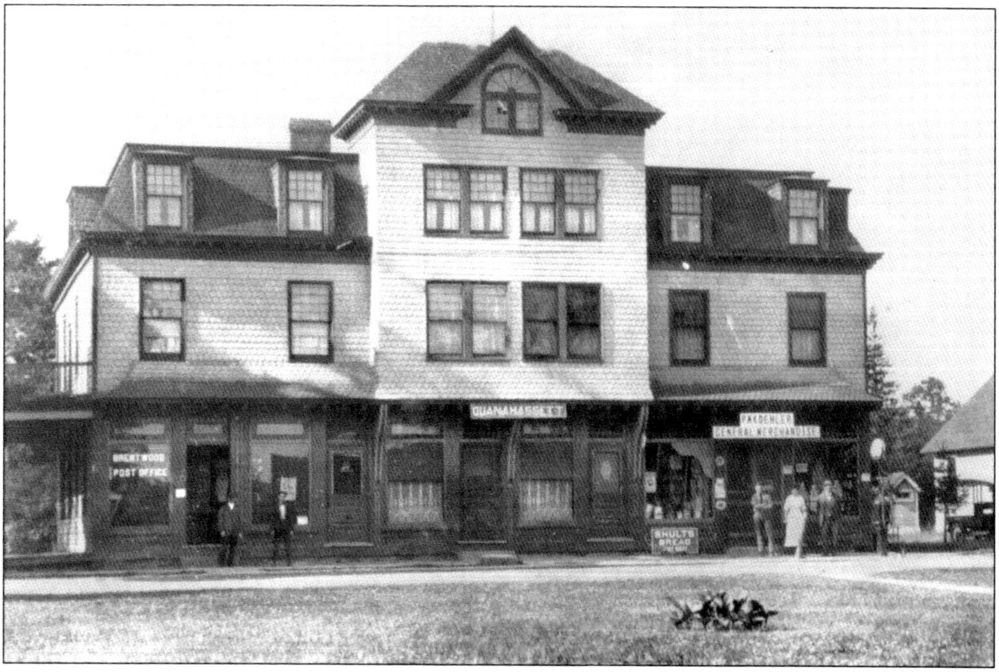

The Quanahassett Hotel was built in 1890 on First Avenue, opposite the train station. The hotel housed a general store operated by the Koehler family, a telegraph office, and the Brentwood Post Office. The congregations of the Presbyterian Church and St. Anne's Catholic Church utilized the hotel while the churches were under construction. The hotel operated until the 1920s and is still standing today. (Courtesy of the Brentwood Public Library.)

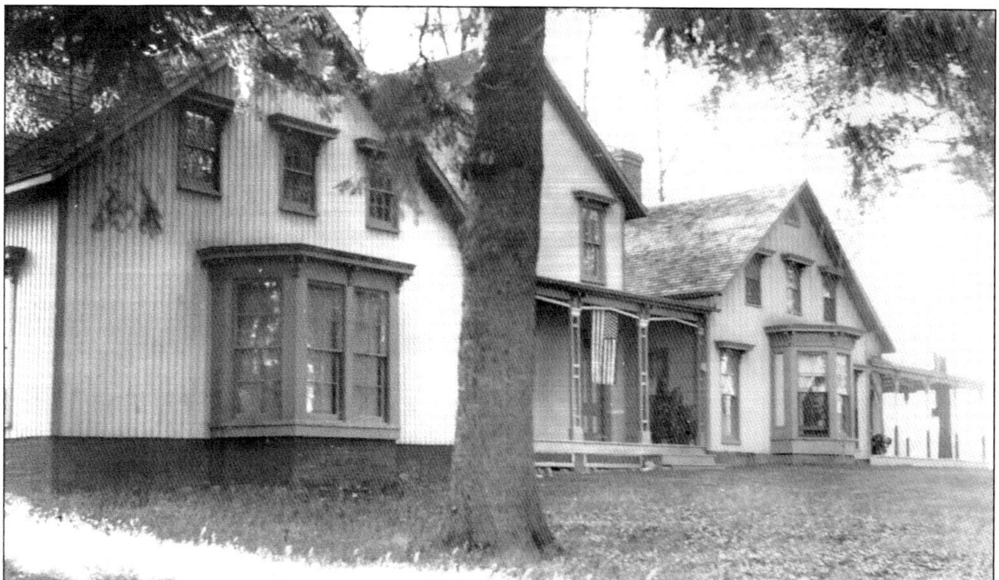

Charles Arbuckle and his brother John, multimillionaires in the coffee trade, purchased the Platt estate in 1885. The south wing, seen here, was built just after the Civil War. The Arbuckle Palace as it was sometimes known, was one of numerous properties the family owned. In the early 20th century, it was briefly a hotel. (Courtesy of the Brentwood Public Library.)

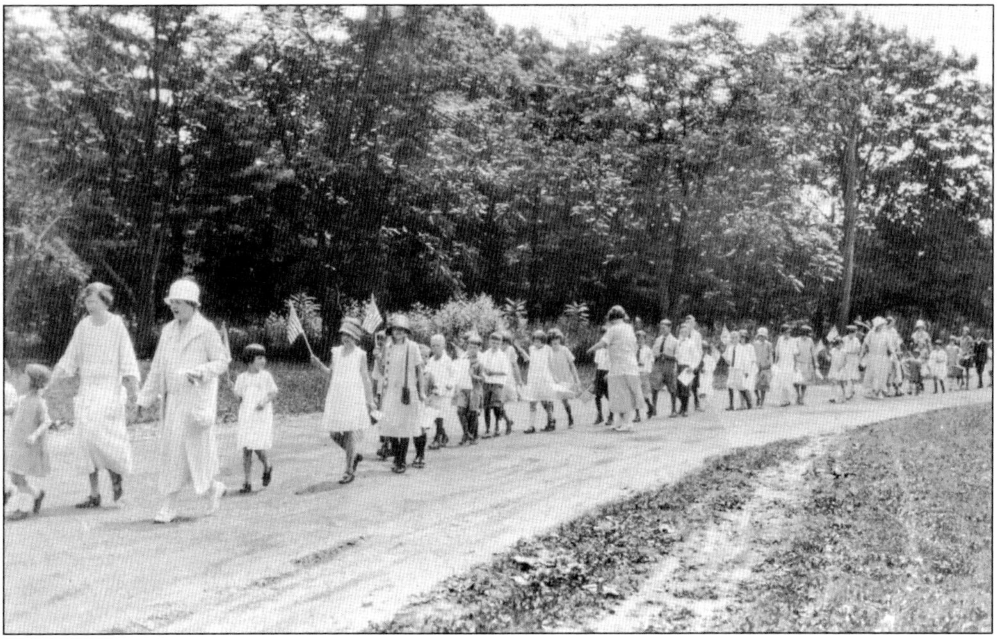

For a town founded on the basis of anarchy, rejecting formal laws and government, Brentwood became one of the most patriotic communities in Islip Town. Here, Brentwood schoolchildren march in Brentwood's Independence Day parade on July 4, 1913, a tradition that continued until the Great Depression. (Courtesy of the Brentwood Public Library.)

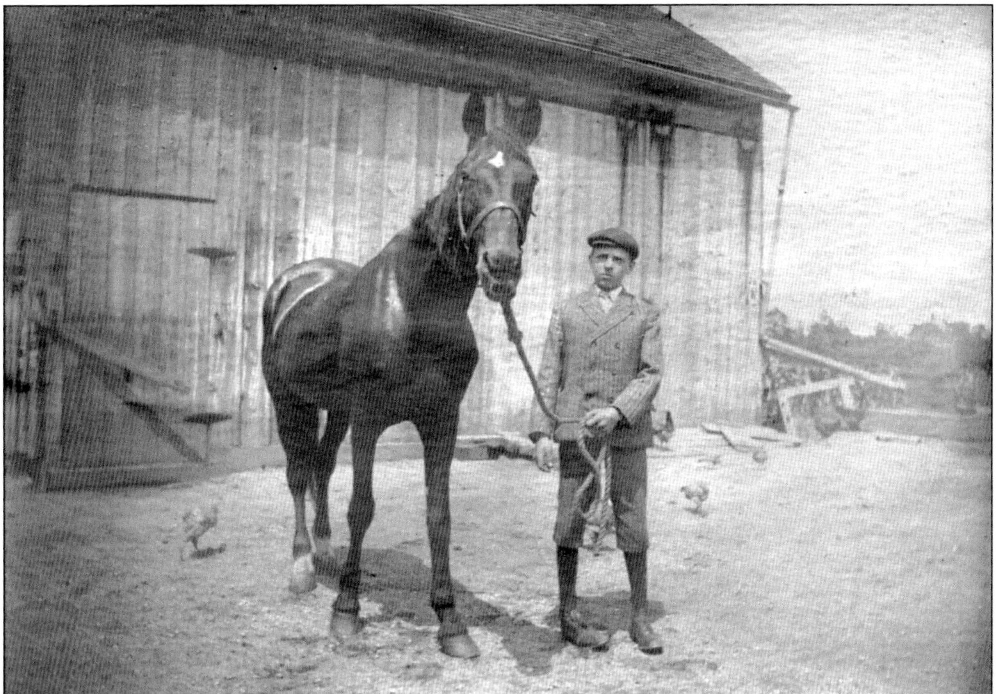

Clemence "Clem" A. Taylor is seen here working at the family barn on Wicks Road around 1900. (Courtesy of Jeanne L. Taylor.)

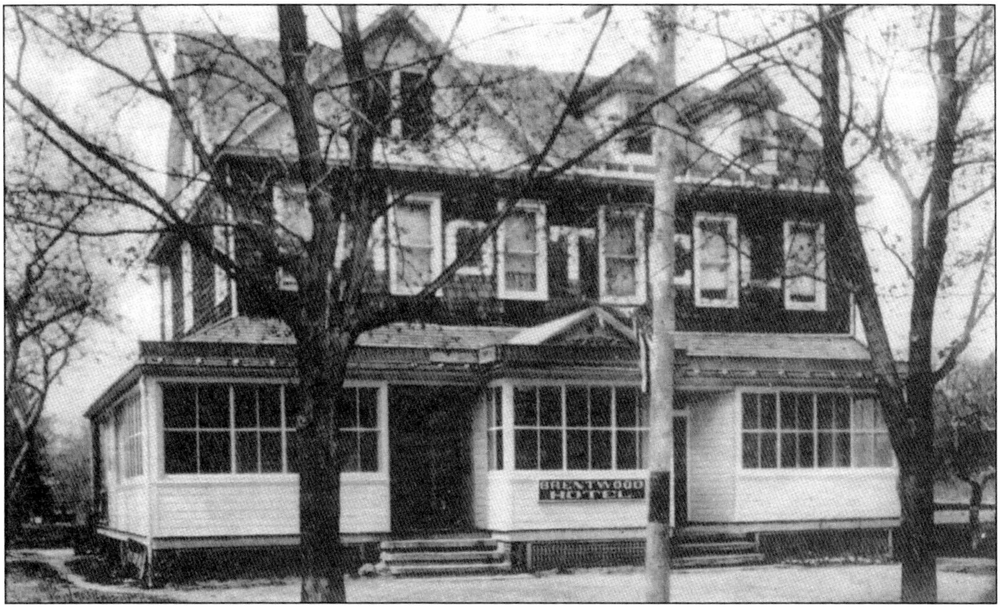

The Brentwood Hotel became extremely popular with visitors and locals alike and became a favorite meeting spot for residents and community organizations. In the 20th century, the hotel had received some minor alterations; notably the wraparound porch had become entirely enclosed, offering additional room and dining space This was advantageous when the hotel became a restaurant. The image above is from a c. 1920s postcard. (Courtesy of the James Fordyce Collection.)

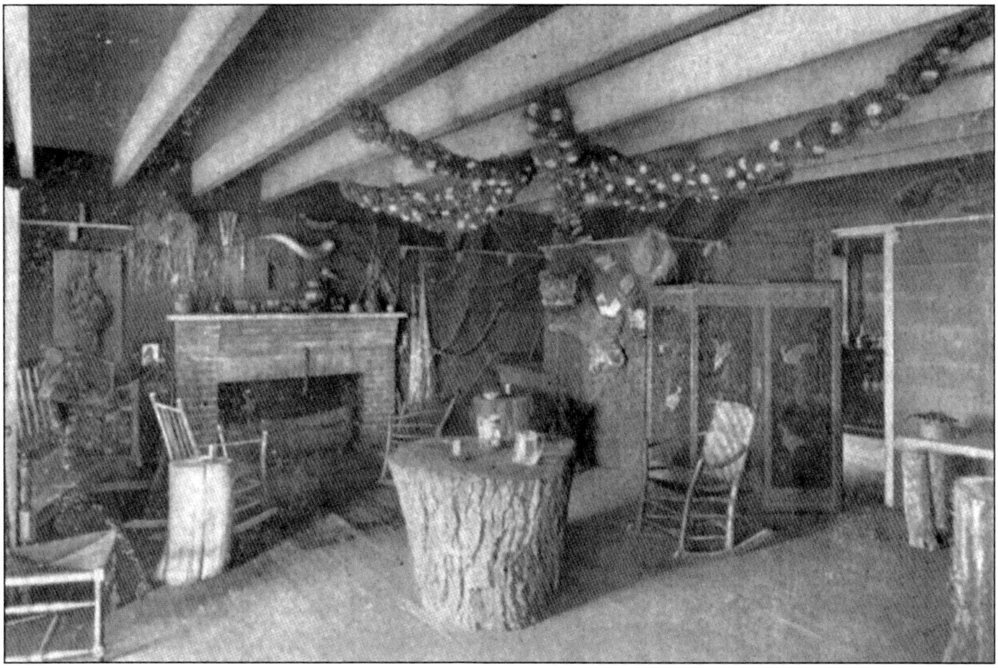

After the Wicks family moved out of Thompson's Station and the facility closed, the former station found a second life as the Piney Woods Inn. The hotel served many visitors who were looking to breathe the air of the pine belt. This interior shot of the café at the Piney Woods Inn at Brentwood is from an early advertisement. (Courtesy of the James Fordyce Collection.)

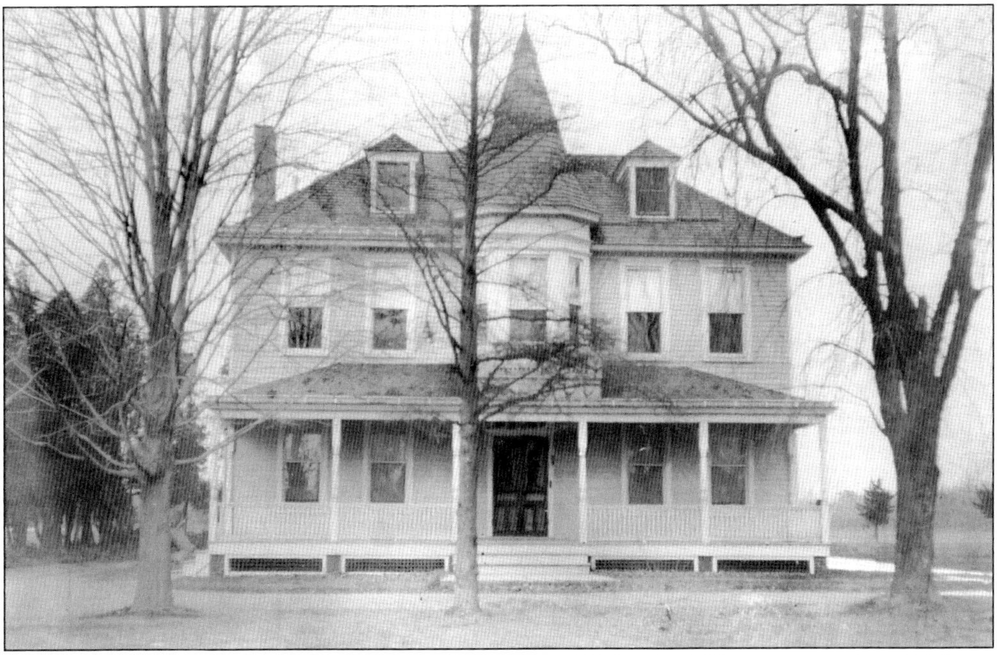

Pictured here in 1900, the Arborlea Inn was built in 1877 by Civil War veteran Capt. William A. Maury on the north side of Suffolk Avenue. The inn quickly became a favorite spot with tourists and locals alike. The inn changed ownership several times and has undergone several renovations. Today, the building remains as an apartment complex called Arborlea Apartments. (Courtesy of the Brentwood Public Library.)

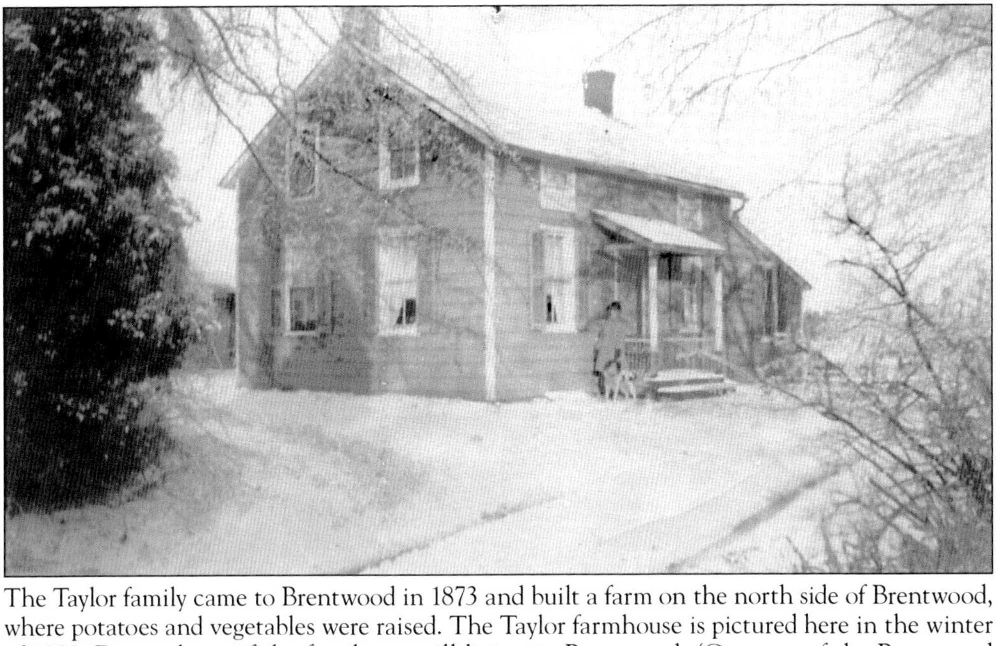

The Taylor family came to Brentwood in 1873 and built a farm on the north side of Brentwood, where potatoes and vegetables were raised. The Taylor farmhouse is pictured here in the winter of 1888. Descendants of the family are still living in Brentwood. (Courtesy of the Brentwood Public Library.)

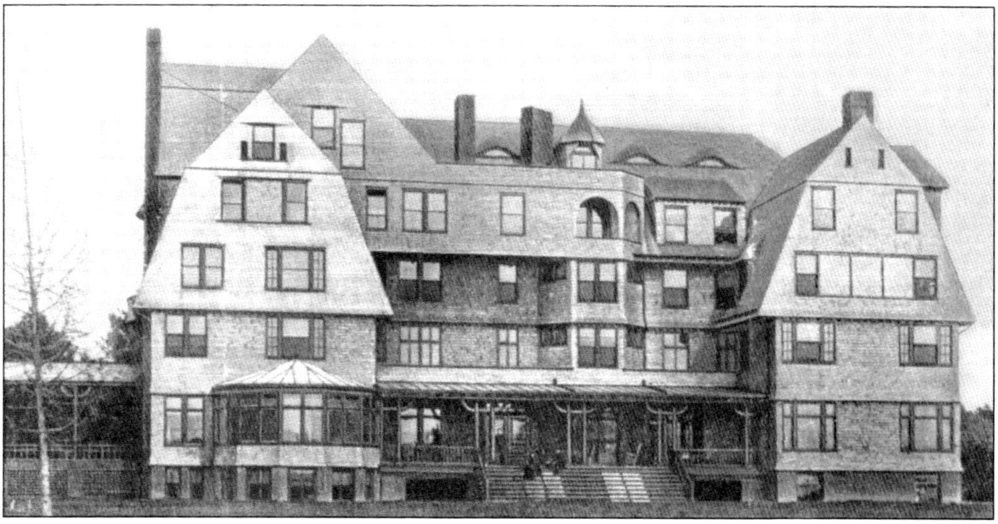

To build a grand and magnificent hotel and resort in the Brentwood Pines, the Studley-Kellam-Hart Syndicate, already operating the Hotel Brentwood, constructed the massive and luxurious Austral Hotel. The Austral had 135 rooms with accommodations for 235 guests. Dr. William Ross was hired on as the physician. The hotel opened its doors in 1888, but by 1892, the company was bankrupt and the grand hotel was forced to close. (Courtesy of the Richard H. Handley Collection of Long Island Americana, Smithtown Special Library District.)

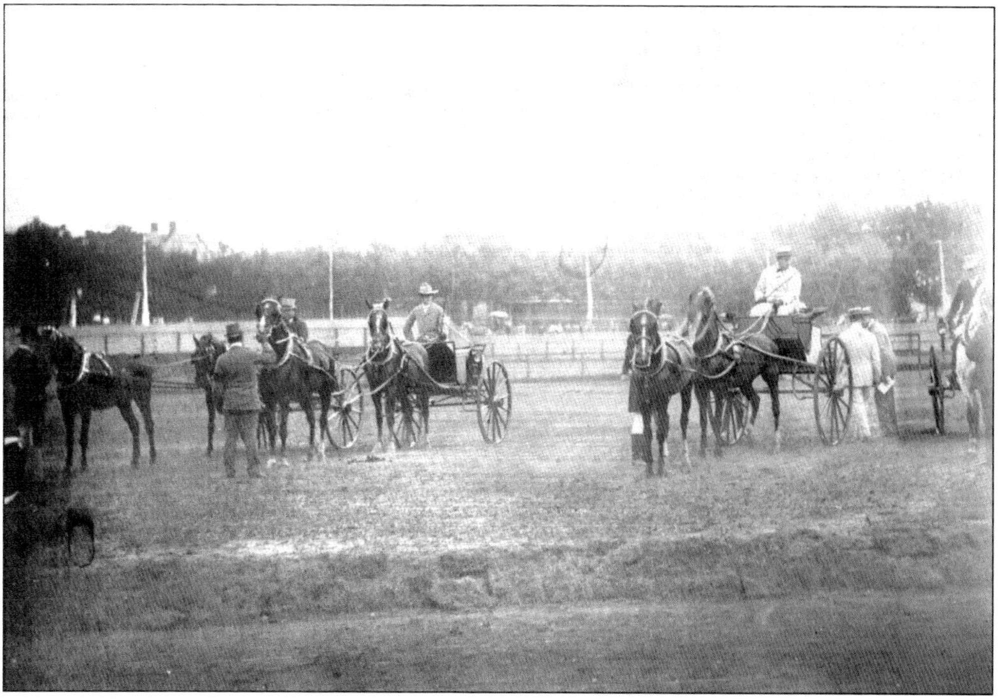

Brentwood's horse racing track was a local hot spot for residents and tourists. A half-mile-long track, it was located just off Wicks Road, a few blocks north of where the Pathmark now sits. This is the only known image of the track with carriages and visitors and the track in the background in either the 1880s or 1890s. The track closed in the early 20th century. (Courtesy of Jeanne L. Taylor.)

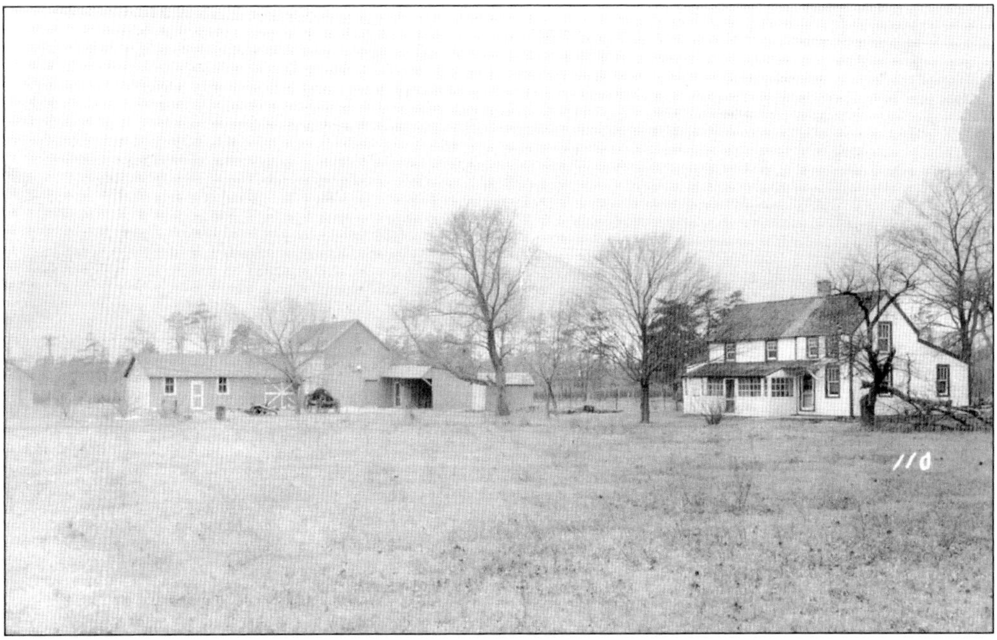

A farm in the Brentwood-Central Islip area is seen here between 1890 and 1905. Farming was one of the main industries of the area, but orchards eventually gave way to Long Island's primary cash crop—potatoes. By 1915, almost all farms in the area were producing potatoes as well as corn, wheat, and other grain stuffs. (Courtesy of the Sr. Anne Pulling Collection, Central Islip Library.)

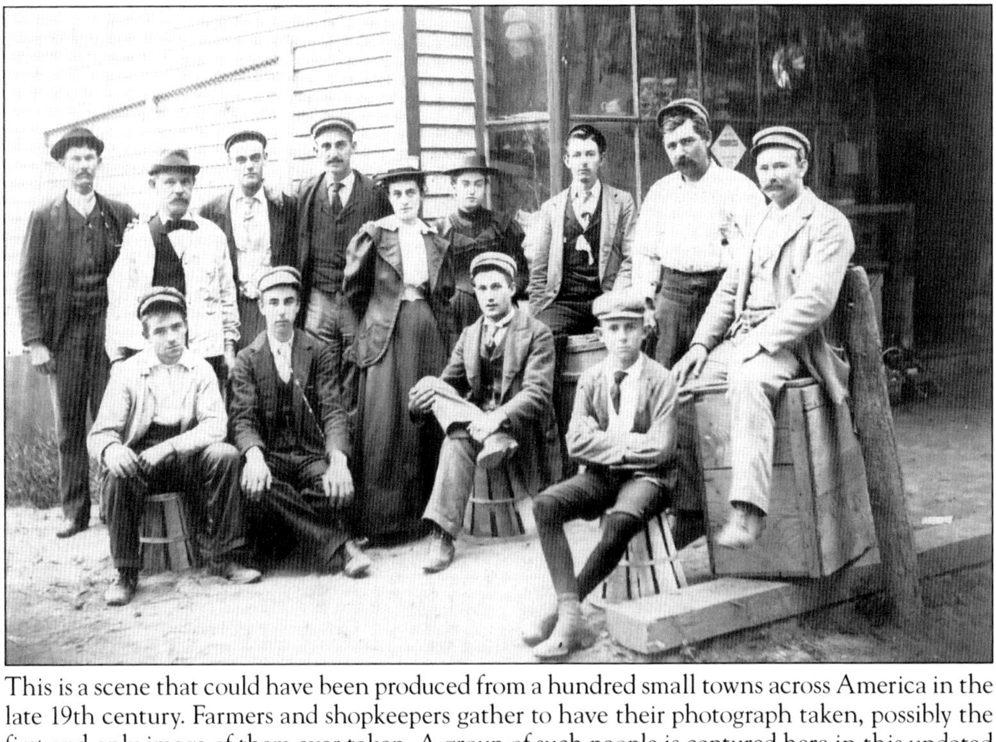

This is a scene that could have been produced from a hundred small towns across America in the late 19th century. Farmers and shopkeepers gather to have their photograph taken, possibly the first and only image of them ever taken. A group of such people is captured here in this undated photograph. (Courtesy of the Brentwood Public Library.)

Three

Into the 20th Century

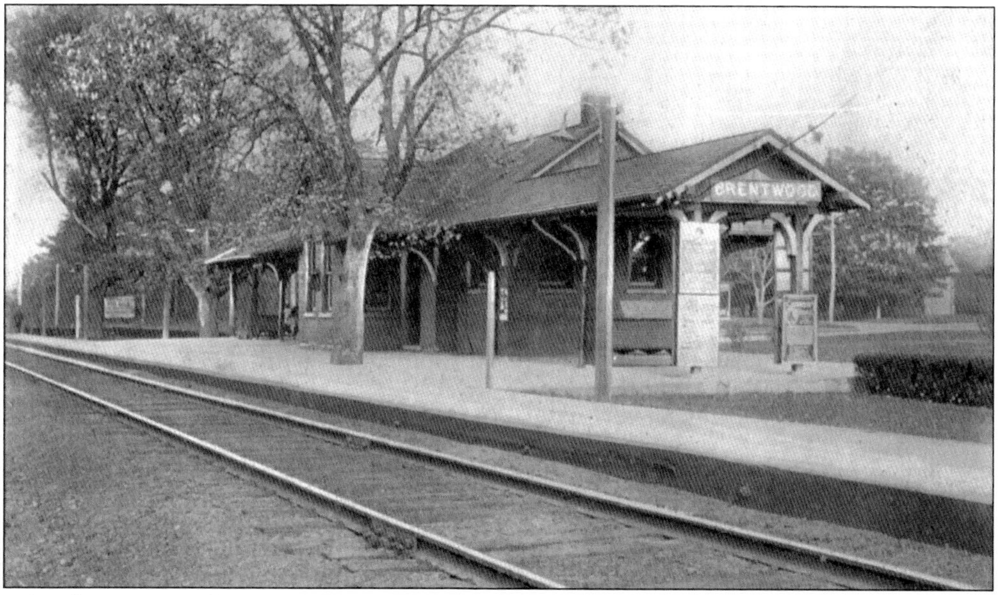

After the Brentwood Railroad Station burned down in 1905, a larger, multiroom brick station was built by the Long Island Rail Road at the same spot on First Avenue. The station operated from 1907 until the 1980s, when the line was electrified and a new modern elevated platform station was built a few yards east down the track. (Courtesy of the Brentwood Public Library.)

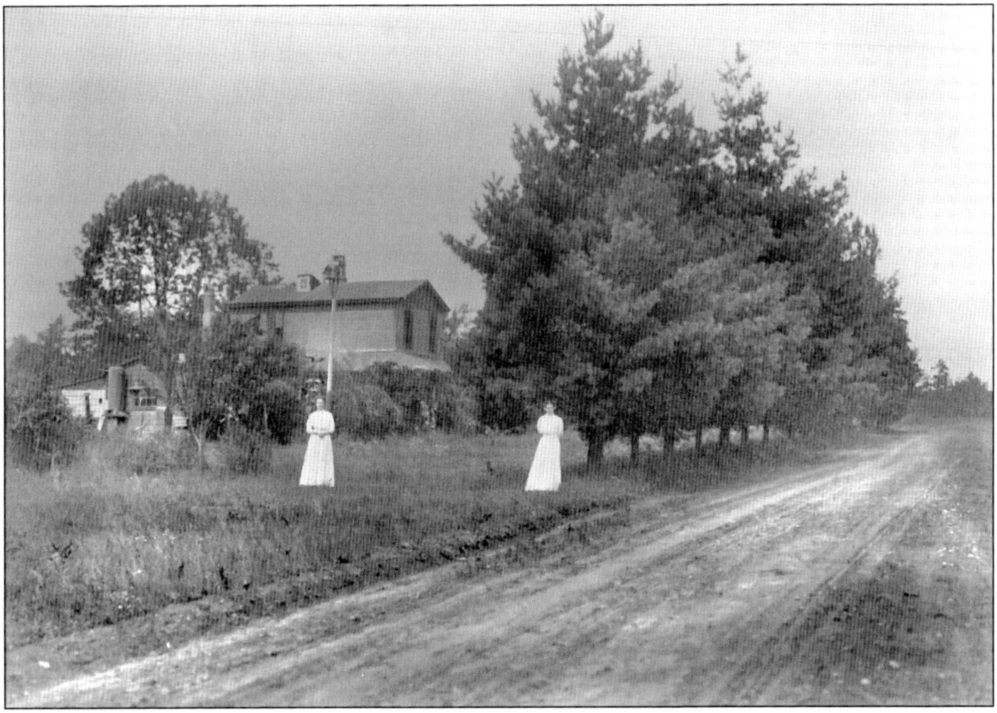

In this view looking north in 1908, members of the Ayling family pose with their home in the background on Madison Avenue. (Courtesy of the Brentwood Public Library.)

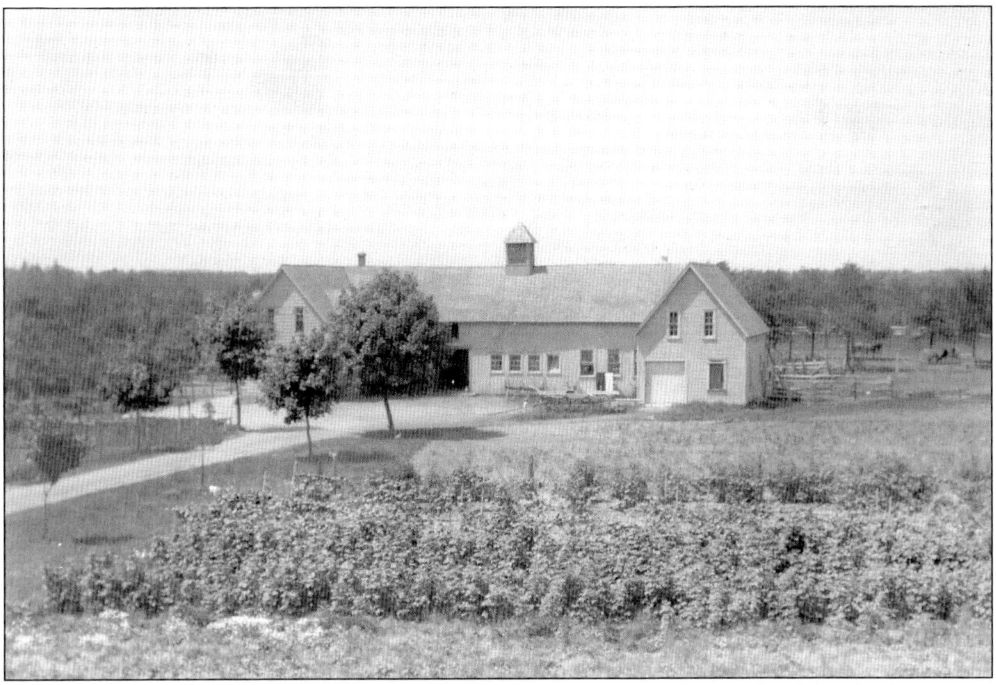

Seen here is Knoll Farm around 1900. Known largely as a horse farm and stable, the farm in its early days also boasted orchards and other produce grown in adjacent fields. (Courtesy of the Brentwood Public Library.)

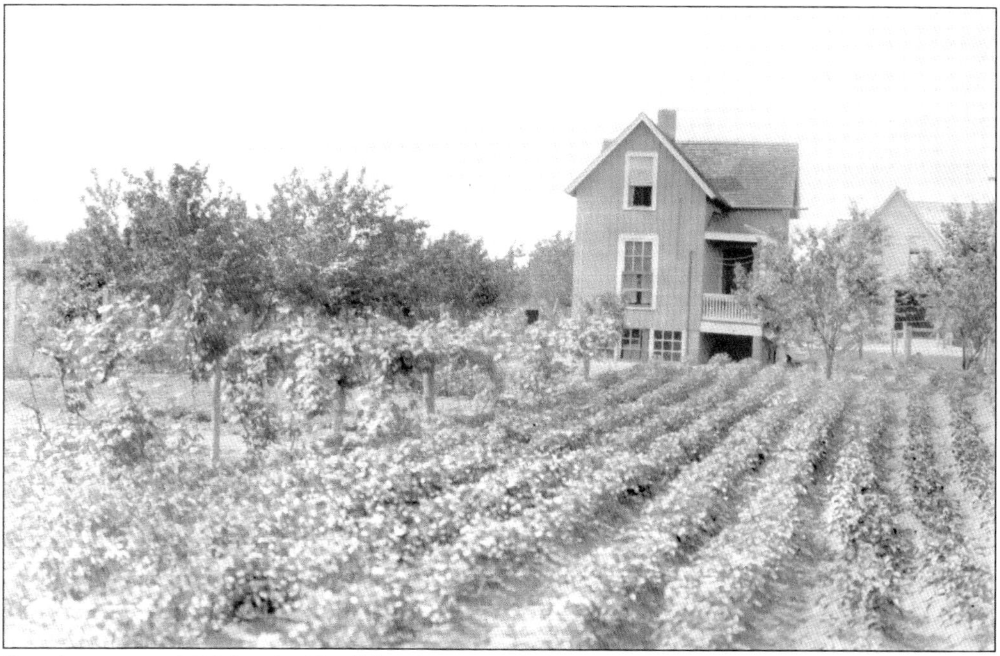

Seen here around 1900 is the Knoll farmhouse with the barn in the background and the planting field with orchards behind the house. (Courtesy of the Brentwood Public Library.)

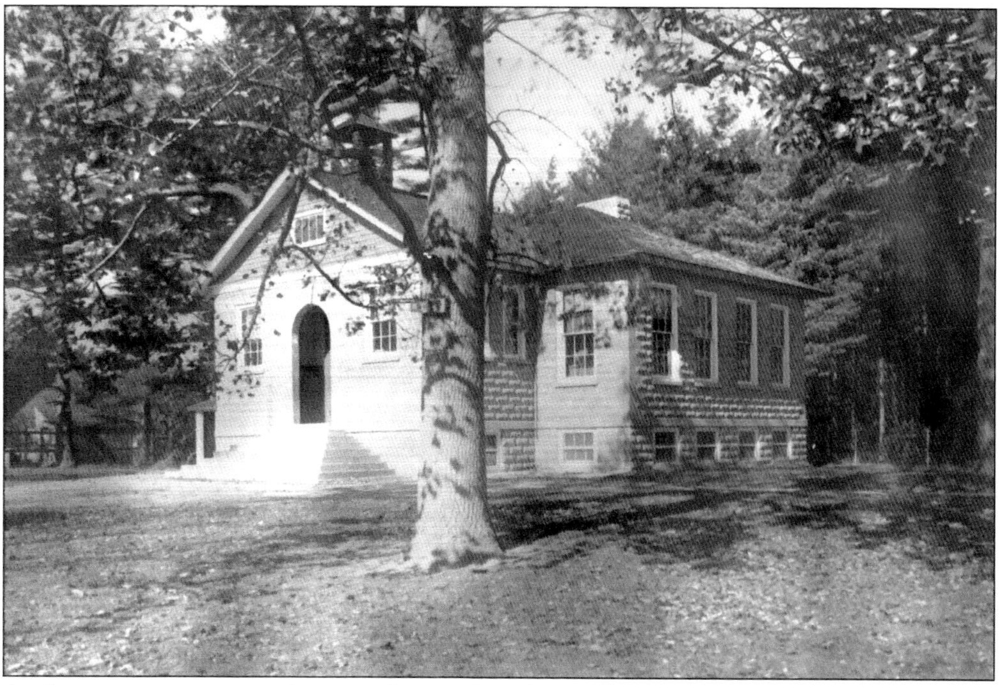

As the community grew, it became obvious that the small one-room schoolhouse had outlived its usefulness and a larger school was needed. The second schoolhouse, also known as Building No. 2, was a two-room elementary school that began holding classes in 1907. It was built at a cost of $5,000 and was located on the corner of Third Avenue and Fourth Street. (Courtesy of the Brentwood Public Library.)

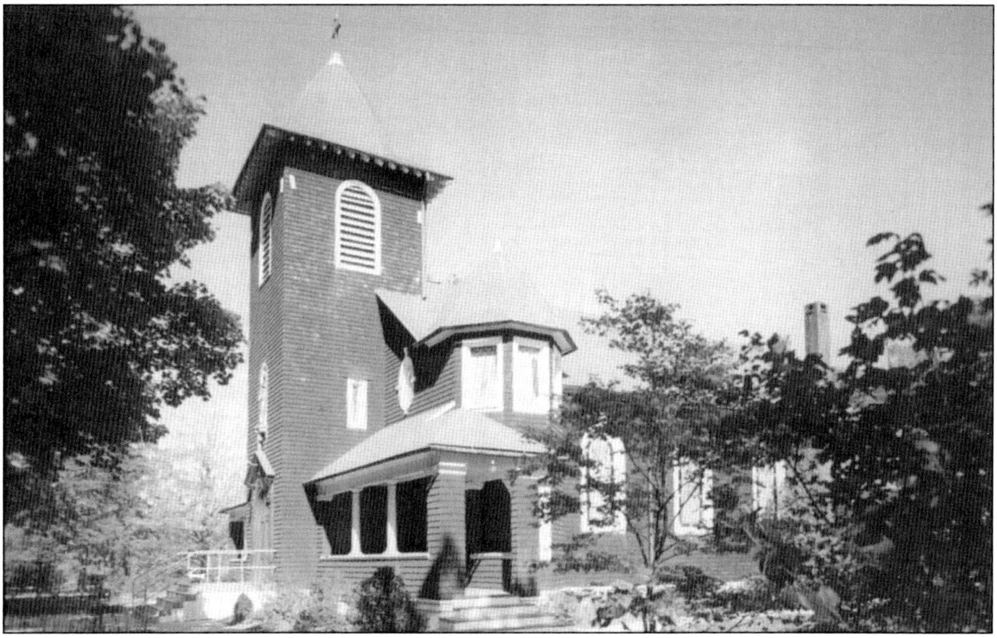

St. Anne's Catholic Church was the first Catholic congregation in Brentwood and traces its origins back to 1895. The Van Nostrand family helped organize the Brentwood Catholics and oversaw the construction of the church in 1897. Originally called St. Anne's in the Pines, the congregation quickly and steadily grew through the 20th century. The original St. Anne's was demolished to make room for a larger modern structure in 1970. (Courtesy of the James Fordyce Collection.)

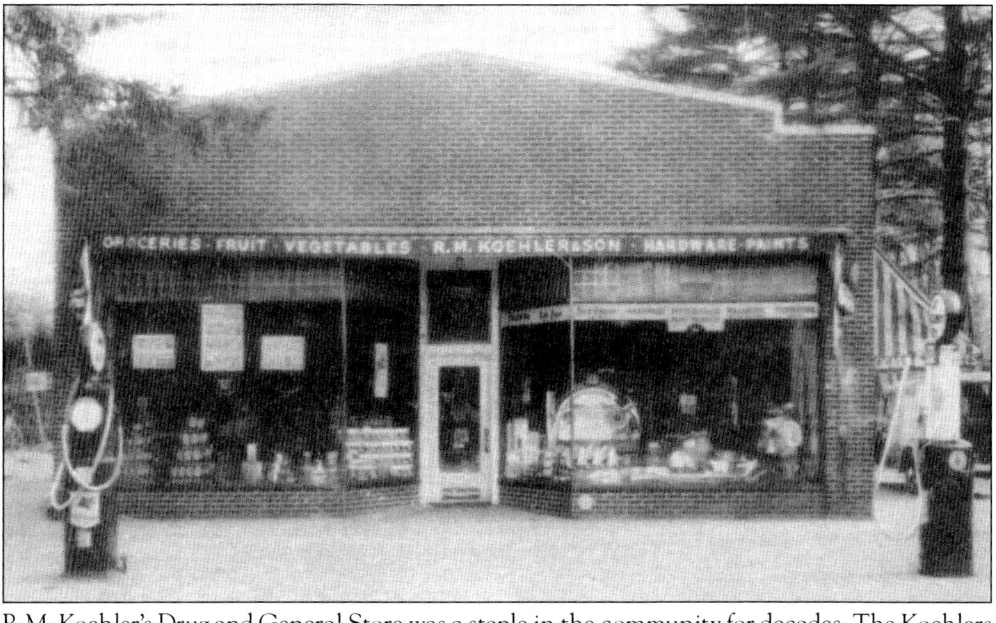

R.M. Koehler's Drug and General Store was a staple in the community for decades. The Koehlers moved their store out of the Quanahassett Hotel on First Avenue and built this general store on Brentwood Road. The store sold groceries, hardware, gasoline, and other products. The Koehlers had postcards of Brentwood produced and sold in their store. Numerous renovations later, the building still stands today. (Courtesy of the James Fordyce Collection.)

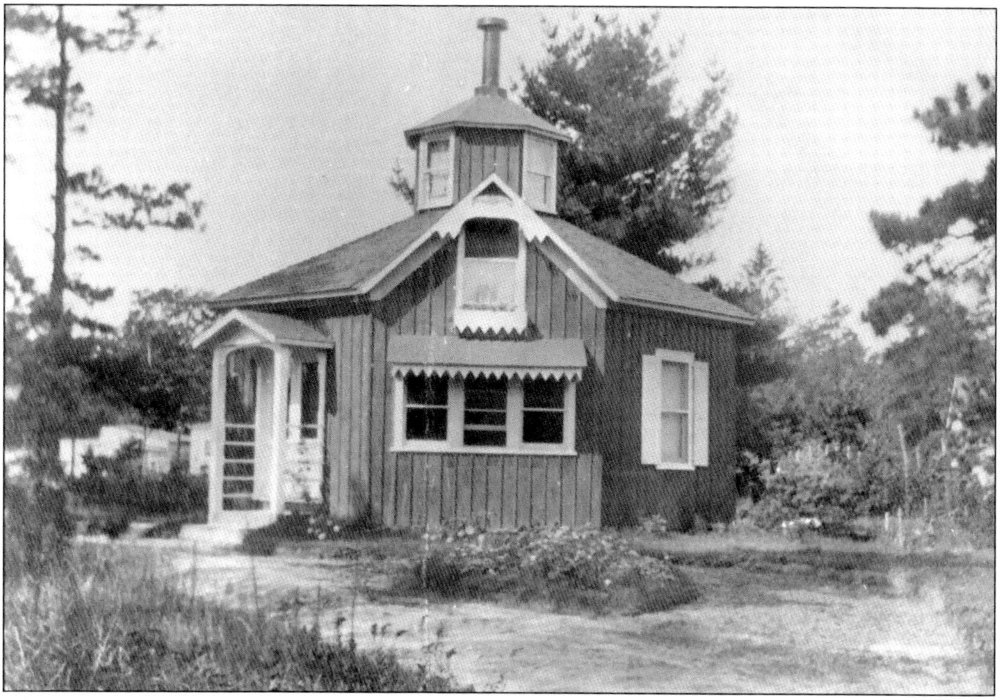

This image is of the former one-room octagon schoolhouse around 1910; once it ceased operations, it was moved and became a private residence. It would remain a private home for the better part of the 20th century before being abandoned and falling into disrepair. (Courtesy of the Brentwood Public Library.)

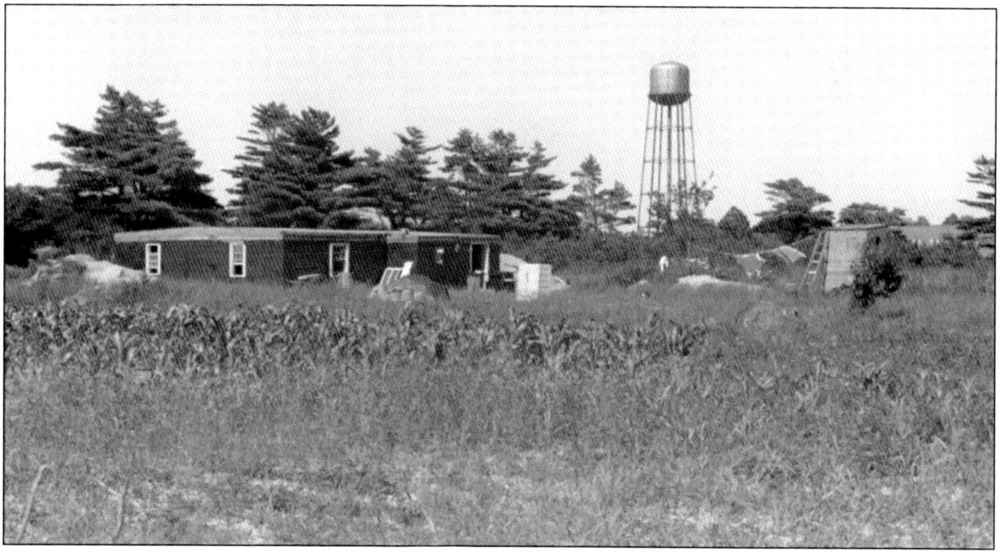

This 1930s image captures Depression-era Brentwood. The Great Depression took its toll on many farms and businesses in the area, and a small "Hooverville" developed along the railroad tracks and the Pine Aire Drive/Third Avenue Corridor. This view of the shanty town is looking east from Fifth Avenue toward the area that today contains the Hess gas station, Brentwood Legion Ambulance, and Brentwood Youth Activities baseball fields. (Courtesy of the Brentwood Public Library.)

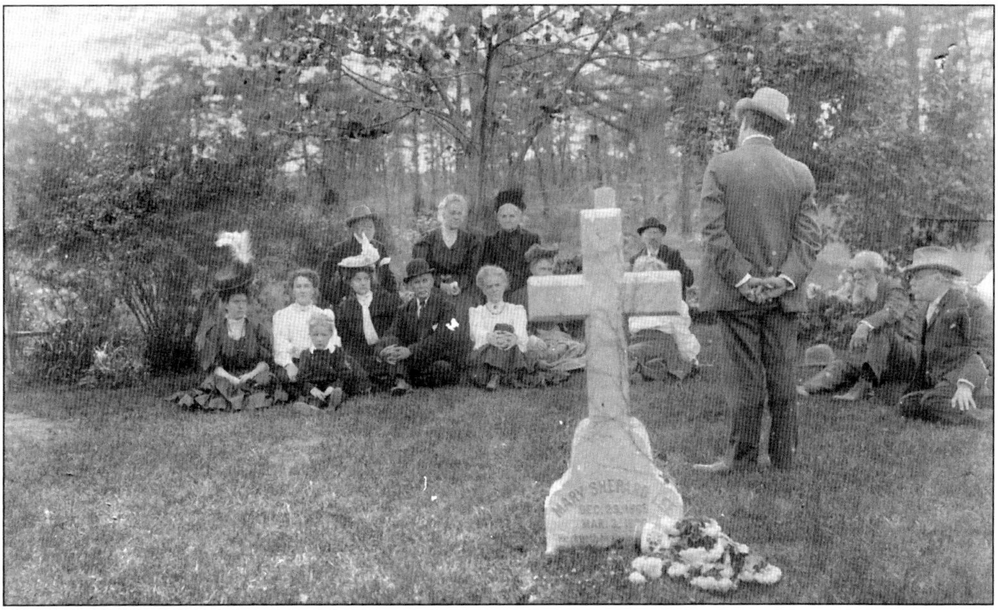

Original settler Edward F. Linton, who was a child at Modern Times, addresses Brentwood residents at the Brentwood Cemetery on Decoration Day (Memorial Day) on May 30, 1905. Here, he eulogizes the original colonists of Modern Times. That eulogy speech was entitled *Fifty Years After*. (Courtesy of the Brentwood Public Library.)

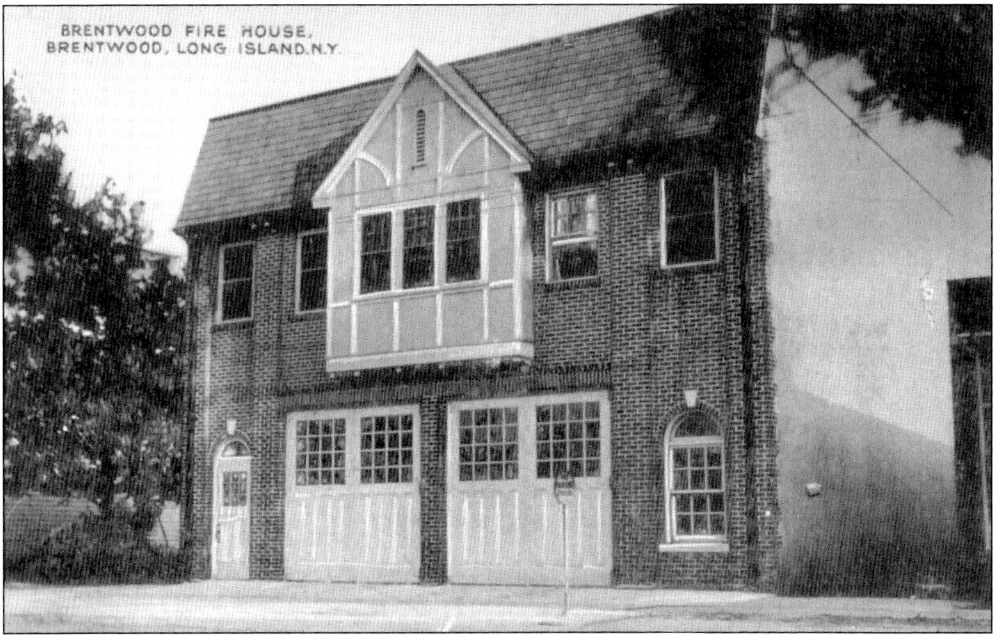

Brentwood Fire Department's first station is seen here, after renovations to house fire trucks and additional office space. The building is located on First Avenue and is seen here in a 1920s postcard. The building was also used as a community meeting place, which included use by the American Legion Post 1006 and St. Luke's Roman Catholic Church. The department headquarters building was erected behind this original structure. The building is a store today. (Courtesy of the James Fordyce Collection.)

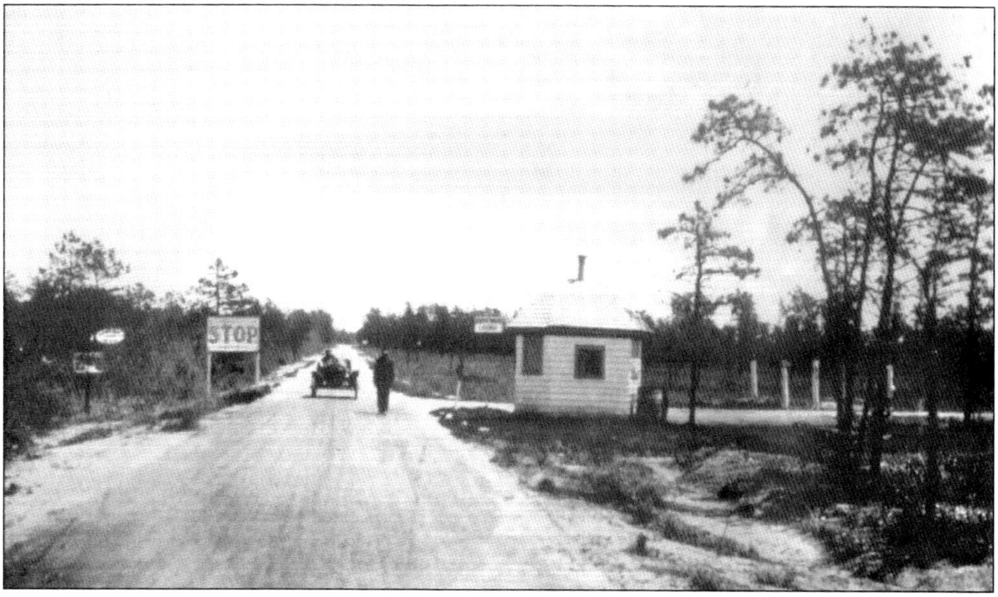

Vanderbilt's Motor Parkway formed Brentwood's northern border. Looking east is the Brentwood Toll Lodge with Washington Avenue directly behind it. Resident Thomas O'Rourke worked as the toll collector and is seen standing in the middle of the road in this 1911 photograph. This was the first of four Brentwood toll lodges and operated from 1911 to 1915, before it was moved several miles west to the intersection of Motor Parkway and Commack Road. (Courtesy of Al Velocci, Virginia MacMurray.)

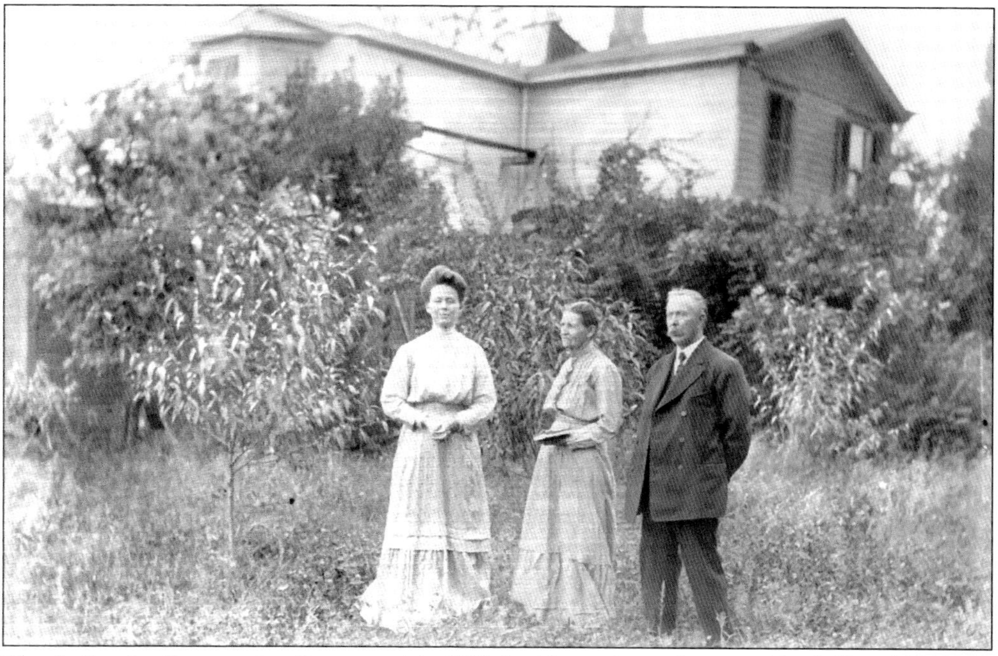

The Ayling family moved to Brentwood in 1893, building a home between Garfield and Madison Avenues. Mary Ayling (left) is seen in this 1914 image with her mother, Jesse May Ayling, and her father, Charles Graham Ayling, who worked for the Brentwood Realty Company and was a railroad station agent in Central Islip and a cabinet maker. (Courtesy of the Brentwood Public Library.)

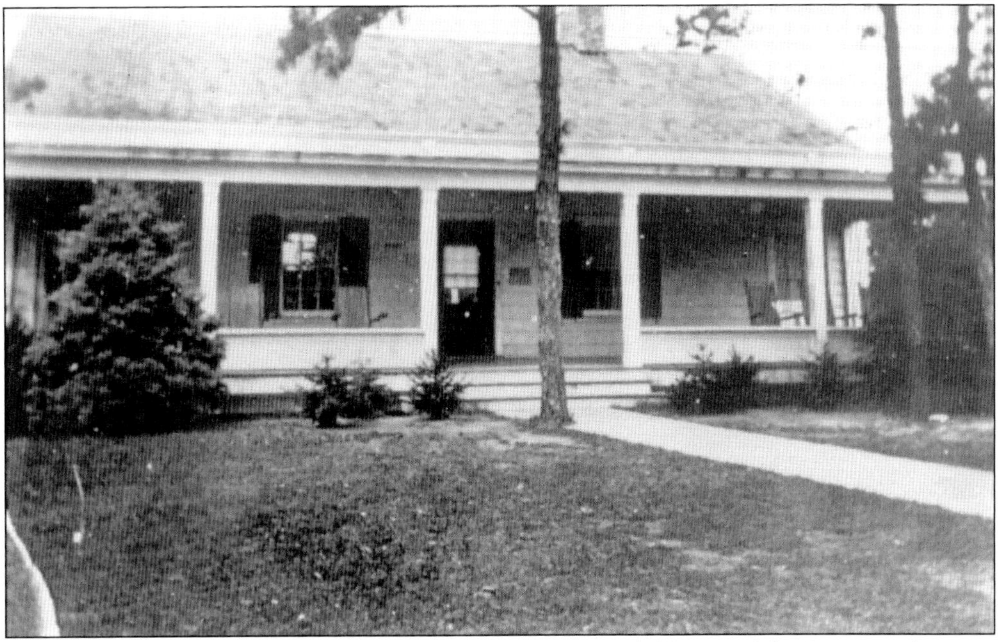

The first clubhouse of the Brentwood Golf and Country Club, built in 1920, is seen here. Although the clubhouse has changed, the Brentwood Country Club still attracts golf professionals today. (Courtesy of the Brentwood Public Library.)

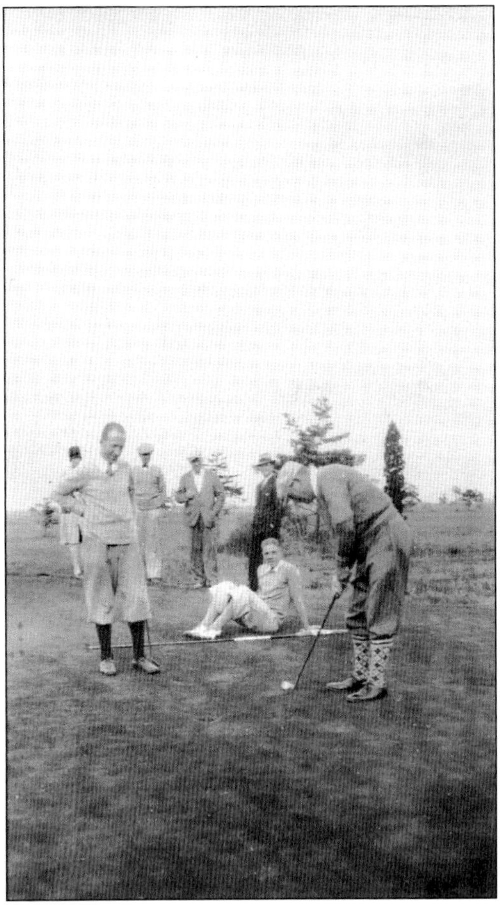

Golfers at Brentwood Country Club in 1925 are seen here. (Courtesy of the Brentwood Public Library.)

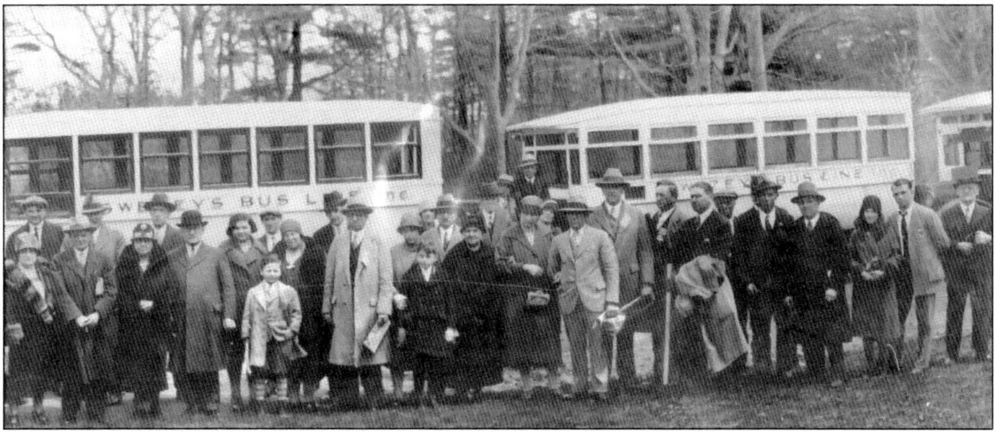

Brentwood Realty would host arrival ceremonies when new buyers arrived on specified days. New residents would take the train out and be picked up by buses that would take them to their new houses in Brentwood. In this scene near the train station, new immigrants are posing for a formal photograph before being brought to their new homes. (Courtesy of the Brentwood Public Library.)

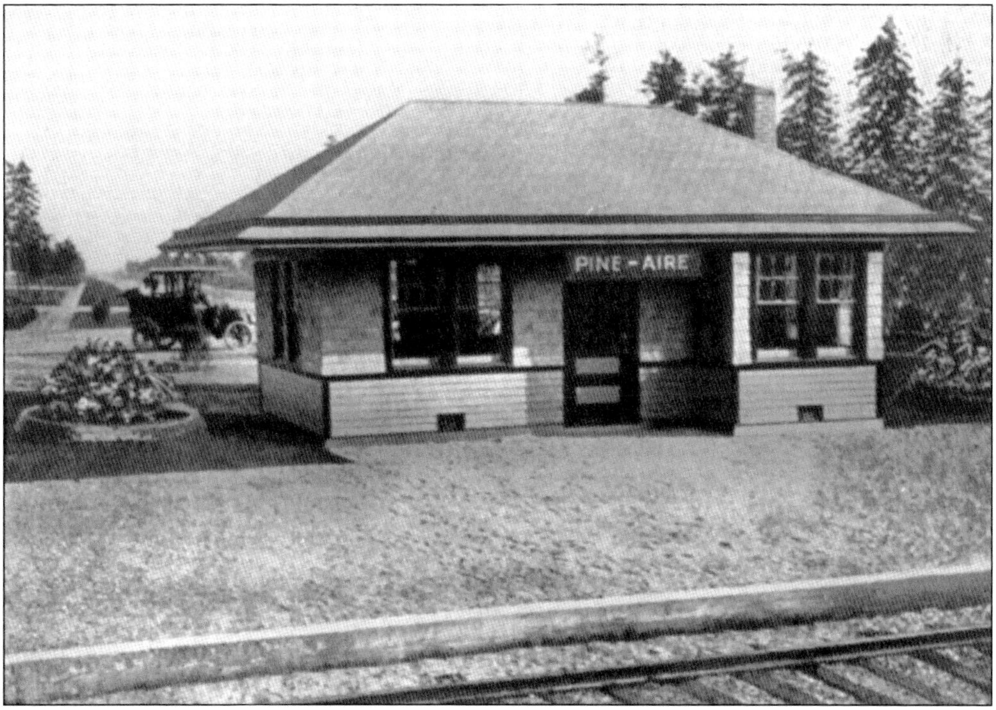

The Pine Aire Train Station was built at the intersection of Manatuck Boulevard and Pine Aire Drive, close to the original location of Thompson's Station. The Pine Aire Station was one of several train stations located in Brentwood and served the people in the western section of Brentwood. The building itself was eventually demolished, but the station continued to operate as a platform until the 1970s. This photograph was taken around 1910. (Courtesy of the Brentwood Public Library.)

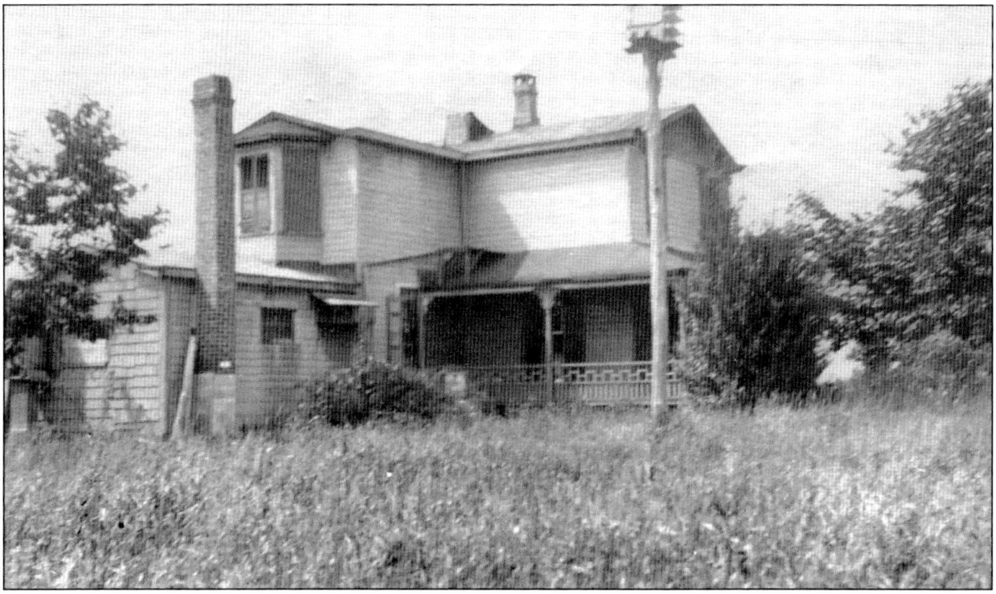

Seen here in 1924 is the Henry Kopf house on Madison Avenue, between Garfield and Le Grand Streets. It was demolished in 1962 to make room for the Long Island Expressway. (Courtesy of the Brentwood Public Library.)

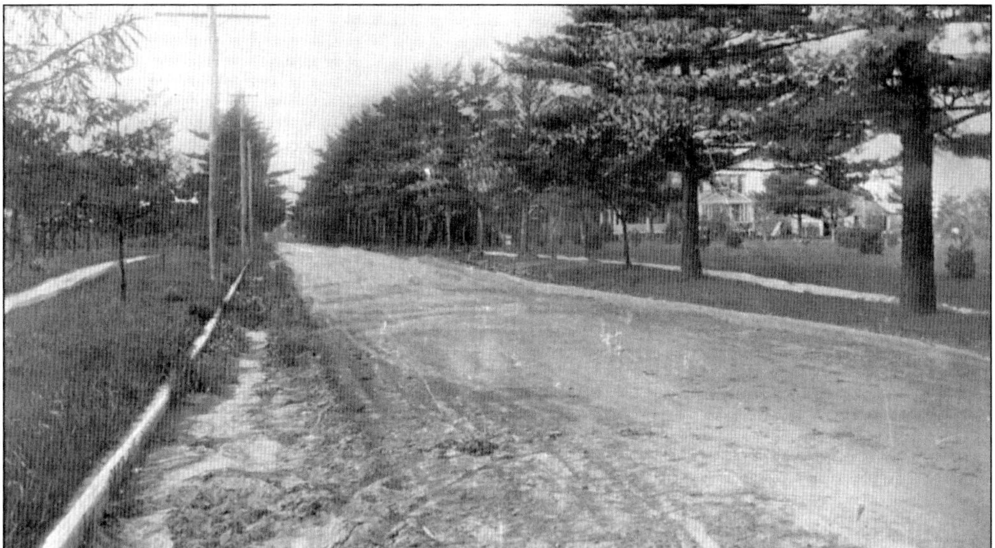

Seen here is a postcard image of Washington Avenue looking north in the 1920s. (Courtesy of the James Fordyce Collection.)

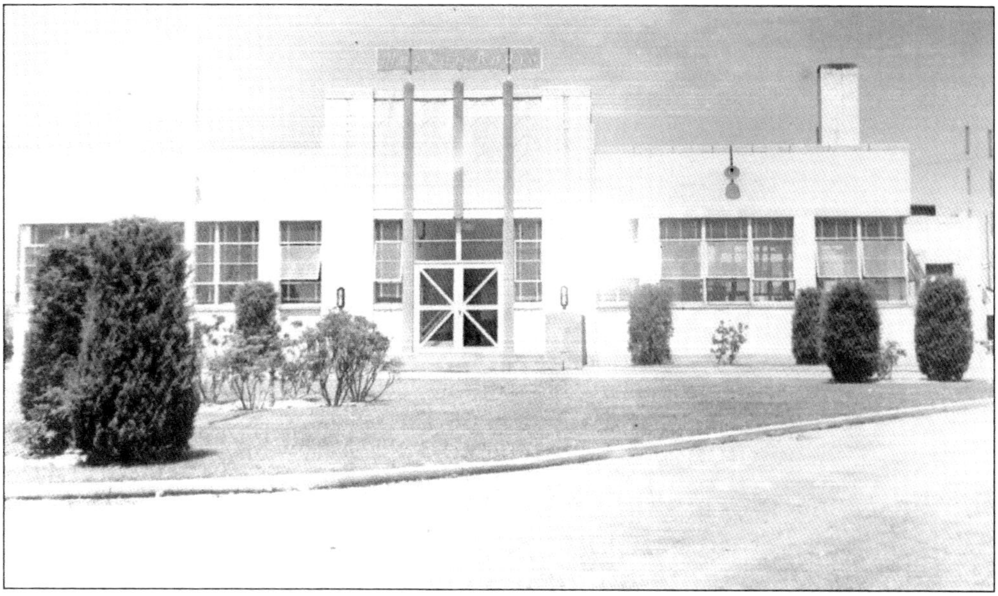

When Mackay Radio outgrew its Sayville location, construction began on a new station in North Brentwood in 1934 on a 1,100-acre site. The Brentwood Mackay Radio station went on the air in May 1935. The facility used radiotelegraph transmitting point-to-point communications worldwide. Traffic included telegrams, news and press, government correspondence, and military communiques. CBS operated *Voice of America* in a rear wing. It became ITT Worldcom and closed on August 31, 1986. (Courtesy of George Flanagan.)

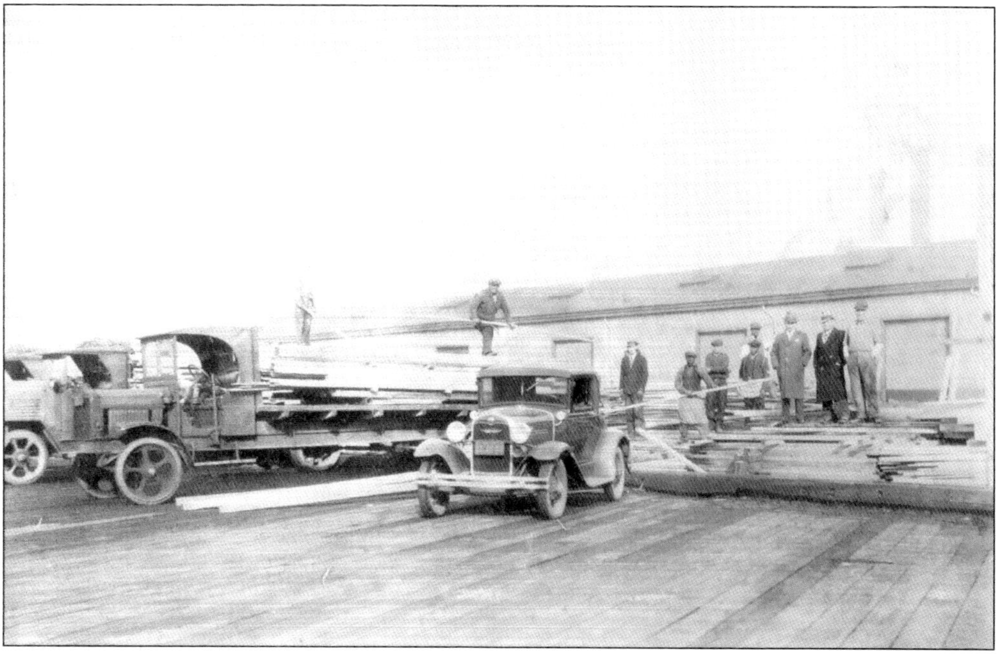

The Pilgrim Transportation Company was established in 1929 by proprietor William J. Jennings on Crooked Hill Road. It was one of many building supply and contracting companies in the area. Jennings's company was one of many subcontractors brought in to help build Pilgrim State Hospital. (Courtesy of Michael J. Grant Jr.)

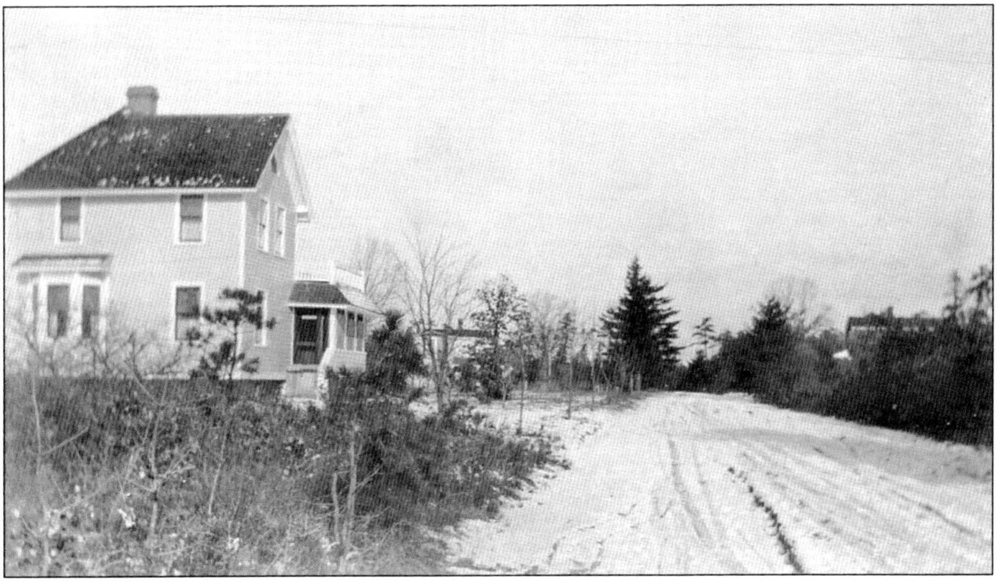

Mr. and Mrs. Alvah Blanchard's home on Madison Avenue between Arthur and Garfield Streets is seen here in 1913. (Courtesy of the Brentwood Public Library.)

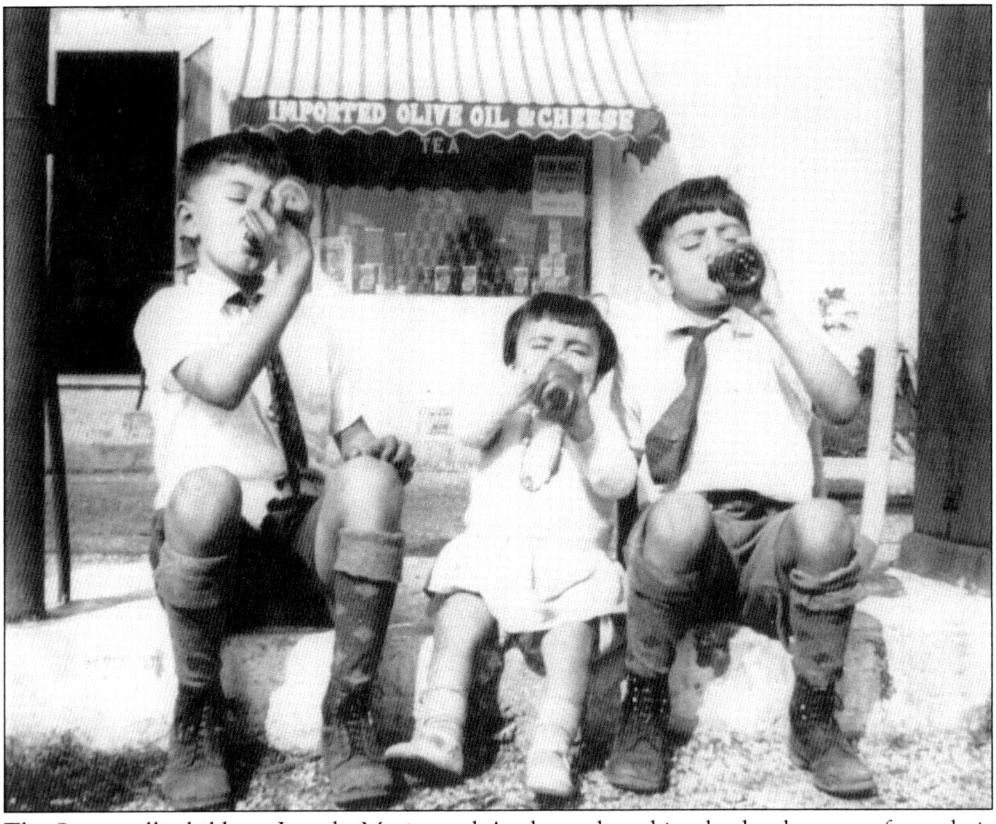

The Scimonelli children, Joseph, Marie, and Anthony, knocking back a beverage from their father's deli, which they are sitting in front of in 1935. Anthony Scimonelli would go on to open and run the Brentwood Plumbing Supply Store. (Courtesy of the Brentwood Public Library.)

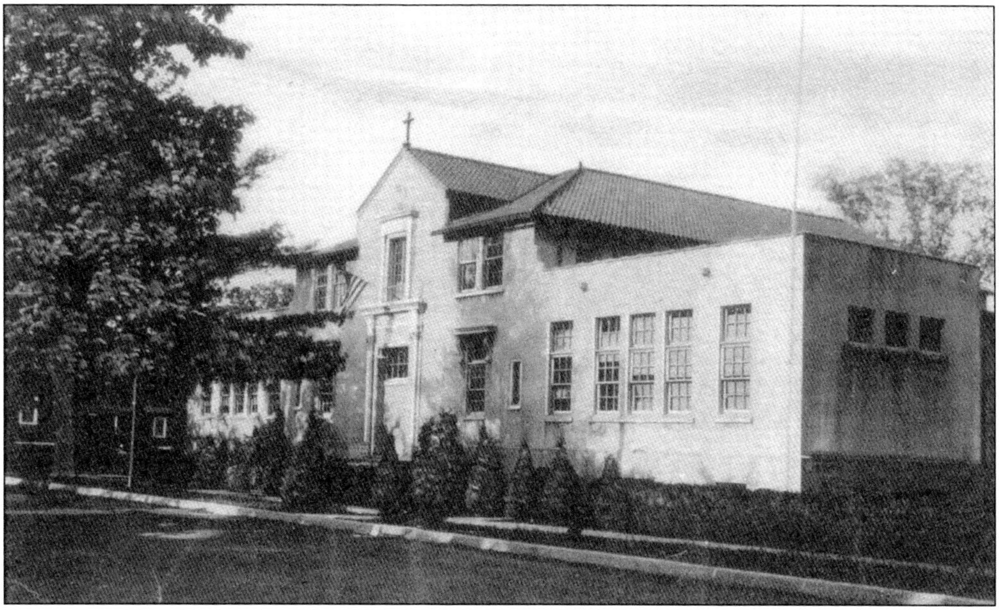

St. Anne's Parochial School opened on September 10, 1923, and offered elementary education to boys and girls. It served as an alternative to the small Brentwood Public School District or St. Joseph's Academy, which was an all girls' school. The school also offered Sunday school and catechism classes. The school closed and was demolished in the mid-1990s. (Courtesy of the James Fordyce Collection.)

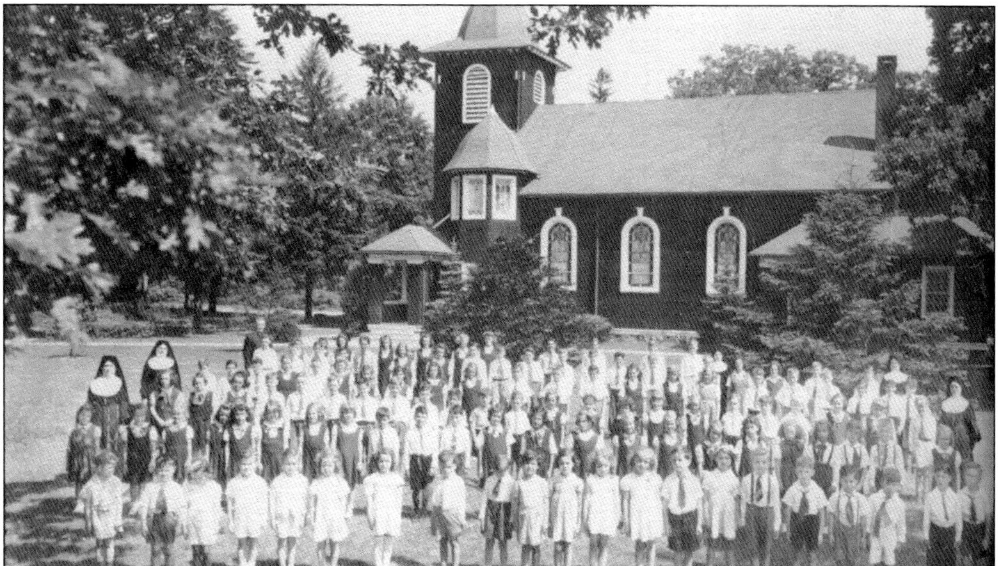

St. Anne's elementary school class poses on a late spring day in the mid-1930s. Sisters from the convent next door worked as teachers and instructors. (Courtesy of the Brentwood Public Library.)

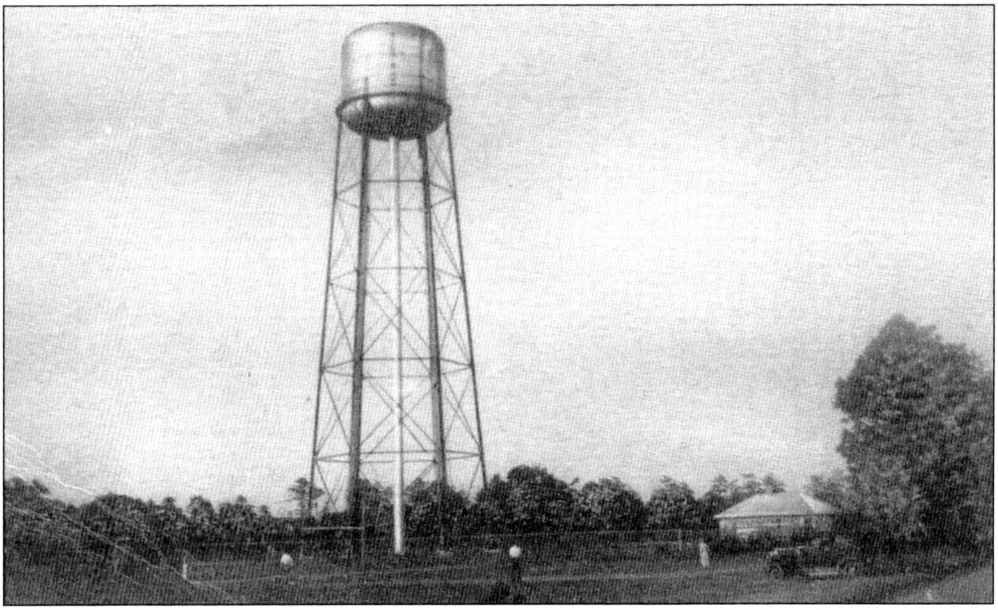

The Brentwood Water District was organized in the early 1930s, and the community received the first of six water towers at that time, seen here in a postcard from the mid-1930s. The original water tower on Third Avenue has long become an icon and symbol of Brentwood. (Courtesy of the James Fordyce Collection.)

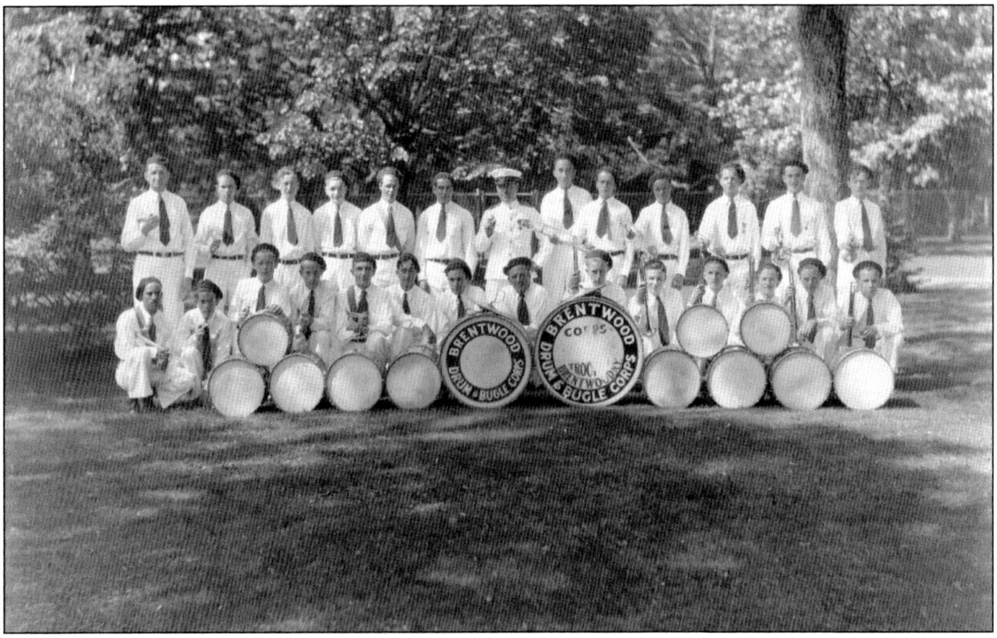

The Brentwood community band, known as the Brentwood Drum and Bugle Corps, is seen here in 1935. The band can trace its origins back to Suffolk County's first brass band organized by Modern Times residents Joseph Owram and Josiah Warren. The Drum and Bugle Corps was the first community band in the modern era, preceding the high school's "Green Machine" or the fire department's "Wanderers." The band eventually folded. (Courtesy of the Brentwood Public Library.)

Dr. William H. Ross, MD, (1862–1953) came to Brentwood in 1890 as the physician of the Austral Hotel. Although the hotel failed, Dr. Ross loved the town so much that he stayed and opened a private practice, becoming Brentwood's primary medical provider for four decades. Ross was an active philanthropist; he was a member of the board of South Side Hospital and Suffolk County Sanatorium as well as president of the Brentwood Board of Education. (Courtesy of the Ray Welch Collection, Ruth Leboeuf Downer.)

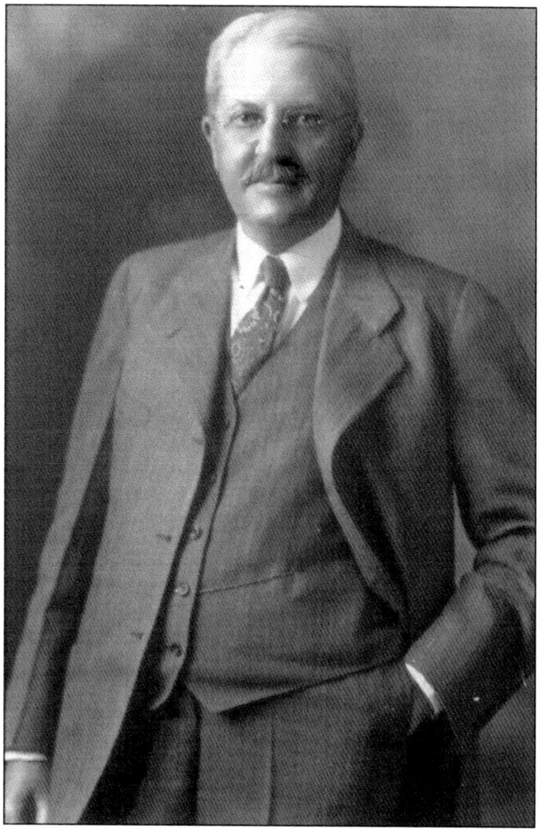

Charles Scimonelli was one of the first Italian immigrants to move to Brentwood. His deli was built on Suffolk Avenue and is seen here in 1934. (Courtesy of the Brentwood Public Library.)

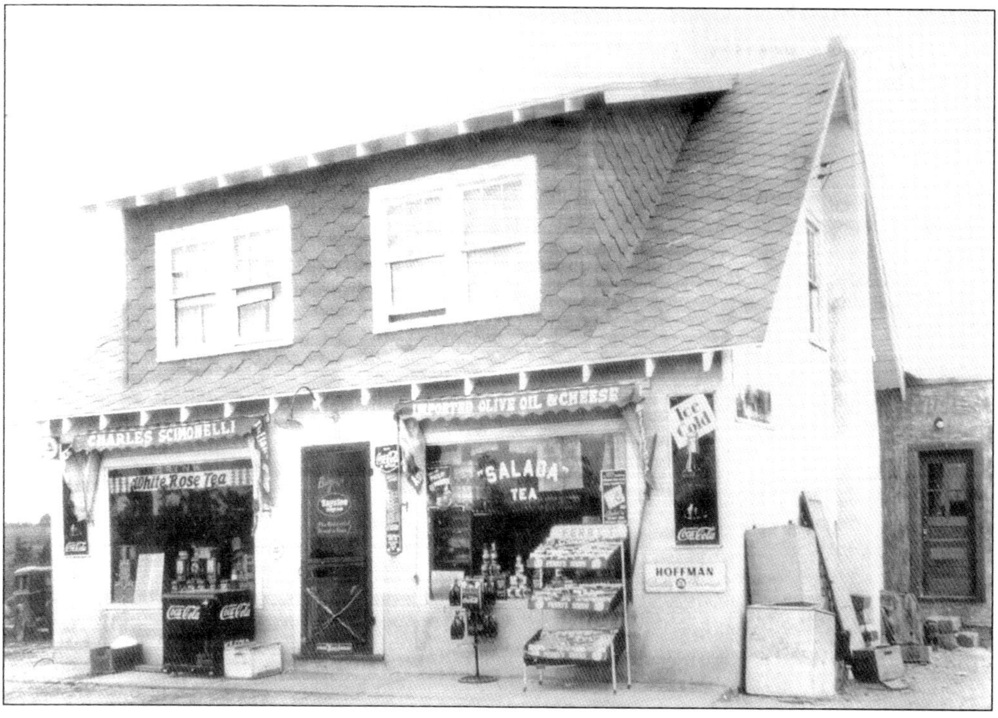

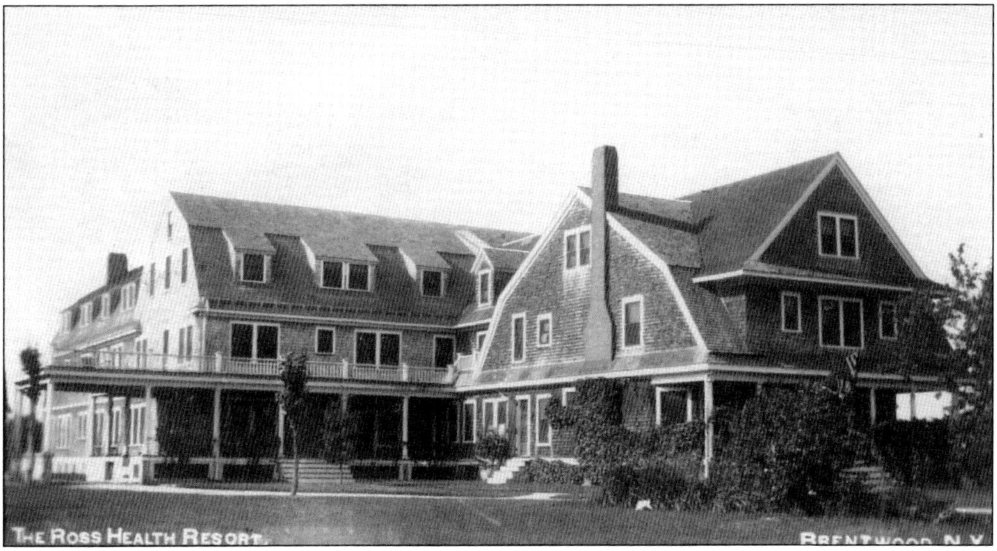

Dr. Ross built his estate called Onetah on the north side of Washington Avenue. In 1898, Dr. Ross built a clinic on his property, which he expanded in 1904 as the Ross Sanitarium. The sanitarium held 70 rooms and was designed to treat those recovering from serious injury or illness. Part hospital and part spa, the facility housed a surgery, pharmacy, convalescence rooms, recreational facilities, sauna, hydrotherapy, and solariums. (Courtesy of the Brentwood Public Library.)

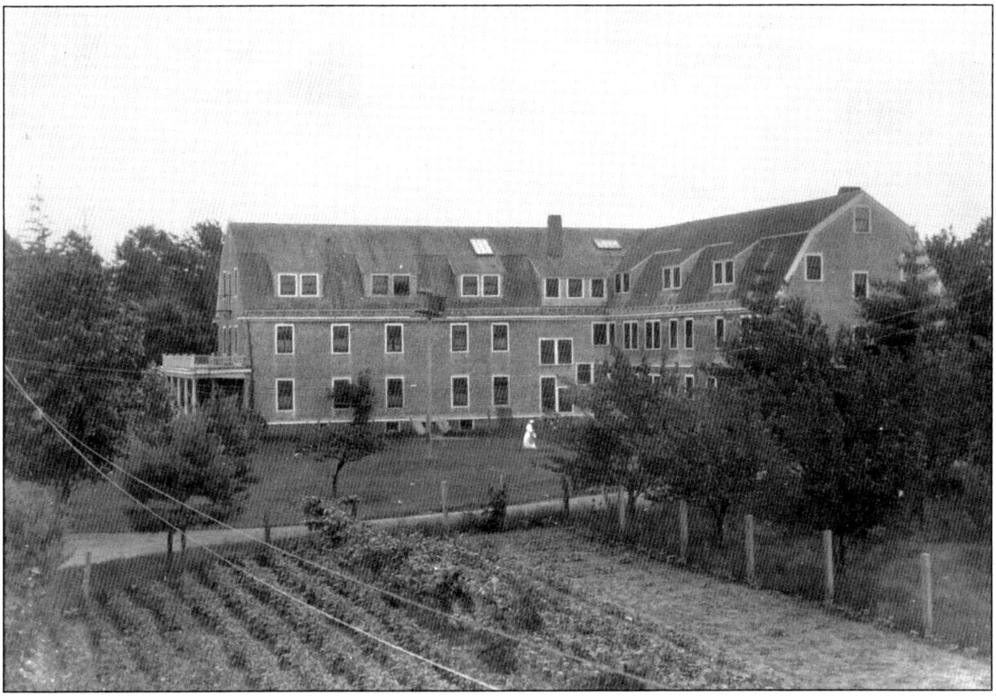

A rare shot of the rear of the Ross Sanitarium shows the buildings, gardens, and orchards. Occupation in fresh air and sunlight were instrumental to a patient's recovery, and many worked in the nurseries. The clinic had many names including Onetah, Ross Sanitarium, and Brentwood Sanitarium. When the term sanitarium passed out of fashion, the facility was renamed the Brentwood Health Resort. (Courtesy of the Brentwood Public Library.)

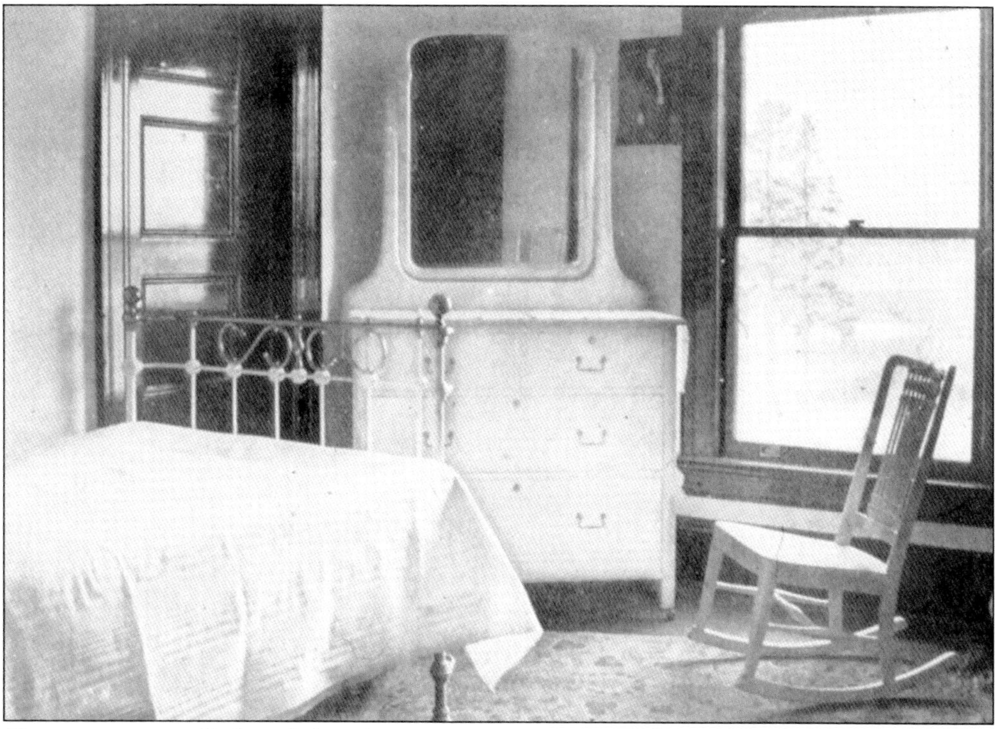

Clients were typically boarded in their own private rooms at the Ross Sanitarium, seen here in this c. 1910 photograph. The health center served not just the Brentwood community as a sort of informal hospital, but attracted clients from across the country looking to convalesce. (Courtesy of the Ray Welch Collection, Ruth Leboeuf Downer.)

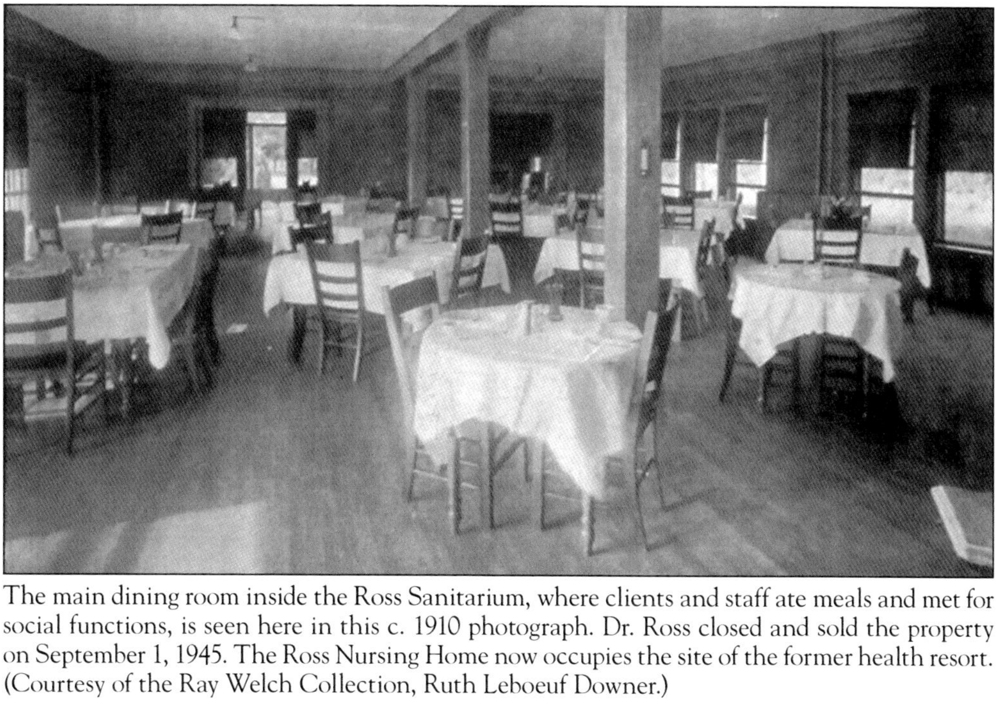

The main dining room inside the Ross Sanitarium, where clients and staff ate meals and met for social functions, is seen here in this c. 1910 photograph. Dr. Ross closed and sold the property on September 1, 1945. The Ross Nursing Home now occupies the site of the former health resort. (Courtesy of the Ray Welch Collection, Ruth Leboeuf Downer.)

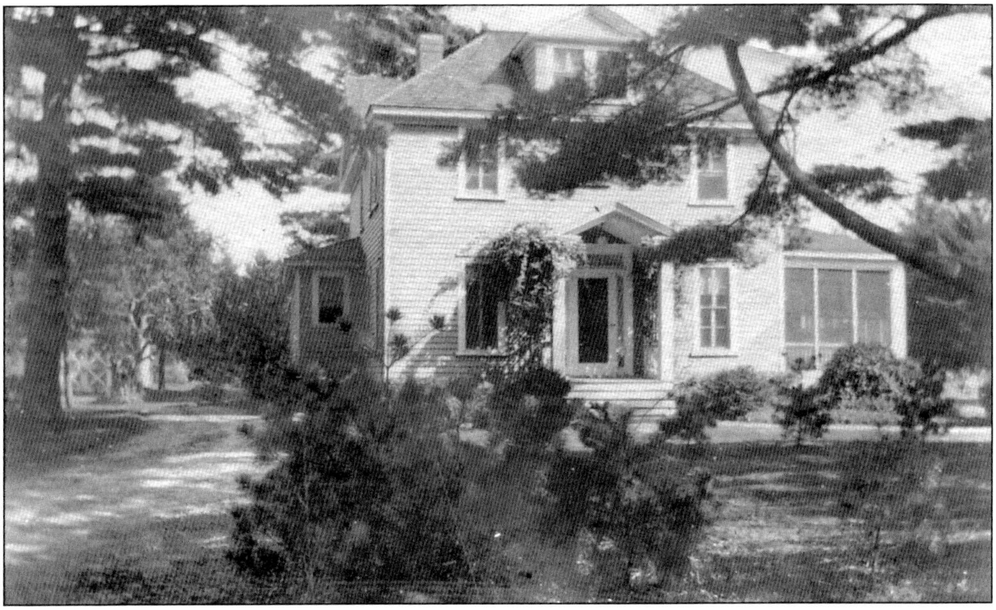

Seen here is the home of Dr. David Raisky, MD, (1891–1949). David fled Belarus because of Jewish persecution, coming to the United States in 1929. Chief of arthritic medicine at Lebanon Hospital in New York City, he purchased Judge Nobel's home as a summer property in 1940 and eventually retired there. Raisky was an accomplished musician and composer, having over 80 musical compositions published in Switzerland and United States. (Courtesy of the Brentwood Public Library.)

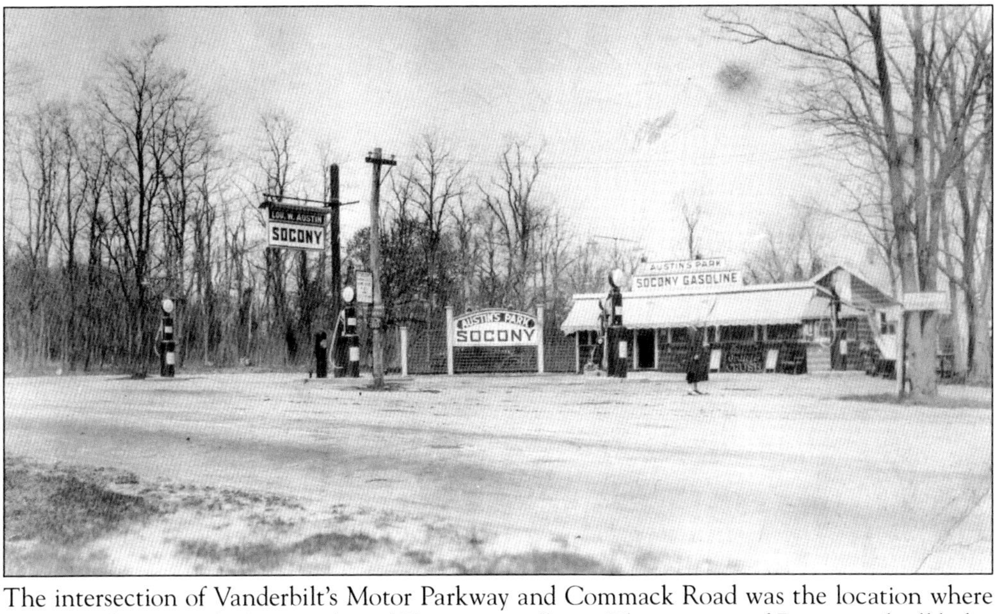

The intersection of Vanderbilt's Motor Parkway and Commack Road was the location where Brentwood, Deer Park, Commack, and Hauppague all met. There, a second Brentwood toll lodge was built on the north side of the road, and Lou W. Austin served as the lodge keeper. When the toll lodge moved to the south side of the road, Lou opened a Standard Oil Company of New York gas station, seen here in 1924. The Bonwit Inn now occupies the site. (Courtesy of the Sr. Anne Pulling Collection, Central Islip Library.)

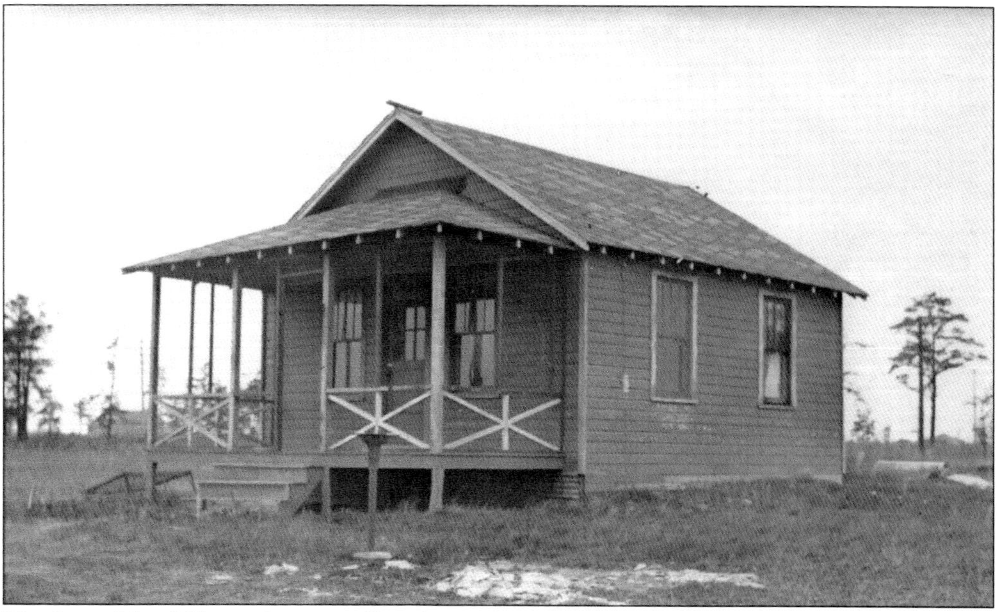

The Long Island Flying Service office, located on the grounds of Brentwood Airport on Islip Avenue, is seen here. Later, it was the home of Capt. Henry W. Bender when he owned the airport. (Courtesy of the Sr. Anne Pulling Collection, Central Islip Library.)

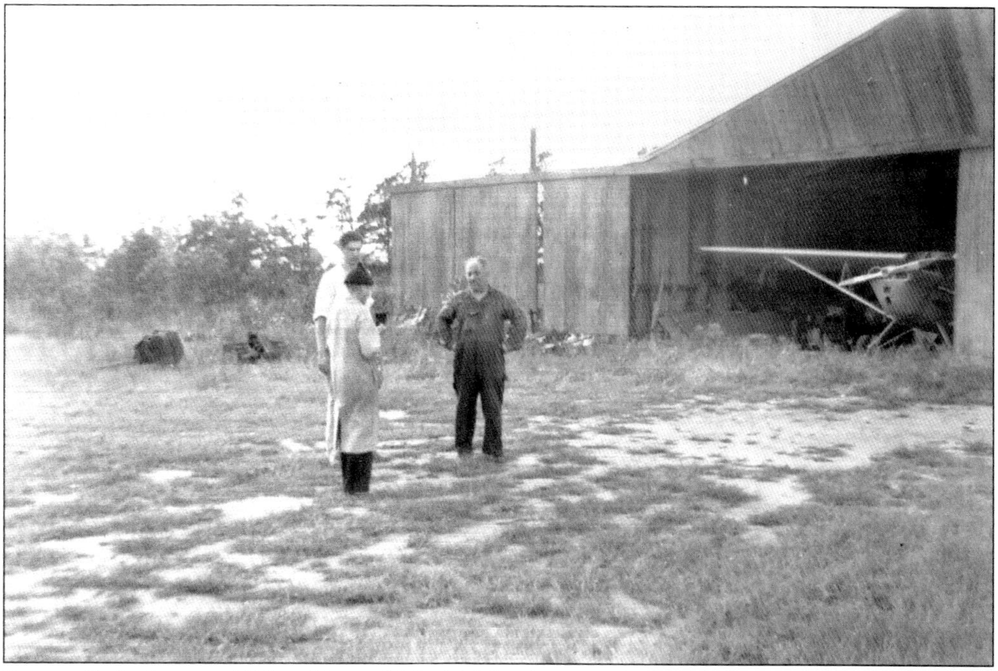

Originally laid out in 1920 as Central Islip Field, it became Brentwood Airport in 1930. In 1936, World War I veteran Capt. Henry W. Bender (center), a pilot and mechanic, took possession of and operated the tiny airport. Known variously as Bender's Field and Bender's Brentwood Airport, it operated until flying ceased in the early 1950s. Long Island Lighting Company bought the property for an office and yard in 1958, which is now the Long Island Power Authority plant. (Courtesy of the Erale family.)

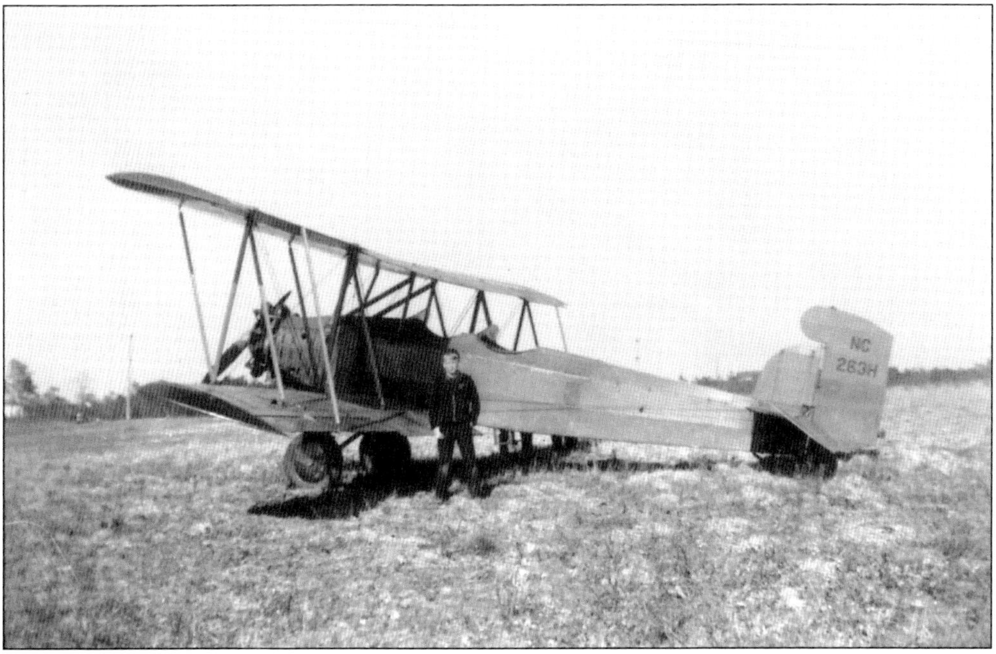

A Curtiss Fledgling biplane is seen at Brentwood Airport in this 1938 photograph. Brentwood Airport had only one dirt runway, which ran north to south and is today Grand Boulevard. A wide array of early aircraft was stored at the field. The airport was used as a junkyard by Capt. Henry W. Bender, who collected a cemetery of old cars, trucks, and airplanes. (Courtesy of the Erale family.)

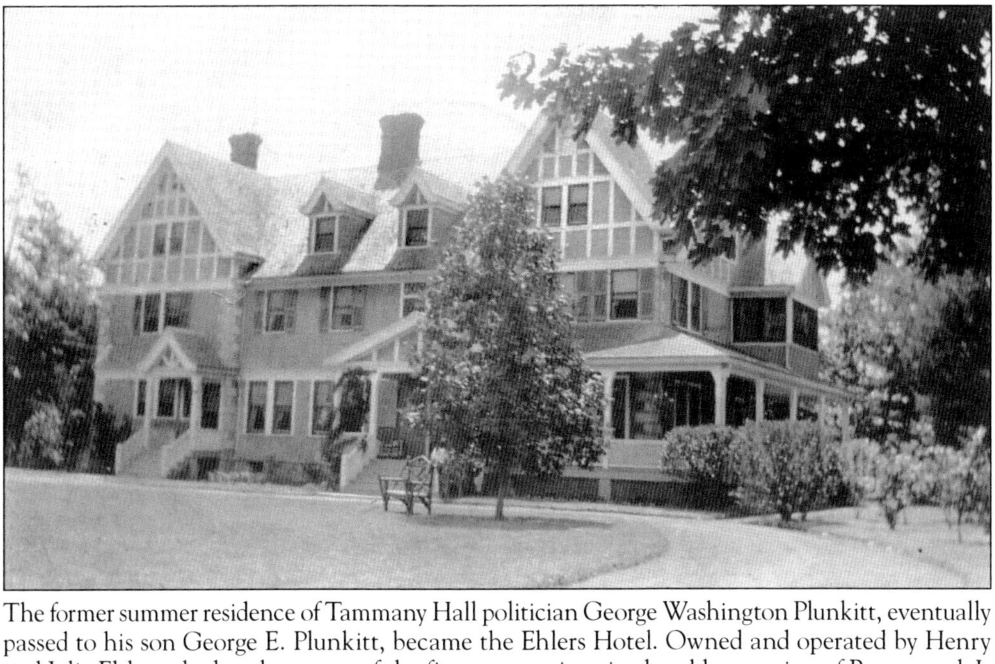

The former summer residence of Tammany Hall politician George Washington Plunkitt, eventually passed to his son George E. Plunkitt, became the Ehlers Hotel. Owned and operated by Henry and Julia Ehlers, the hotel was one of the finest attractions in the oldest section of Brentwood. It is pictured here around 1916. In 1928, the Ehlers Hotel was destroyed by a forest fire. (Courtesy of the Brentwood Public Library.)

Dr. Paul Studenski, PhD, (1887–1961) is seen here. Born and raised in Russia, Paul leaned to fly in France in 1911 and emigrated to the United States that same year. He was a pioneer aviator and was the first pilot to transport mail by air in the South. He had a doctorate in economics from Columbia and taught at New York University. A resident of Brentwood since 1938, he was a consultant for Governor Dewey and Pres. Franklin D. Roosevelt. (Courtesy of the Brentwood Public Library.)

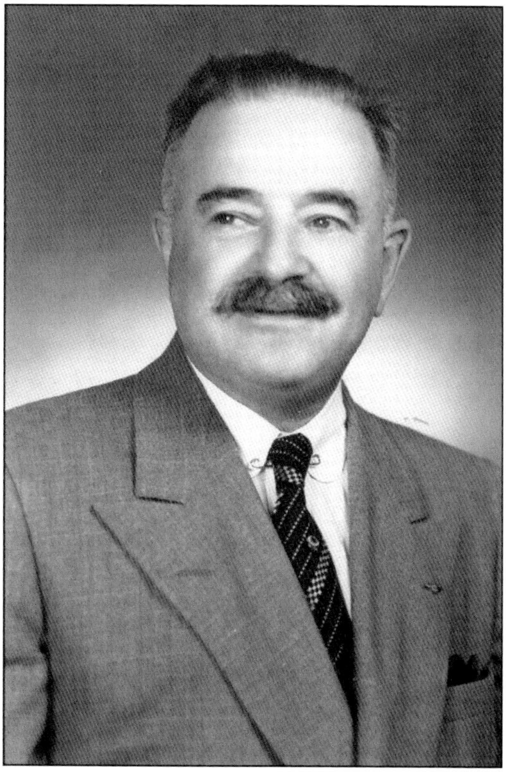

Before the creation of the Suffolk County Police Department, each town had its own police force. The Town of Islip Police was supplemented by a police auxiliary that was assigned to cover various areas. Precinct 2 under the leadership of Capt. Lou Schneider was responsible for patrol in the areas of Bay Shore and Brentwood around 1940. (Courtesy of the Suffolk County Police Museum.)

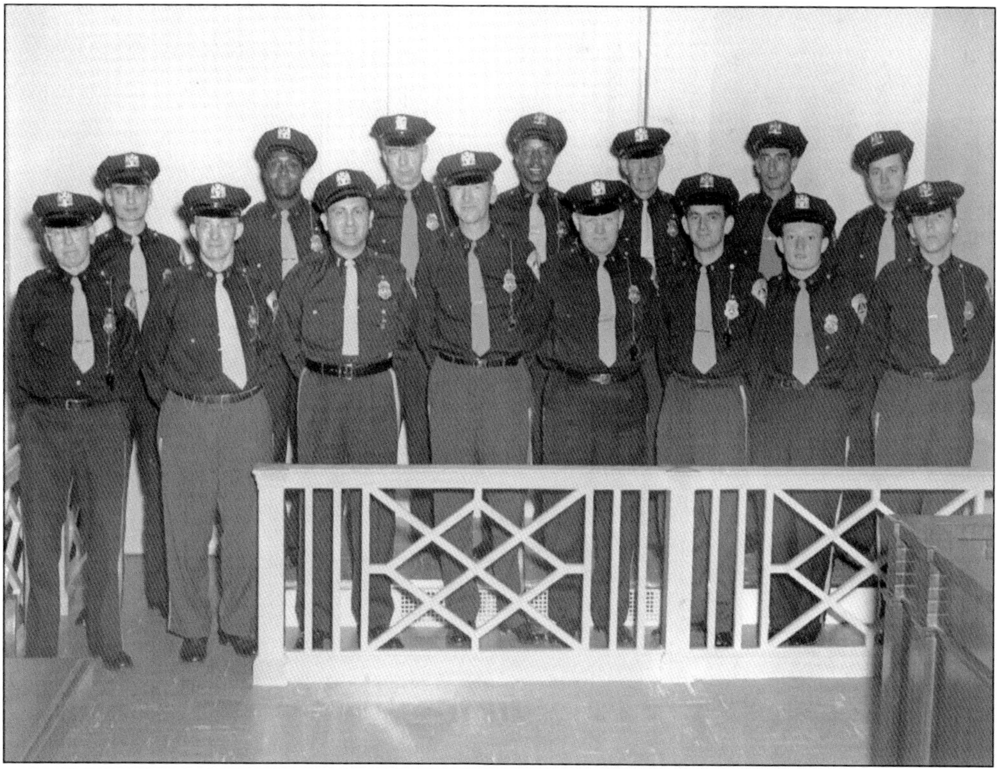

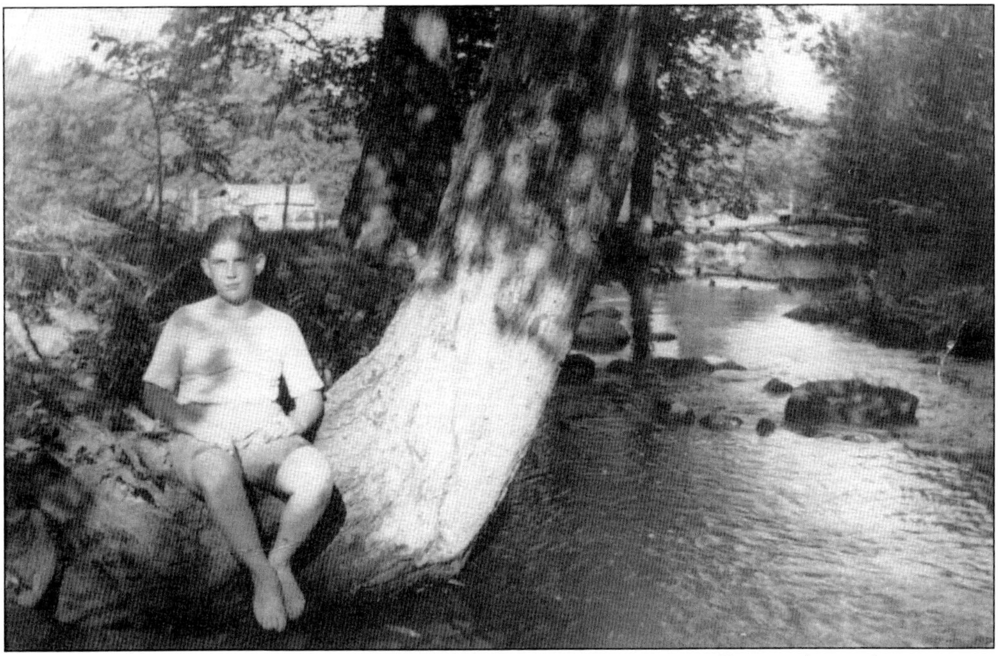

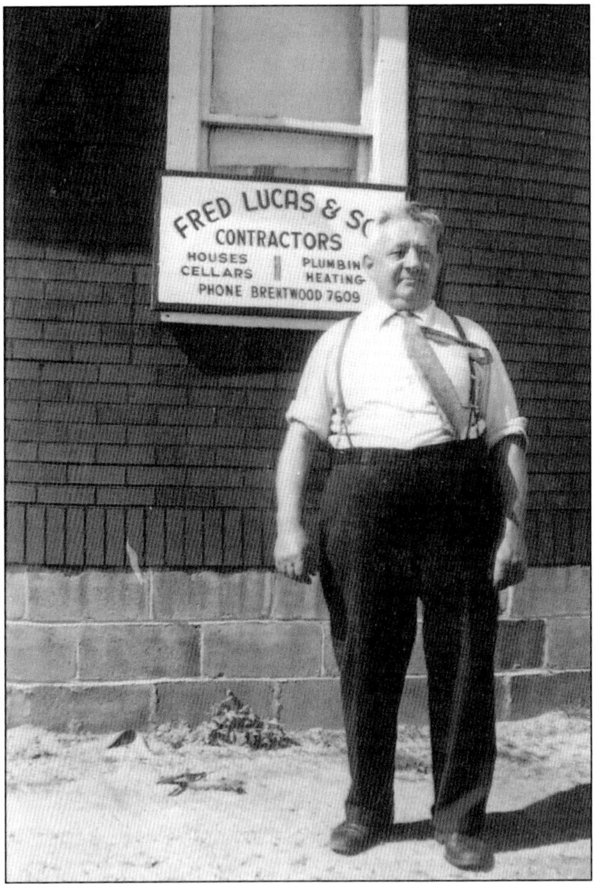

Louis William Schwarz (1928–1983) poses by Brentwood Creek in 1939. Fed from an underground spring near the Brentwood Country Club, the creek runs south, emptying into the Great South Bay. An original source of water for the settlers of Modern Times and early Brentwood, today the creek runs underground near its source, and where it is visible, it is heavily polluted, muddy, and in some areas developed over. (Courtesy of the Schwarz-Wouk family.)

Fred Lucas, one of the first plumbers in Brentwood, is seen here. He had his office in his home on Fifth Avenue around 1940. (Courtesy of the Brentwood Public Library.)

Four

THE MOTHERHOUSE OF THE SISTERS OF ST. JOSEPH

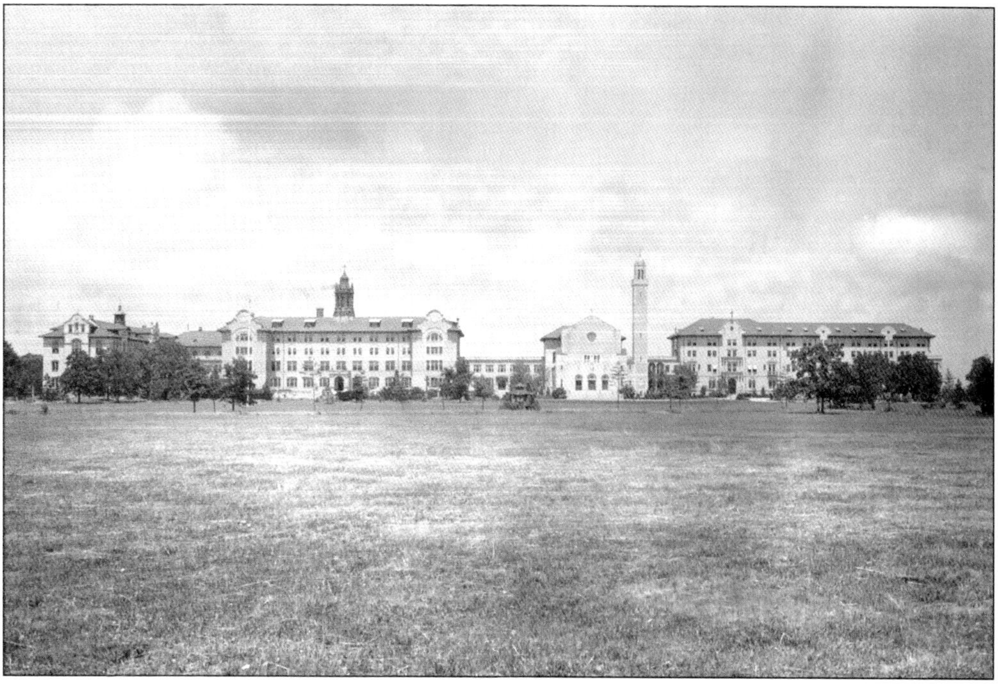

The need for more spacious quarters prompted the Sisters of St. Joseph to move their motherhouse, located at a convent in Flushing, Queens, to a location with more property. In 1896, the Sisters purchased the former Austral Hotel and Pearsall residence of Pine Park, which at that point was the bankrupt Hotel Brentwood. Construction of other buildings soon followed. Seen here in the late 1930s is the academy, chapel, and convent. (Courtesy of the Archives of the Sisters of St. Joseph, Brentwood.)

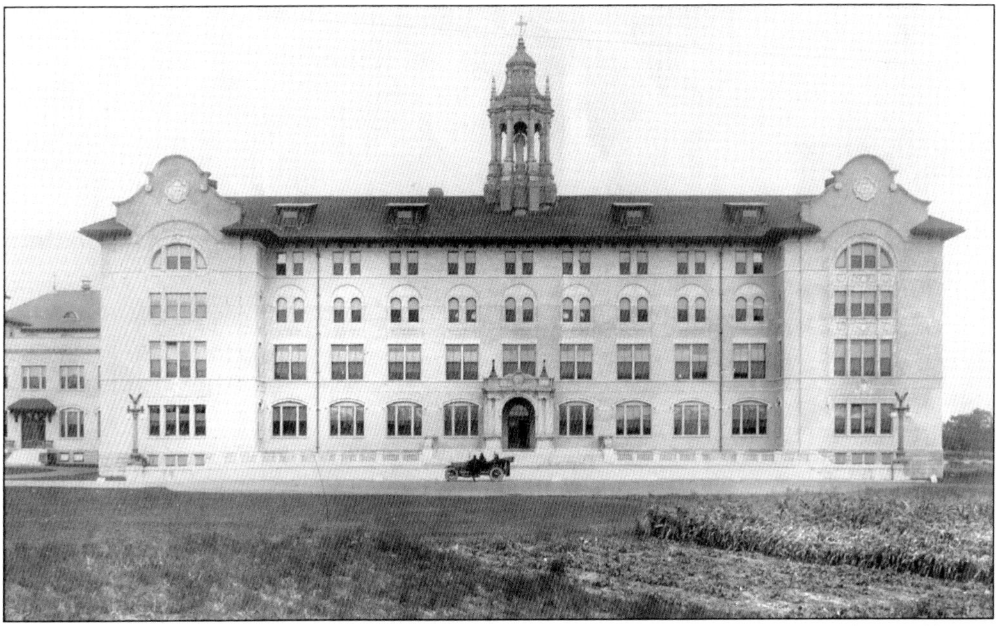

The original academy building, known as St. Louis Hall, opened in 1903. With enrollment climbing at the all girls' school, a new centerpiece was needed for the academy, and St. Joseph's Hall was constructed. It became the iconic symbol of the academy and one of the first buildings built for the new motherhouse. This 1913 shot shows farm fields in front of the school and a statue of St. Joseph can be seen in the cupola. (Courtesy of the Archives of the Sisters of St. Joseph, Brentwood.)

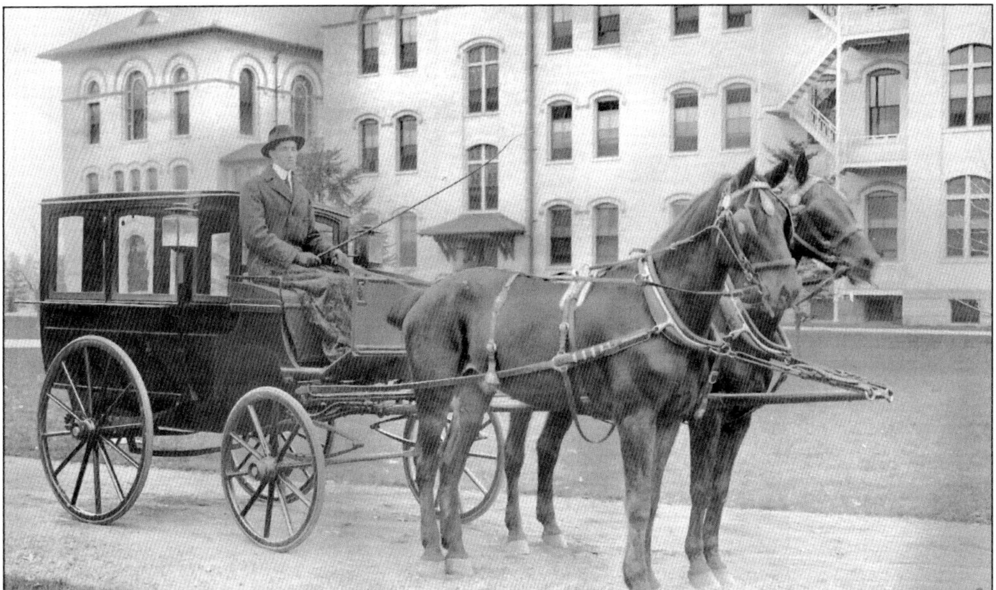

The motherhouse had its own stables, and coaches were used in the early days to bring the Sisters, students, and other faculty and staff to and from the grounds. Here, "Little Pat" (the driver) is seen on the convent grounds sometime in the early 1900s. (Courtesy of the Brentwood Public Library.)

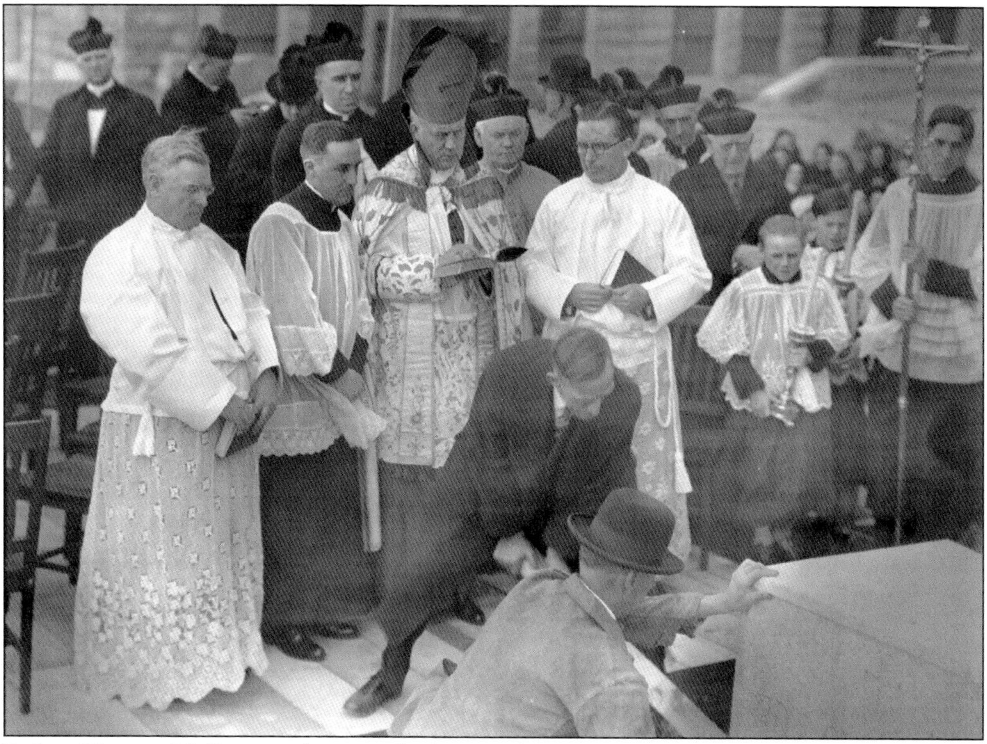

Bishop Thomas Molloy presides over the laying of the cornerstone of the Chapel of the Sacred Heart in 1928. Leaders from across the Diocese of Brooklyn were in attendance as well as members of Brentwood's Catholic population. The Sisters for whom the chapel is being built are barely visible behind the altar boys. (Courtesy of the Archives of the Sisters of St. Joseph, Brentwood.)

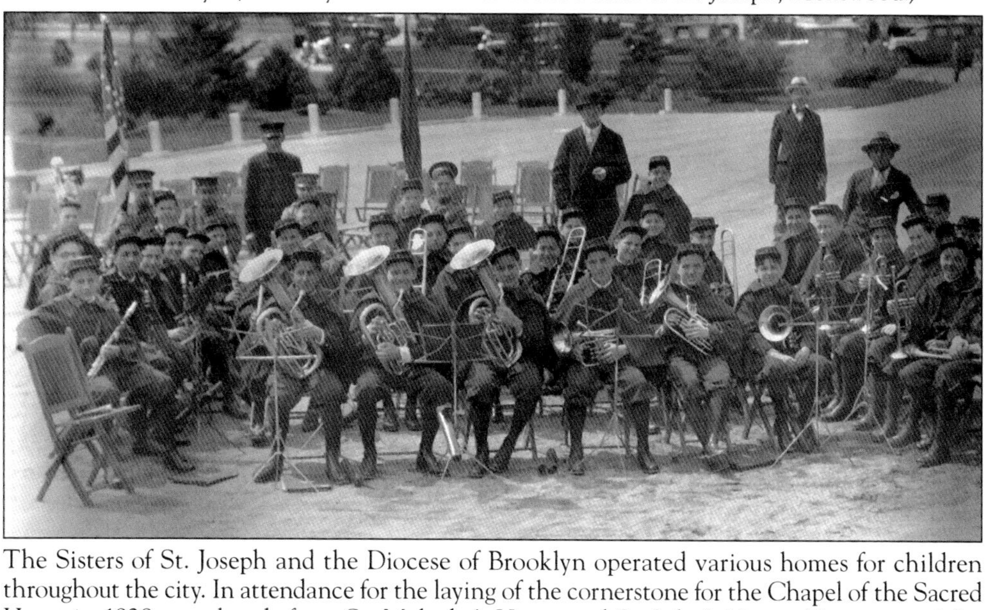

The Sisters of St. Joseph and the Diocese of Brooklyn operated various homes for children throughout the city. In attendance for the laying of the cornerstone for the Chapel of the Sacred Heart in 1928 were bands from St. Malachy's Home and St. John's Home. Here, one of the bands pauses for a moment during the ceremony. (Courtesy of the Archives of the Sisters of St. Joseph, Brentwood.)

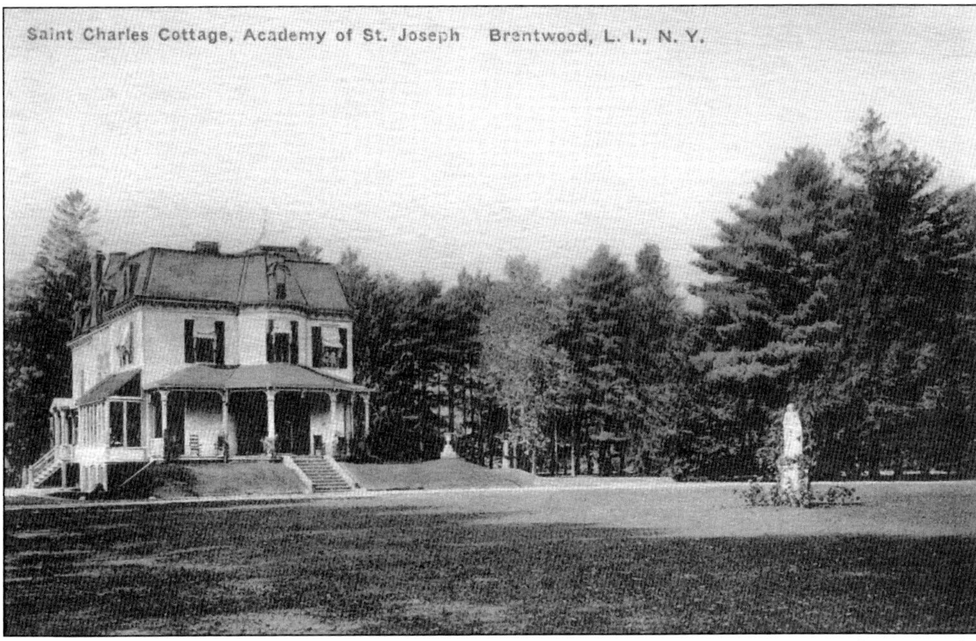

Pine Park, the former Pearsall residence and defunct Hotel Brentwood, was renamed St. Charles Cottage by the Sisters of St. Joseph. The cottage was used as a chaplains' residence. St. Charles Cottage is pictured here in an early-1930s postcard. (Courtesy of the James Fordyce Collection.)

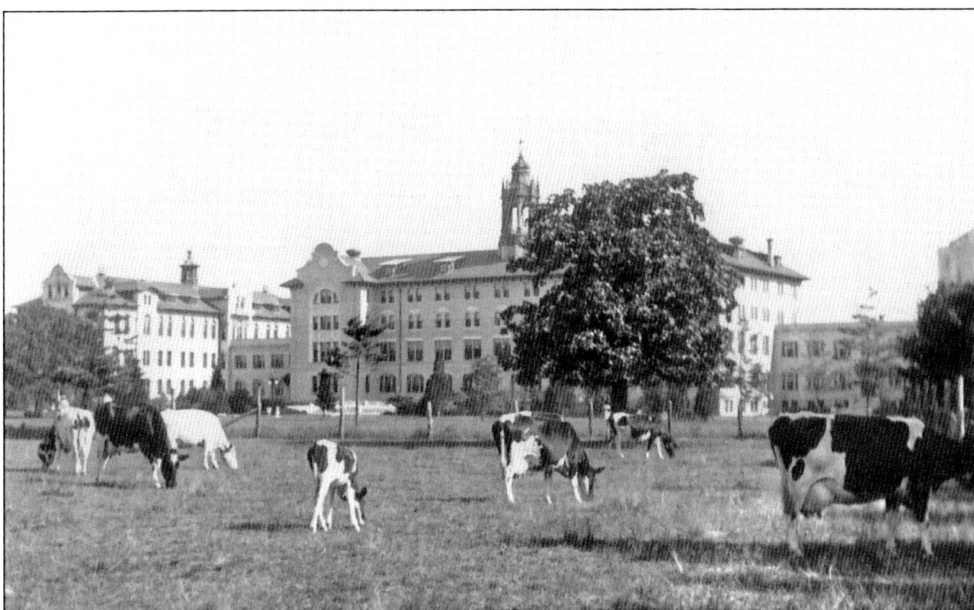

The motherhouse at Brentwood was complete with its own farm, including dairy and livestock. Here, cows are grazing on the fields in front of the complex of buildings in the late 1930s. The original 1903 Elementary Building (St. Louis Hall) and the 1913 Main Building (St. Joseph's Hall) dominate the background. (Courtesy of the Archives of the Sisters of St. Joseph, Brentwood.)

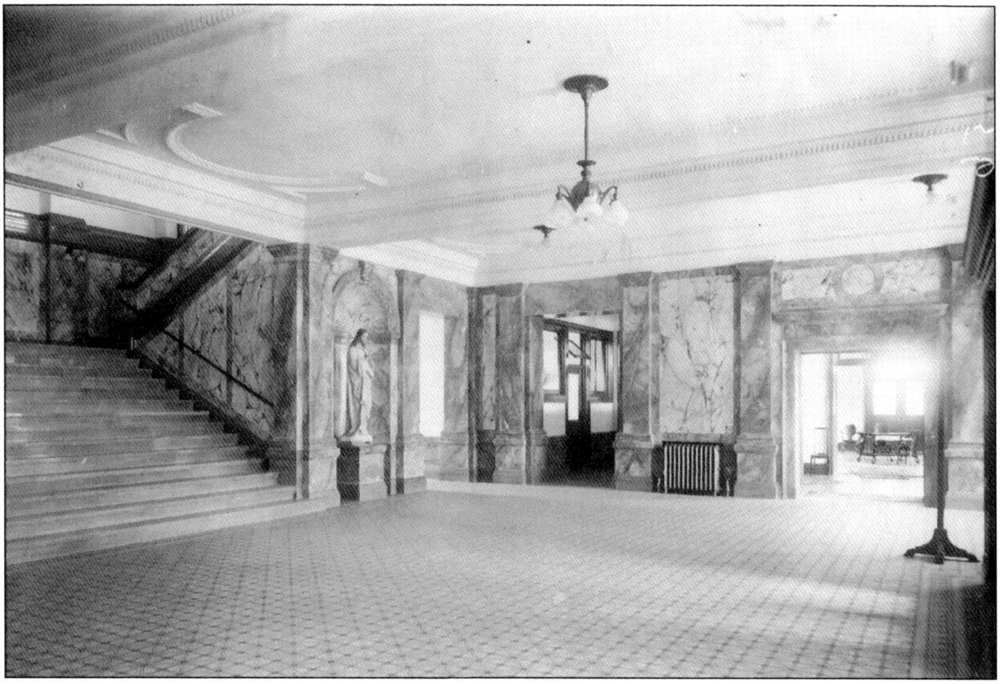

The main entrance and reception hall of the Academy of St. Joseph is seen here around 1940. The photograph belies the sheer grandness of the scene. Apart from the radiator and the chandelier, not much has changed. (Courtesy of the Archives of the Sisters of St. Joseph, Brentwood.)

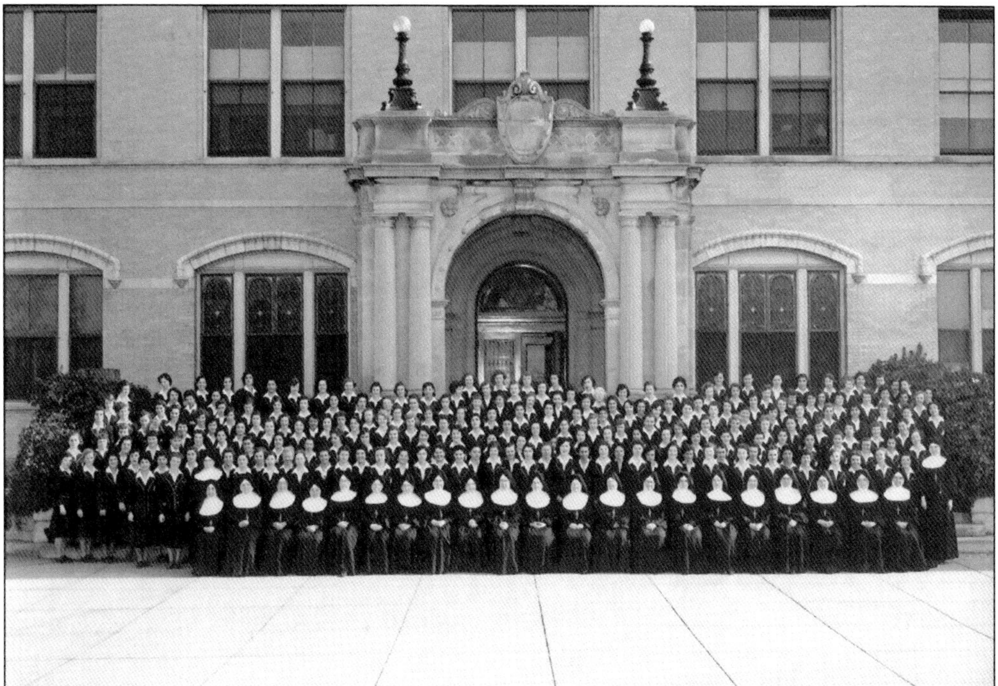

This 1955 photograph depicts the students and faculty of the Academy of St. Joseph in front of the academy building. (Courtesy of the Archives of the Sisters of St. Joseph, Brentwood.)

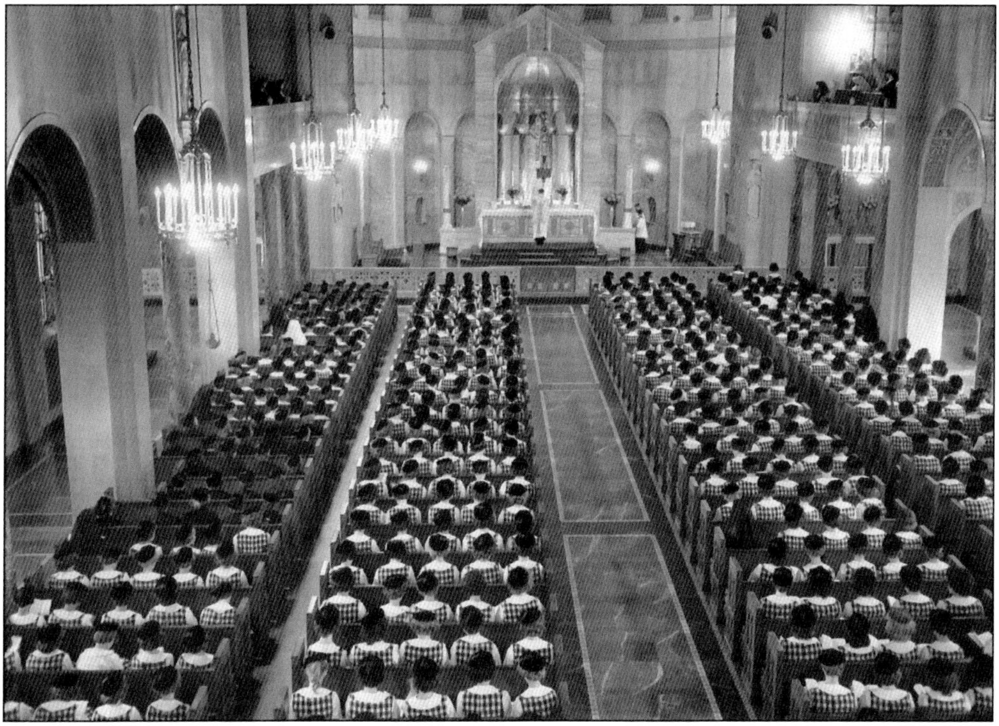

Seen here is the interior of Sacred Heart Chapel with academy students and Sisters at mass around 1960. Although the academy closed in 2009, the Chapel of the Sacred Heart is still used by the Sisters of St. Joseph today. (Courtesy of the Archives of the Sisters of St. Joseph, Brentwood.)

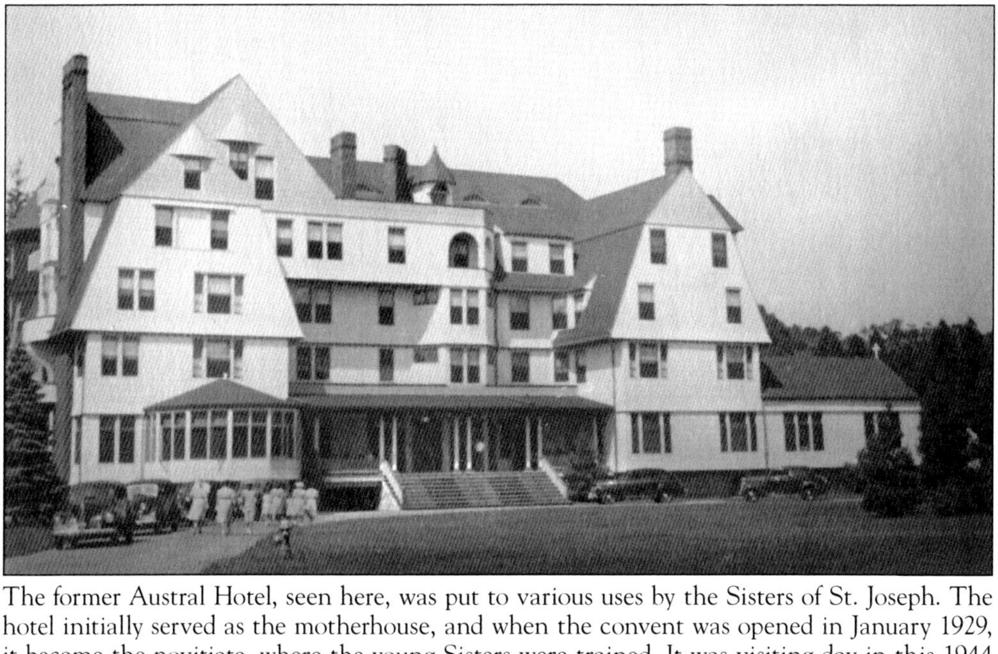

The former Austral Hotel, seen here, was put to various uses by the Sisters of St. Joseph. The hotel initially served as the motherhouse, and when the convent was opened in January 1929, it became the novitiate, where the young Sisters were trained. It was visiting day in this 1944 photograph. Note the crosses on the roof. The building was demolished in 1960. (Courtesy of the Archives of the Sisters of St. Joseph, Brentwood.)

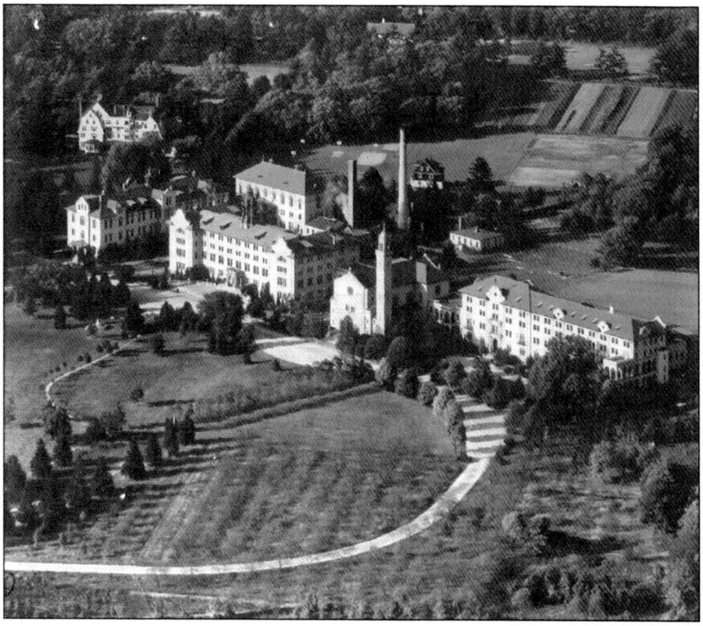

This late-1940s aerial shot shows the grounds and layout of the motherhouse at Brentwood. The former Austral Hotel, being used as the novitiate, is in the upper left corner. The academy's cluster of buildings is to the left of the Chapel of the Sacred Heart, and the convent is to the right of the chapel. The powerhouse, laundry, and industrial buildings are in the rear. The motherhouse was self-sufficient. (Courtesy of the Brentwood Public Library.)

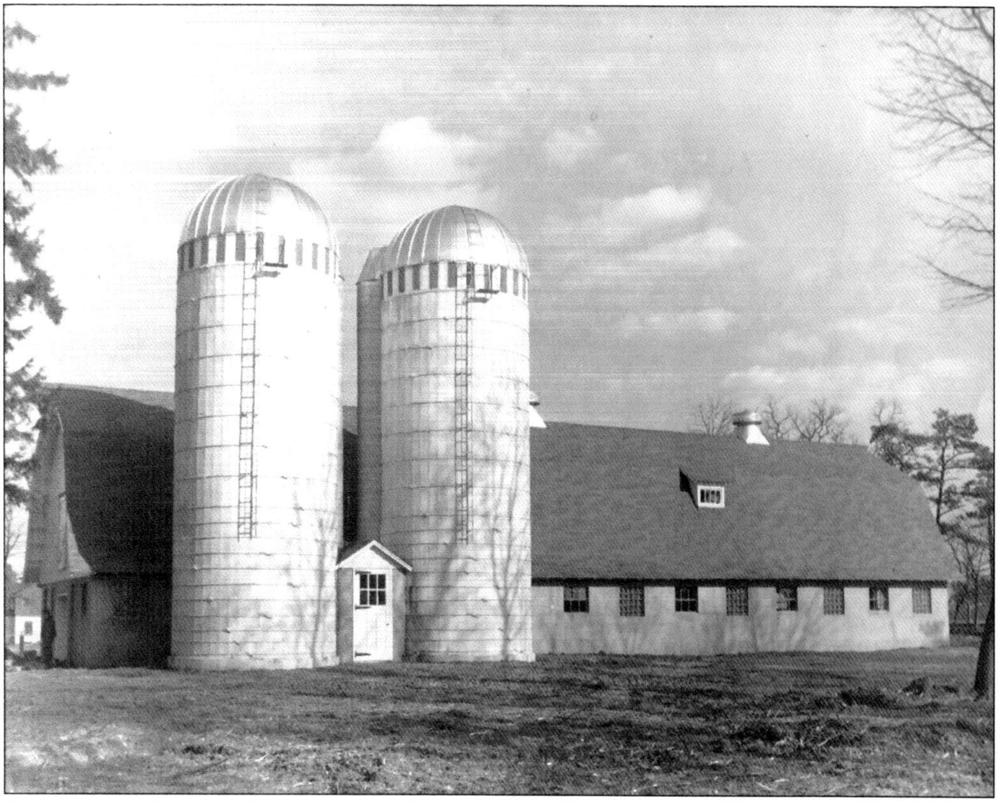

St. Joseph's had its own farm, equipped for growing and harvesting produce and raising livestock. The farm helped the convent remain self-sufficient and added to the picturesque vision of the property. The dairy farm is pictured here in 1950. (Courtesy of the Archives of the Sisters of St. Joseph, Brentwood.)

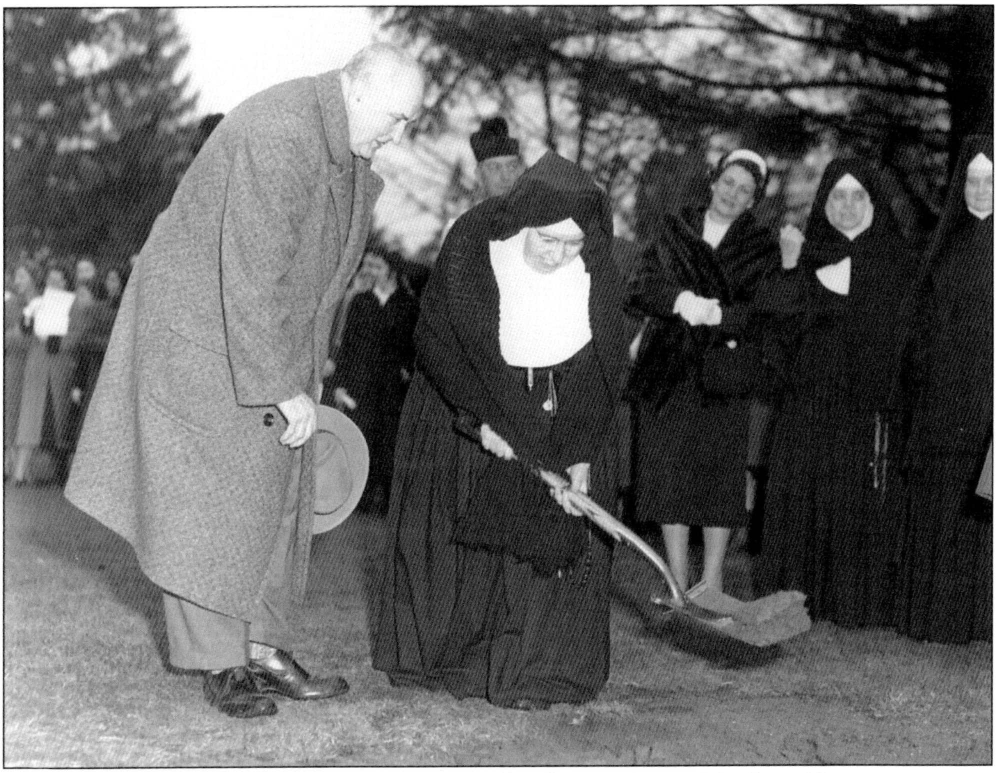

Pictured here is the ground-breaking ceremony for the Academy of St. Joseph's gymnasium on March 19, 1953. Sister Natalie Maria, a faculty member, holds the shovel. (Courtesy of the Archives of the Sisters of St. Joseph, Brentwood.)

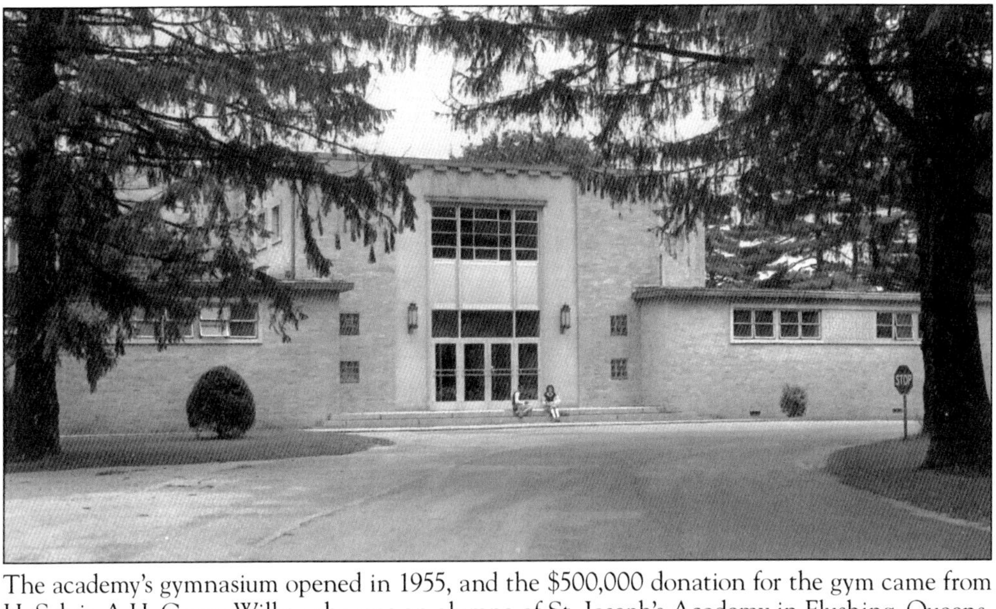

The academy's gymnasium opened in 1955, and the $500,000 donation for the gym came from H. Sylvia A.H. Green Wilks, who was an alumna of St. Joseph's Academy in Flushing, Queens. She had inherited the money from her mother, Hetty Green, one of the wealthiest women in the world. (Courtesy of the Archives of the Sisters of St. Joseph, Brentwood.)

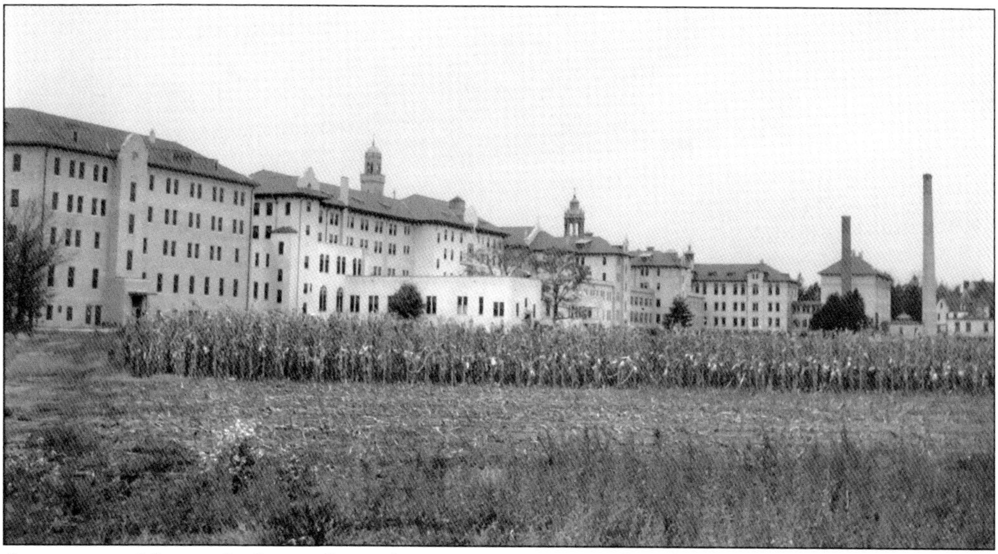

A rear view of the motherhouse shows the novitiate, convent, chapel, and academy. The smokestacks belong to the industrial building, which includes the powerhouse and laundry. Corn can be seen growing in the rear fields. The presence of the novitiate indicates that the photograph is post-1955. (Courtesy of the Archives of the Sisters of St. Joseph, Brentwood.)

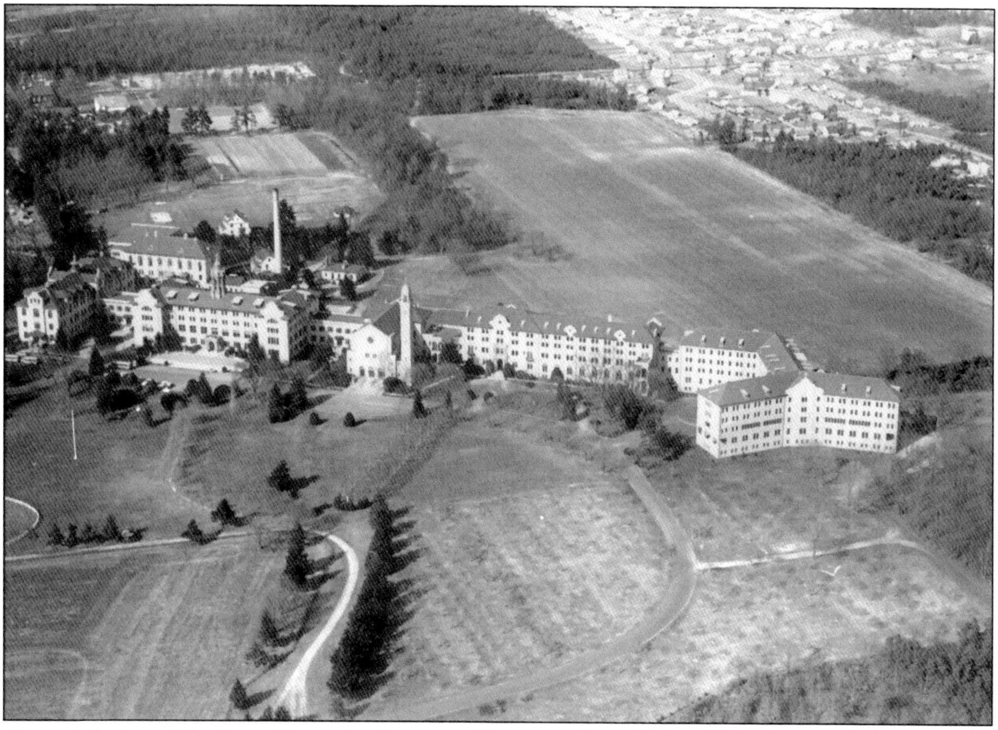

An aerial view of St. Joseph's motherhouse in Brentwood at its height in the mid-1960s is shown. The former Austral Hotel is gone, but the new novitiate wing has been added to the convent buildings. St. Anne's Catholic Church can be seen in the uppermost left corner, while sprawling East Brentwood takes shape on the right side of the photograph. (Courtesy of the Archives of the Sisters of St. Joseph, Brentwood.)

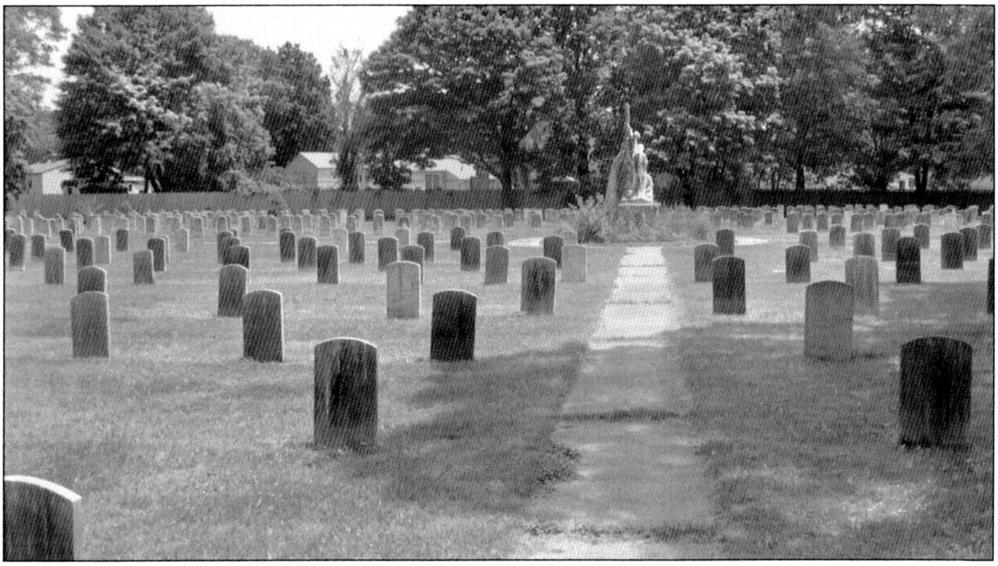

Calvary Cemetery, located on the grounds of the motherhouse, is the final resting place for over a thousand Sisters of St. Joseph. Some of the Sisters buried here are veterans of military service during armed conflicts. Additionally, the cemetery holds two priests who served as chaplains at the convent and a male staff member. (Courtesy of the Archives of the Sisters of St. Joseph, Brentwood.)

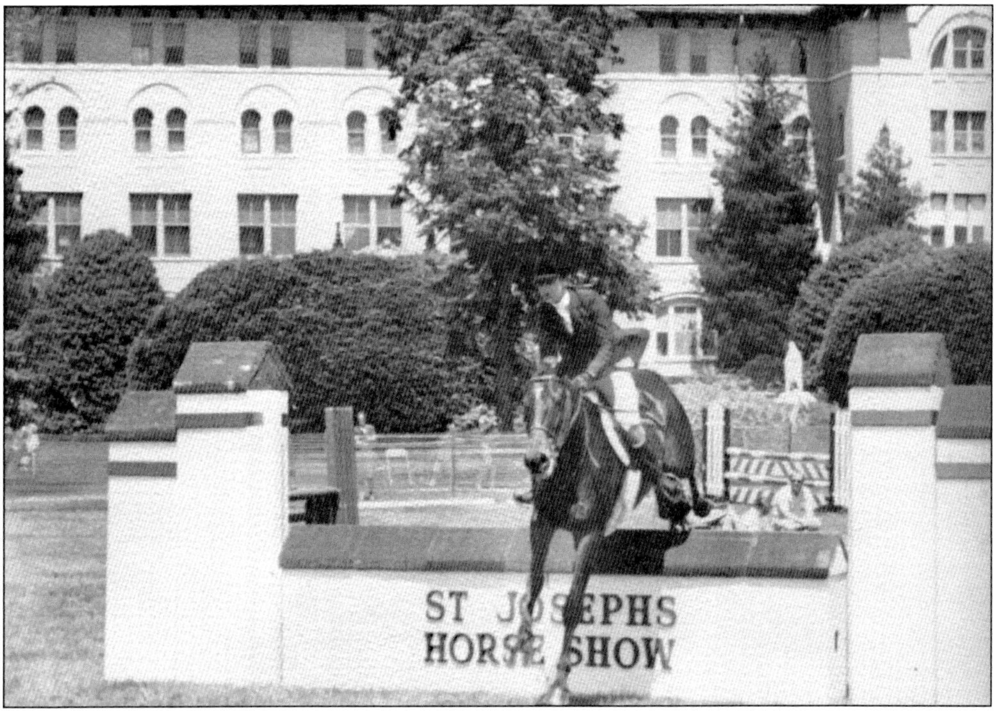

The St. Joseph's Horse Show was a well-known riding competition that took place every summer. Tents were set up on the great lawn in front of the buildings, and horses and riders competed in the splendor and beauty of St. Joseph's grounds. This photograph was taken around 1982. (Courtesy of the Archives of the Sisters of St. Joseph, Brentwood.)

Five

Pilgrim State Hospital

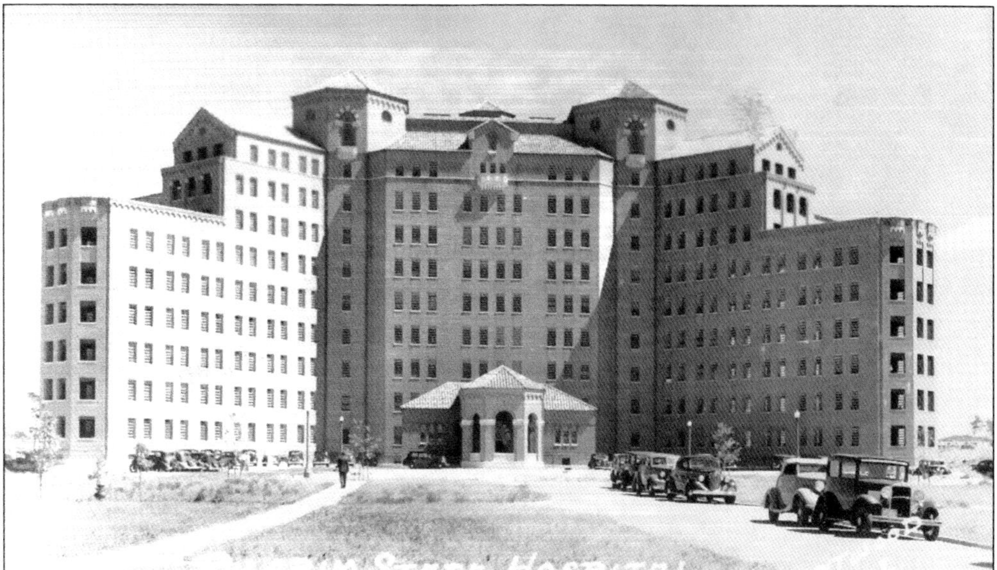

To end the problem of overcrowding at its other hospitals permanently, the State of New York designed and built Pilgrim State Hospital in Brentwood on a massive industrial scale. The hospital was completely contained and self-sufficient. At its height, the hospital housed 13,500 patients, spread out in over 100 buildings, with a staff of 2,500, making it the largest psychiatric hospital in the world. (Courtesy of the James Fordyce Collection.)

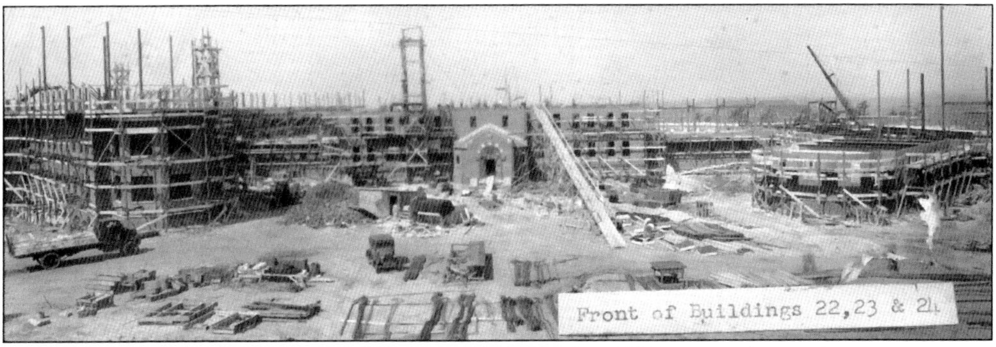

Construction officially began on February 5, 1929. This 1930 image shows the construction of Buildings 22, 23 and 24, the medical-surgical hospital, with the male and female admitting buildings flanking either end of the central surgical building. The hospital officially opened its doors on October 1, 1931. (Courtesy of the Long Island Psychiatric Museum.)

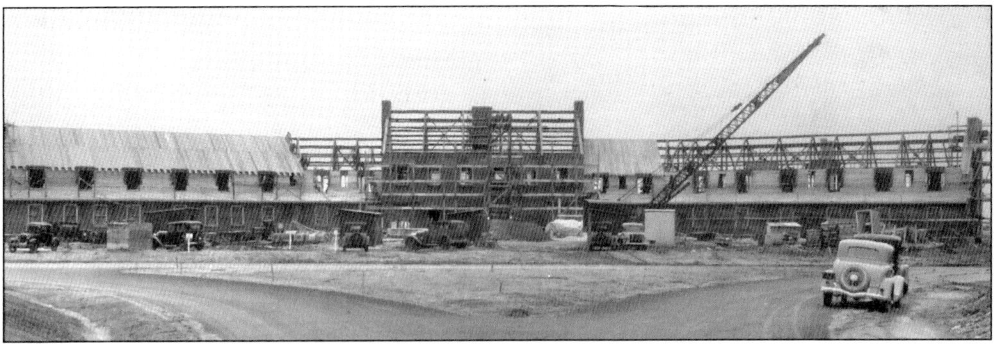

The Works Progress Administration oversaw the construction at Pilgrim State Hospital. Here, a staff house, Building 63, is under construction in the early 1930s. The building, just south of the main hospital complex in the doctor's circle of housing, was used to house professional staff. (Courtesy of the Long Island Psychiatric Museum.)

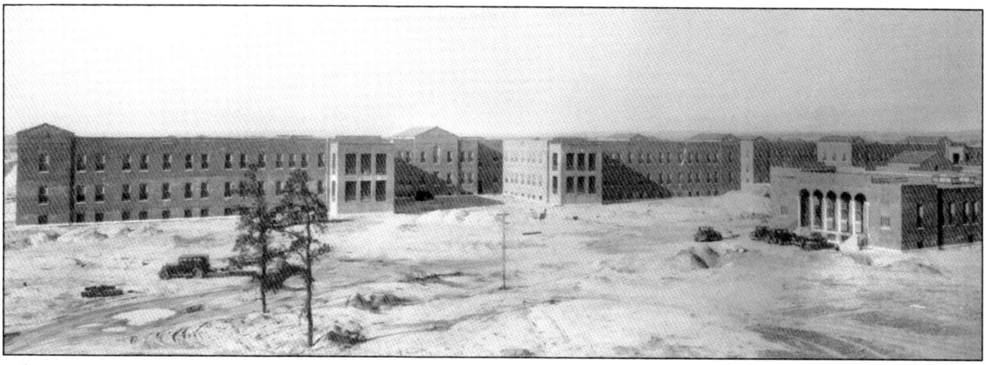

Pilgrim State Hospital patient dormitories are pictured here around 1933 or 1934. Each set of buildings was grouped together, linked by a common kitchen. Patients were assigned to dormitory groups based on their condition and diagnosis. (Courtesy of the Long Island Psychiatric Museum.)

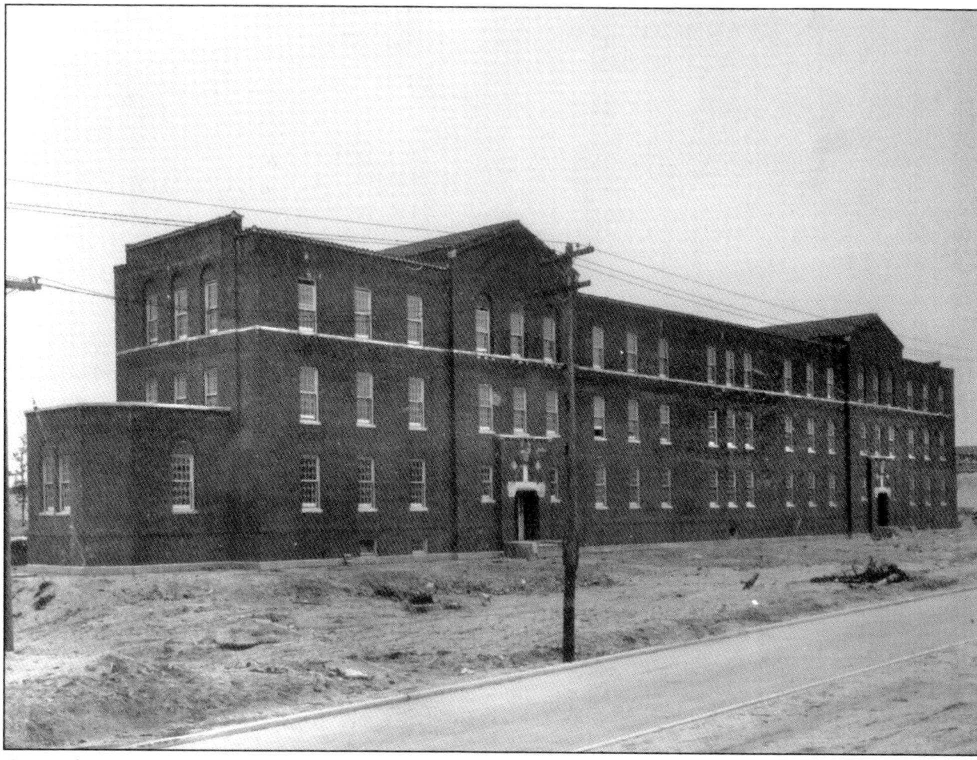

One of numerous buildings on the grounds used for patient treatment is seen here. Typically it would house clinics, offices, therapy rooms, classrooms, and a sheltered workshop where the patients could work on a skill or craft. It provided occupational tasks to distract them from their illness and provided a sense of accomplishment for the patient at creating something useful. (Courtesy of the Long Island Psychiatric Museum.)

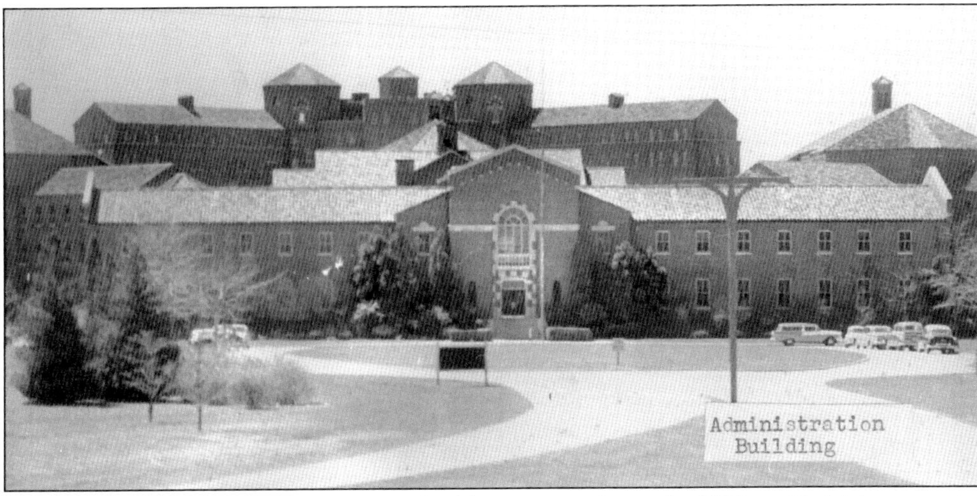

Building 18, the hospital's administration building, was used into the 1980s and held the executive offices and clerical facilities. It also housed the library. Building 25 looms in the distance. (Courtesy of the Long Island Psychiatric Museum.)

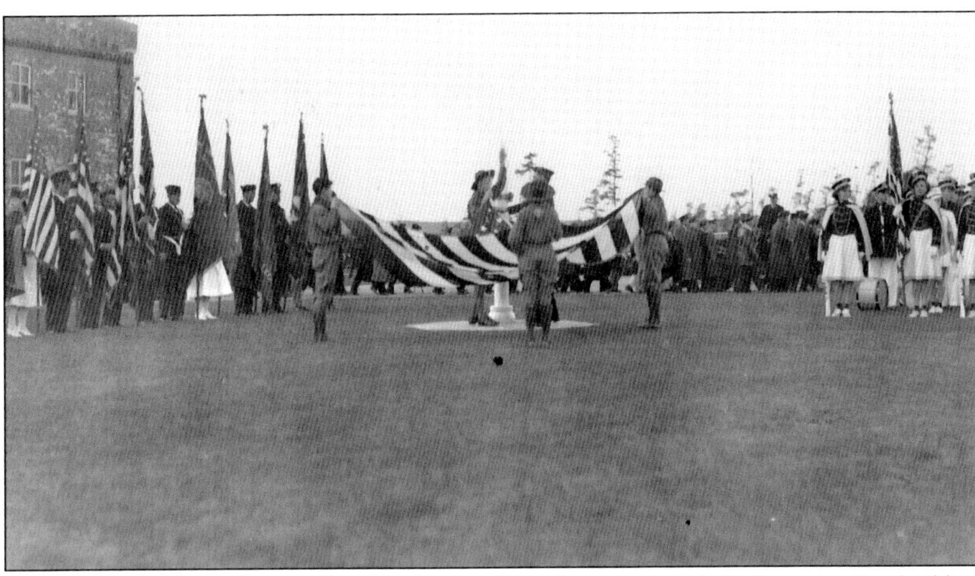

A ceremony marking the installation of a new flagpole at the hospital administration building on November 26, 1940, is seen here. The flag was donated by the Brentwood American Legion Joseph Loeffler Post 1006, whose color guard is present. The flag is being raised by Brentwood Boy Scout Troop 101. (Courtesy of the Brentwood Public Library.)

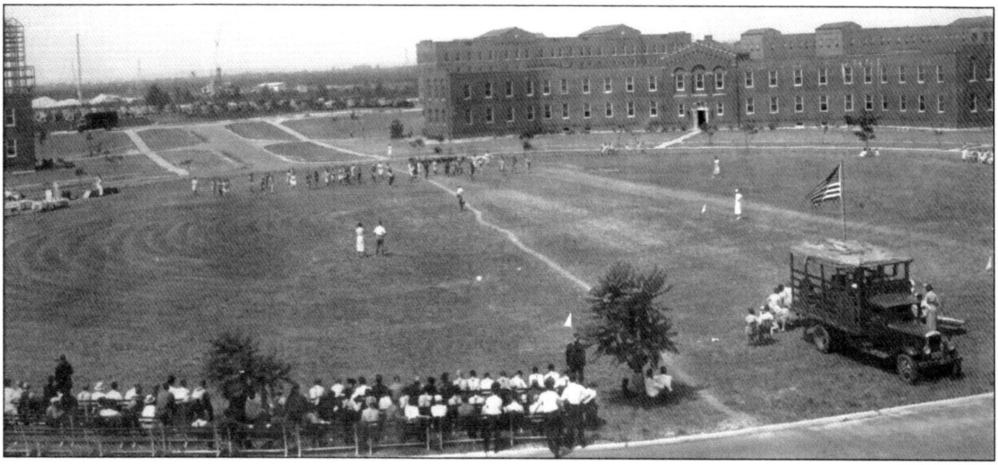

Field days and sporting events during warm weather were an integral part of life for both patients and staff of the state hospitals. It broke up the monotony of institutional life, while exposing patients to fresh air and sunlight, and created a sense of community and belonging between patients and staff. A sporting event is under way near the nurse's residence in this late-1930s image. (Courtesy of the Long Island Psychiatric Museum.)

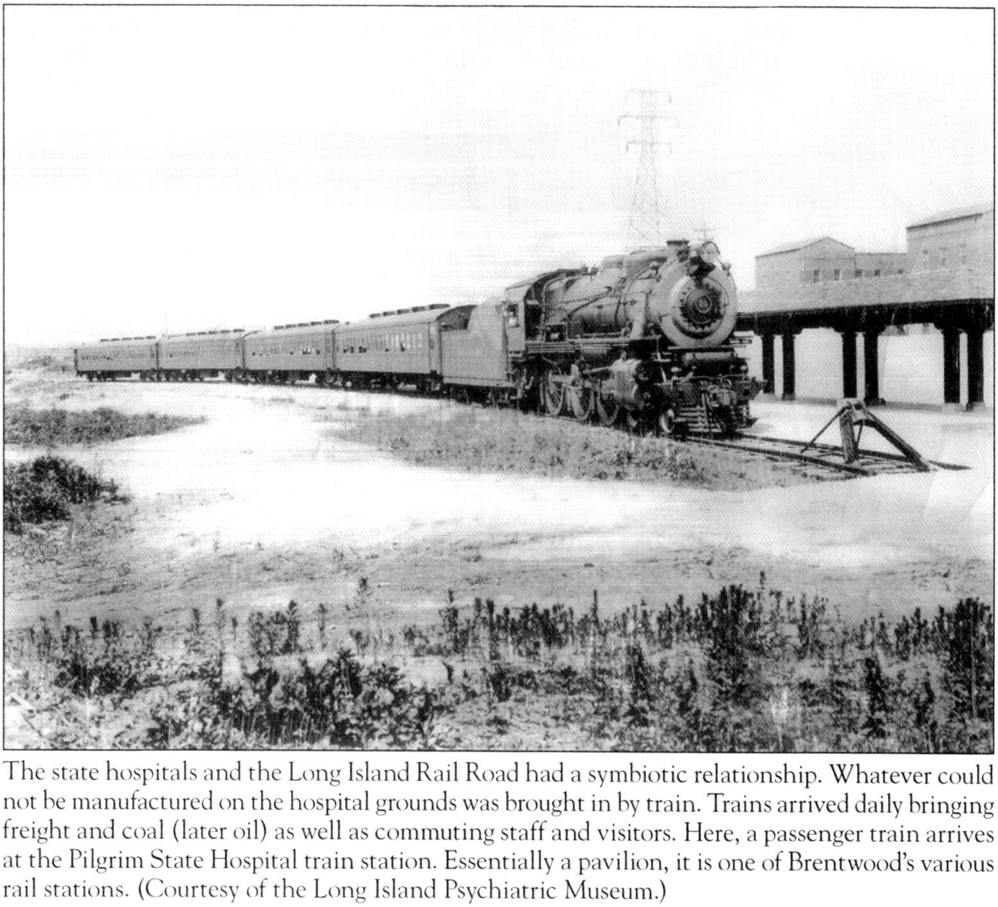

The state hospitals and the Long Island Rail Road had a symbiotic relationship. Whatever could not be manufactured on the hospital grounds was brought in by train. Trains arrived daily bringing freight and coal (later oil) as well as commuting staff and visitors. Here, a passenger train arrives at the Pilgrim State Hospital train station. Essentially a pavilion, it is one of Brentwood's various rail stations. (Courtesy of the Long Island Psychiatric Museum.)

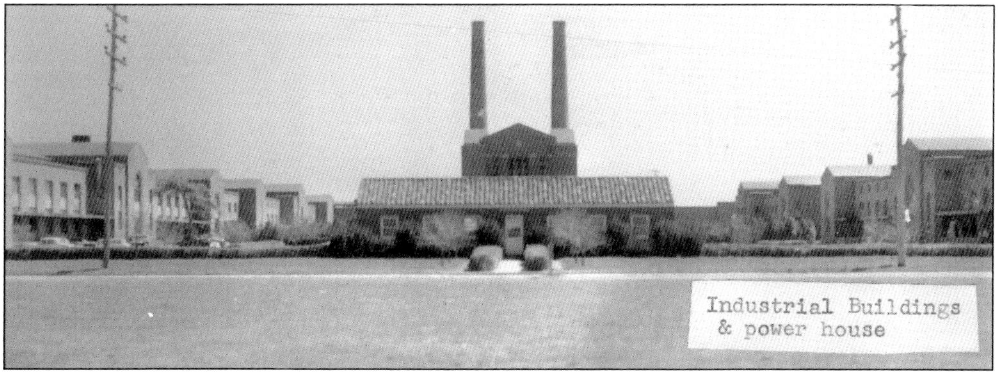

Building 35, Pilgrim's massive powerhouse, rises up in the distance. Industrial buildings, including shops, laundry, and warehouses, line the roads leading to the powerhouse. Building 17, the hospital's greenhouse, had two long glass-enclosed rooms for plant growing in the rear of the building, pictured in the center of this image. (Courtesy of the Long Island Psychiatric Museum.)

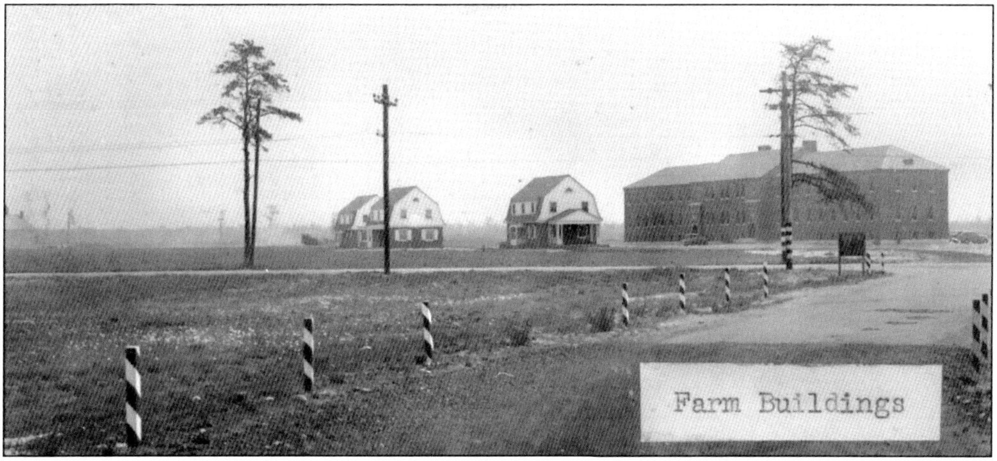

The term farm colony was applied to the various Long Island state hospitals because of their massive farms, and Pilgrim was no different. These farms produced the majority of the food consumed at the hospital, and the patients performing occupational therapy would work the farms various fields and nurseries. Shown here is Pilgrim's farm and its various buildings and sheds, which are today part of the Suffolk County Community College's Brentwood campus. (Courtesy of the Long Island Psychiatric Museum.)

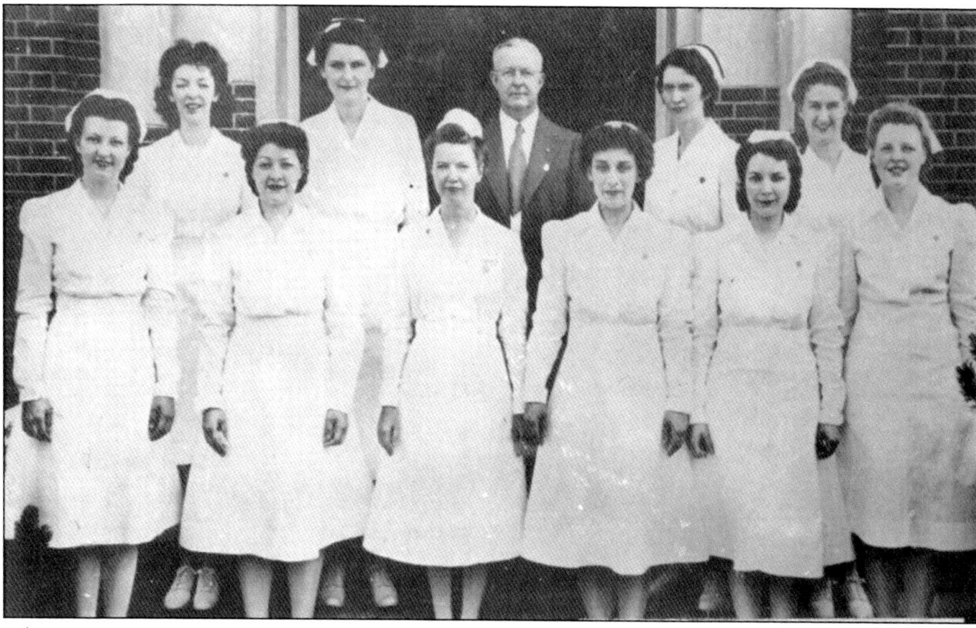

Pilgrim State Hospital had its own nursing school, where students were trained on-site and rotated into the working environment. The Psychiatric Nursing School produced a steady stream of skilled nurses directly into the mental health industry. Pilgrim's school became nationally recognized as a premier educational facility. Here, Dr. Harry J. Worthing, MD, the hospital's director, is with the first graduating class on June 25, 1943. (Courtesy of the Long Island Psychiatric Museum.)

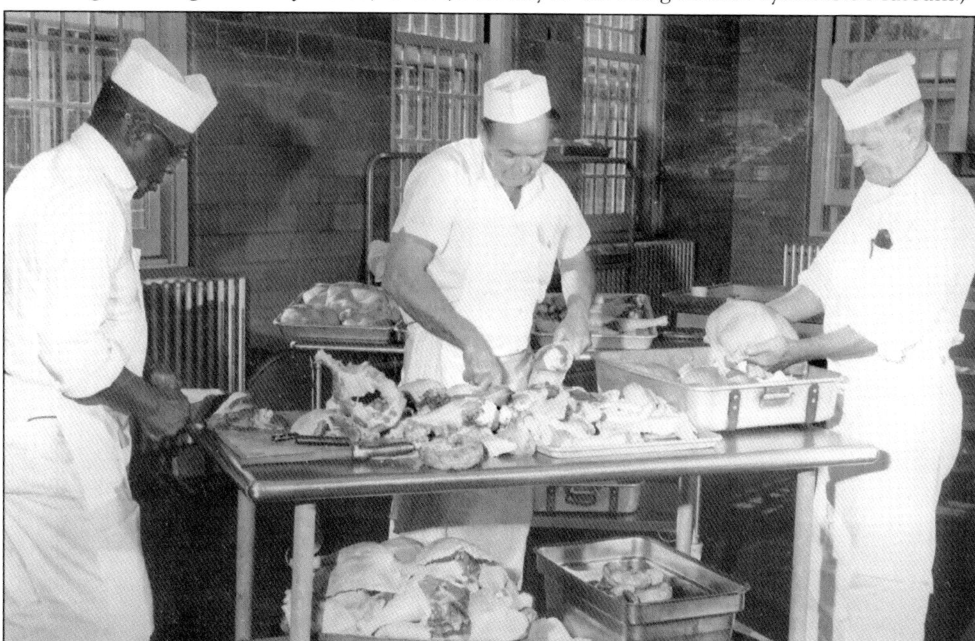

Kitchens were located throughout the various hospital buildings. Each day, the kitchen staff, with the assistance of some patients assigned to kitchen duty, would turn out thousands of meals. Some patients were served on the wards while others were served in dining halls. Here, a kitchen staff is preparing chicken dinners. (Courtesy of the Long Island Psychiatric Museum.)

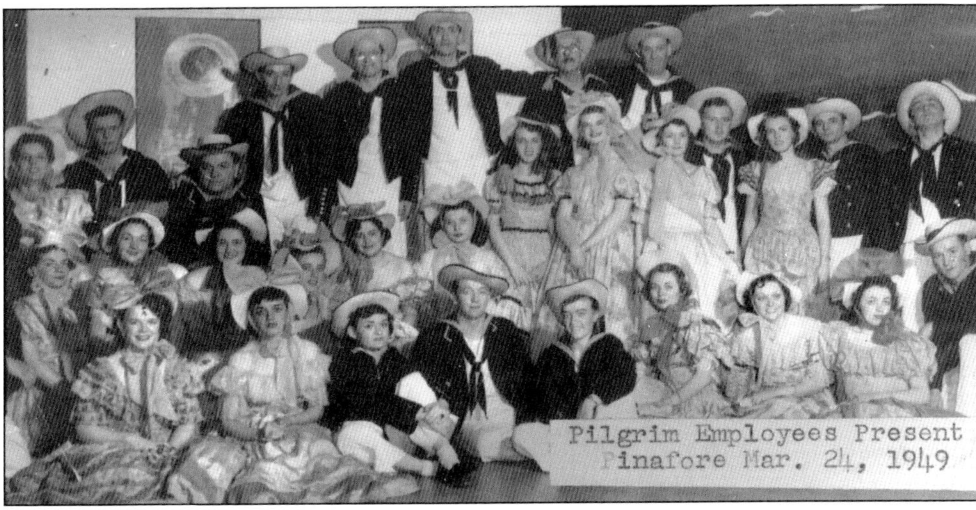

In the early days of the hospital's existence, the majority of the staff resided on the hospital grounds. Pilgrim had a large theater where shows, recitals, concerts, and other entertainments were given by both staff and patients for the residents of the hospital and the local community. This cast photograph of *HMS Pinafore* was staged and performed by Pilgrim employees and their children on March 24, 1949. (Courtesy of the Long Island Psychiatric Museum.)

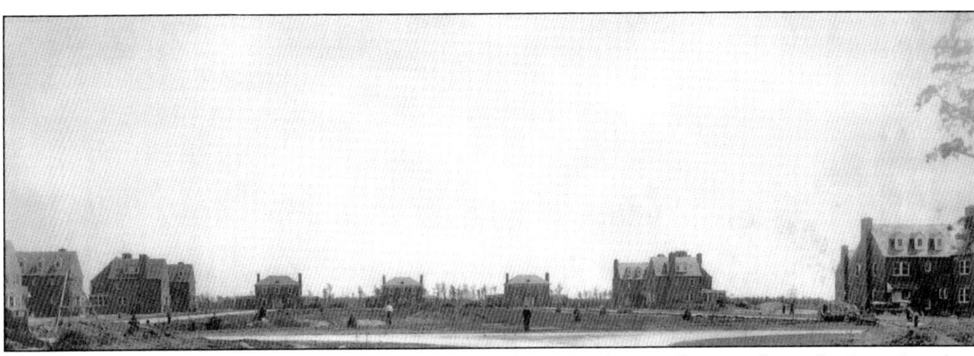

The primary doctors and department heads lived on the hospital grounds with their families, approximately a half-mile from the main complex. This 1935 image shows the doctor's circle, a ring of houses where physicians and psychiatrists resided just after the hospital's opening and the families moved in. Trees and grass would be planted over time, and the section grew into a quaint, exclusive community. (Courtesy of the Long Island Psychiatric Museum.)

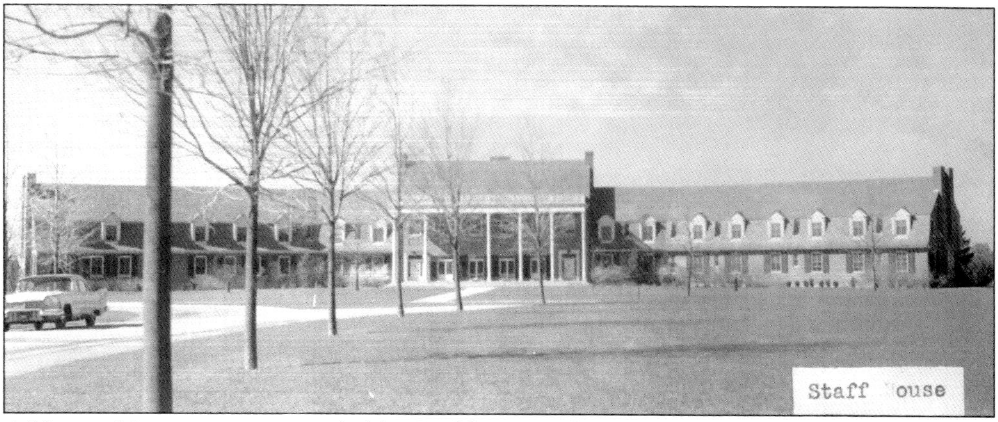

Additional housing was provided by Building 63, the staff house. While the doctors had their own houses for their families, the staff house provided apartment-style housing for the hospital's professionals, including secretaries, aides, and other assistants. The staff house also provided a community recreation center for the employees. (Courtesy of the Long Island Psychiatric Museum.)

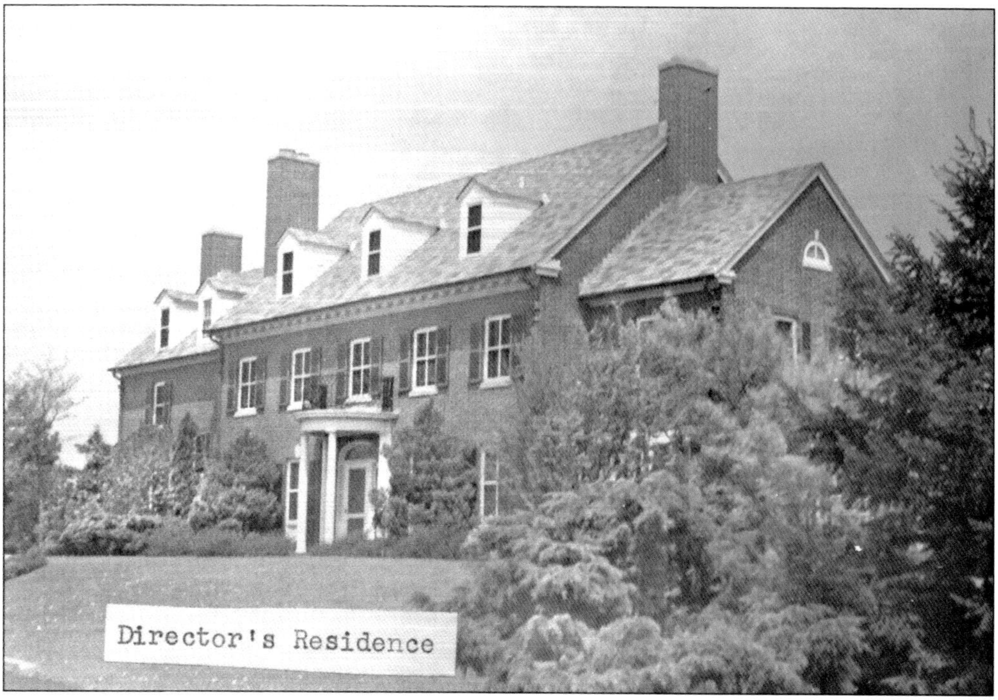

This modest residence was Building 54, the director's house, first occupied by Dr. William J. Tiffany, MD, in 1931. The position was sometimes referred to as a superintendent, and the name for the house reflected this. Just outside the doctor's circle, the residence housed a successive line of Pilgrim State Hospital directors and their families well into the 1970s, when living off the grounds became more fashionable. (Courtesy of the Long Island Psychiatric Museum.)

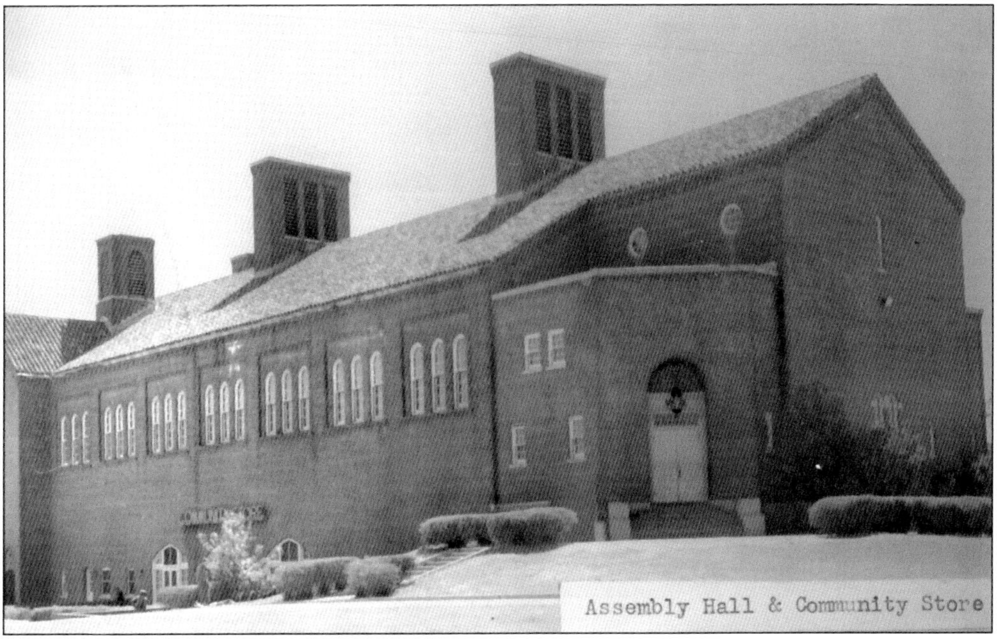

Building 26, the hospital's Assembly Hall and community store, was used by both patients and staff. The building had many purposes, from holding shows, dances, lectures, and other social meetings to a shopping center where patients, employees, and local community residents could buy a variety of items, many manufactured at the hospital. (Courtesy of the Long Island Psychiatric Museum.)

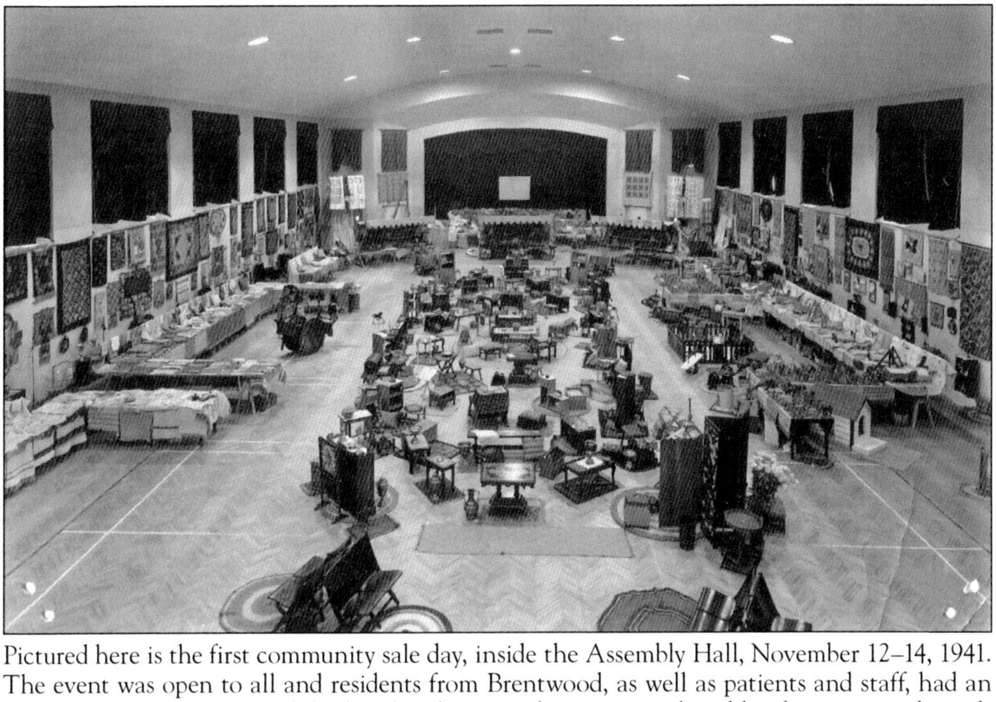

Pictured here is the first community sale day, inside the Assembly Hall, November 12–14, 1941. The event was open to all and residents from Brentwood, as well as patients and staff, had an opportunity to buy many of the handmade items that were produced by the patients through occupational therapy. It gave the patients a sense of pride and accomplishment for their contribution to society. (Courtesy of the Long Island Psychiatric Museum.)

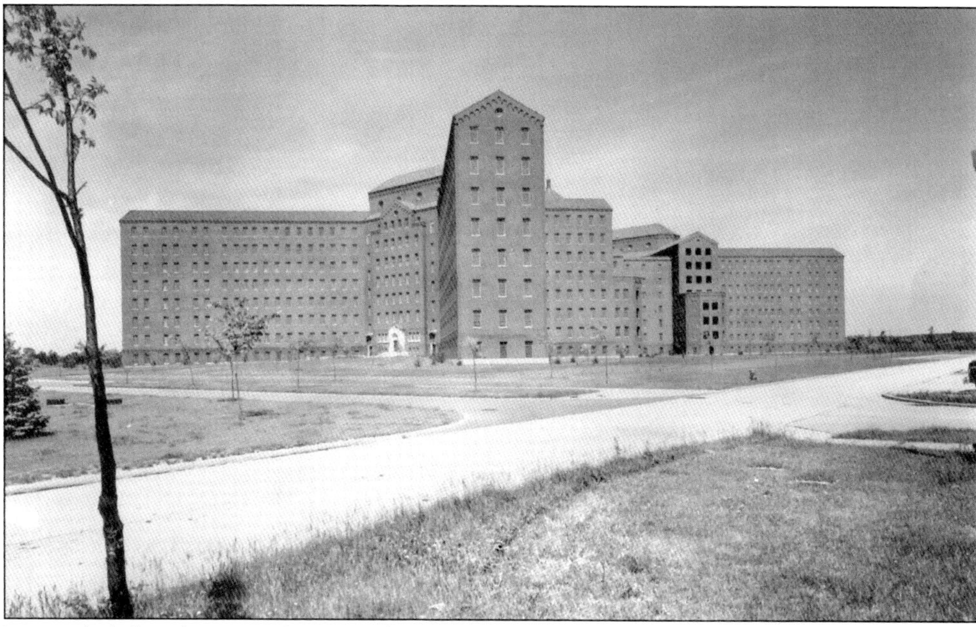

Not included in the original master plan, the massive "80s complex" was constructed in the late 1930s. Buildings 81, 82, and 83 are seen here in 1940 and formed a monstrous facility that was to help alleviate overcrowding. When America entered World War II, the federal government took control of the "80s complex," along with Edgewood State Hospital a mile south, and named it all Mason General Army Hospital. (Courtesy of the Long Island Psychiatric Museum.)

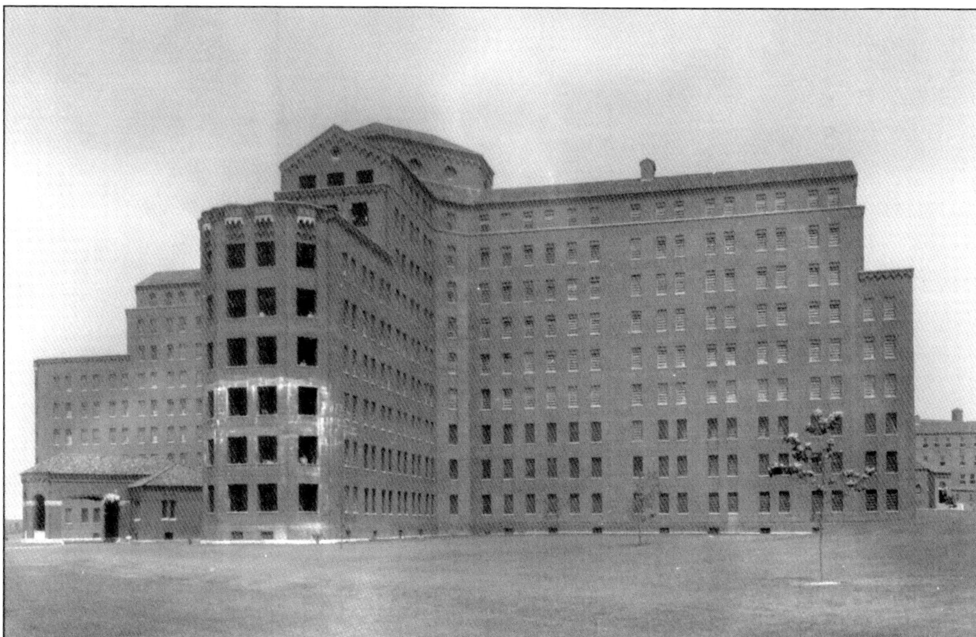

Building 25, one of the largest on the property, is used as the hospital's primary geriatric facility. It has also housed violent patients and the chronically sick. This image is from around 1940. Building 25, along with the "80s complex," have become the defining iconic symbols of Pilgrim State Hospital. (Courtesy of the Long Island Psychiatric Museum.)

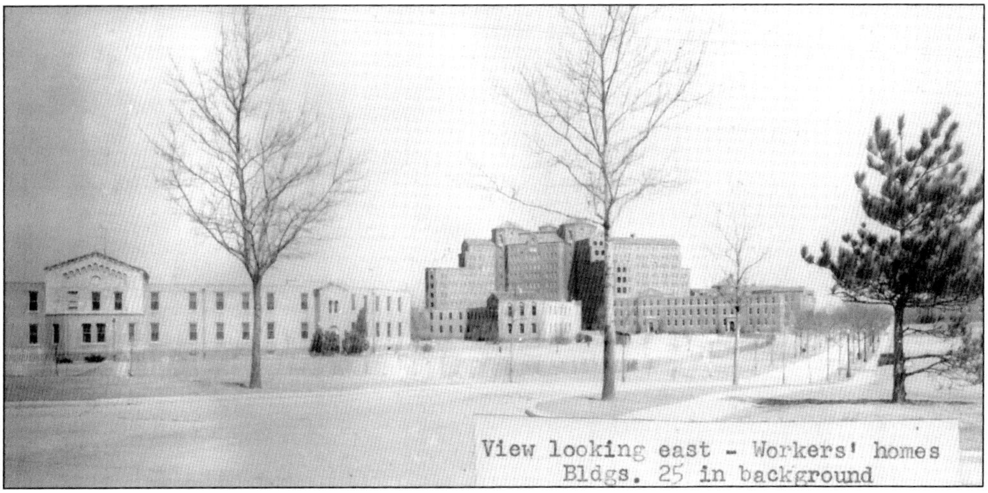

A c. 1950s view, looking east from the intersection H Road and B Road, shows semicircular Buildings 72 and 69, both part of the nurse's circle of housing, with Building 42 just beyond them. Building 25, Pilgrim State Hospital's geriatric unit, looms in the distance and dominates the scene. (Courtesy of the Long Island Psychiatric Museum.)

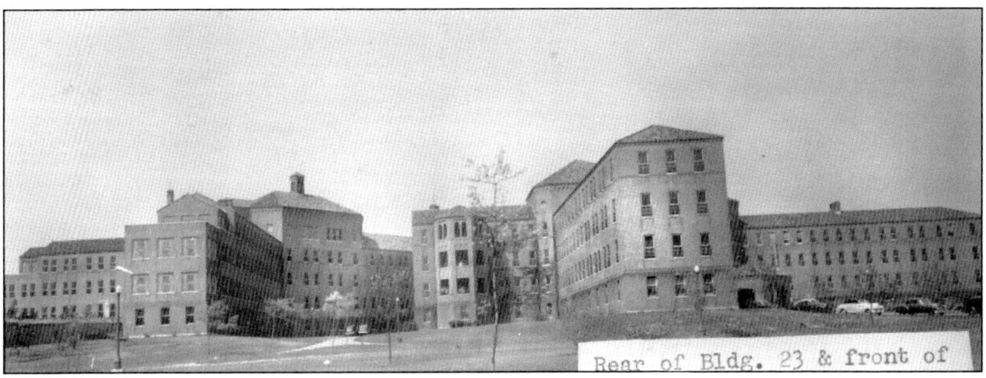

A 1950s image captures the rear of Building 23 and a side profile showing the front of Building 22 near the hospital's main entrance. Building 23 was the hospital's medical-surgical facility, known as med-surge. It housed an emergency room, infirmary, operating theaters, and recovery rooms as well as Pilgrim's primary morgue and forensic laboratories. Building 22 was the admitting ward, which was used for intake, observations, and processing. (Courtesy of the Long Island Psychiatric Museum.)

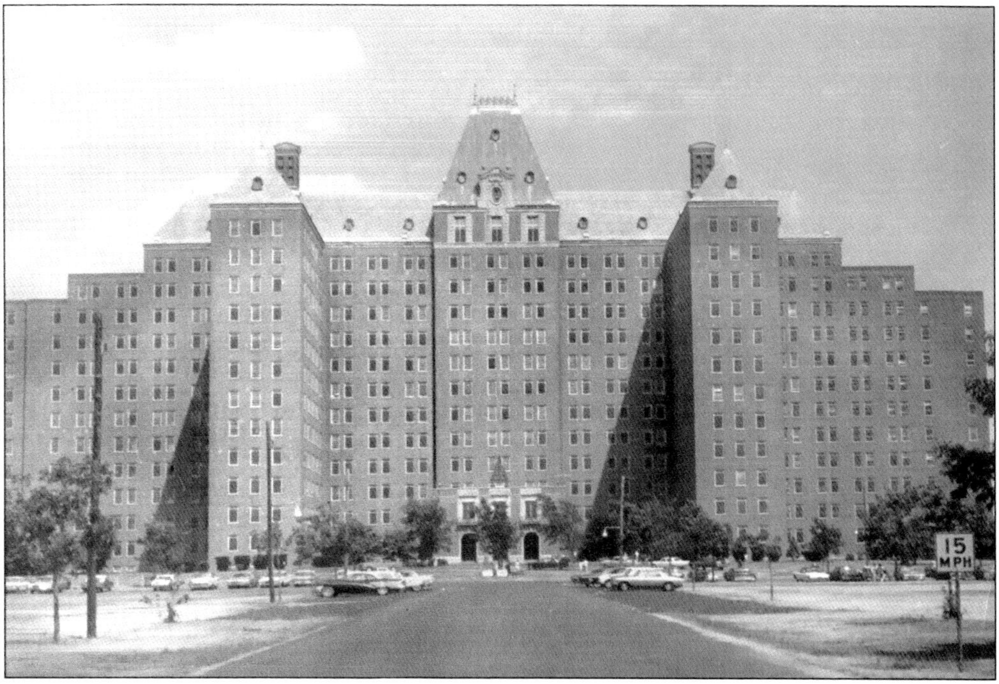

Building 102 at the Edgewood State Hospital, a mile south of Pilgrim, was for a time the tallest structure on Long Island. This facility, built on land that spans Deer Park and Brentwood, was intended to rival Pilgrim in size. Building 102 was Edgewood's largest and primary building, thus becoming an iconic symbol of that hospital. It housed the infirmary and medical-surgical units, dental facilities, library, and acute patients. (Courtesy of the Long Island Psychiatric Museum.)

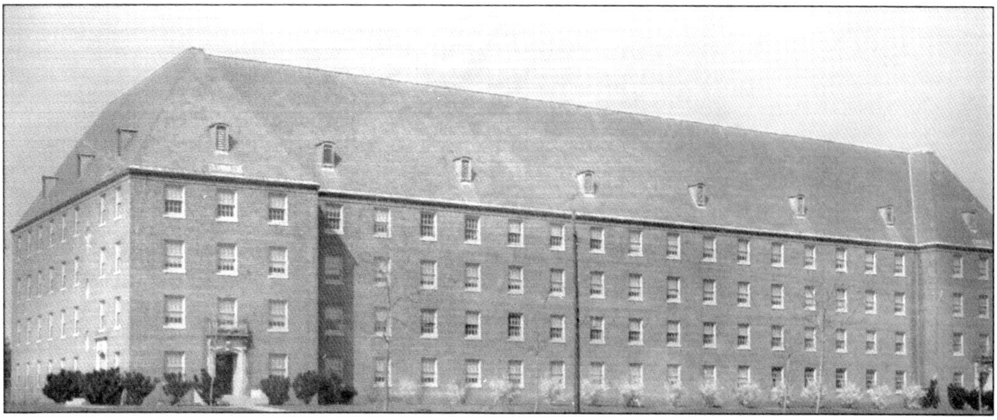

Originally, Building 140 provided apartments for employees and was designated for use for married couples housing. Edgewood State Hospital would never be built to its intended size. It became a subunit of Pilgrim State Hospital and treated the mentally ill suffering from tuberculosis. When employee housing was moved to Pilgrim, Building 140 was used for the Tubercular Continuing Care Unit. (Courtesy of the Long Island Psychiatric Museum.)

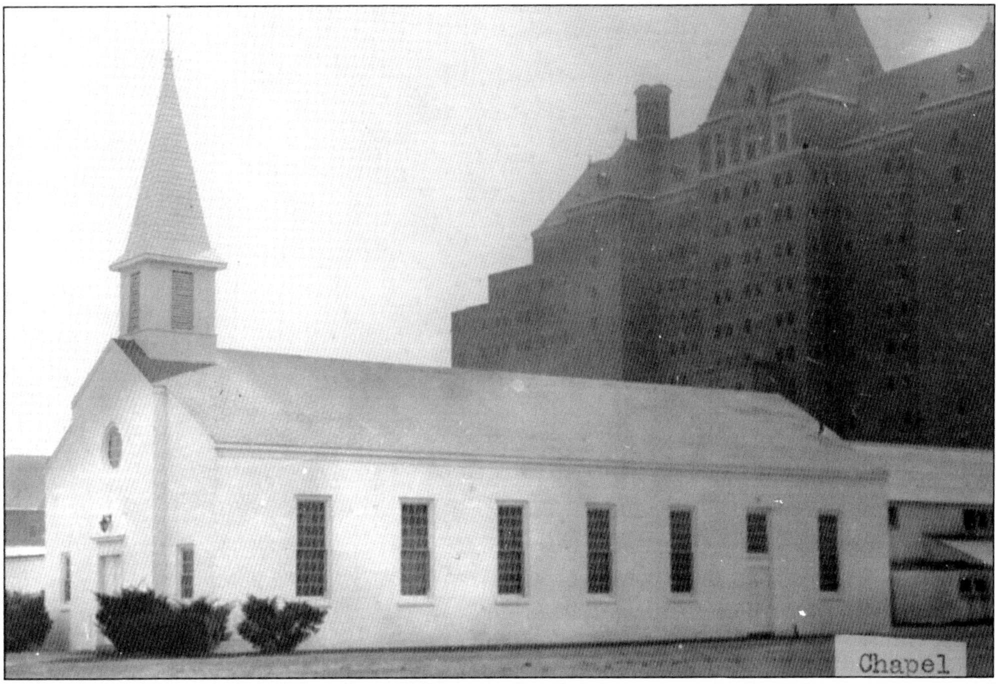

During World War II, the entire Edgewood Hospital and the "80s complex" at Pilgrim was operated as Mason General Army Hospital, treating soldiers suffering from battle fatigue. The Army built this small chapel for use by its patients and staff. When it became Edgewood once again, the hospital continued to use the chapel until it closed in the 1970s and all services transferred to Pilgrim. (Courtesy of the Long Island Psychiatric Museum.)

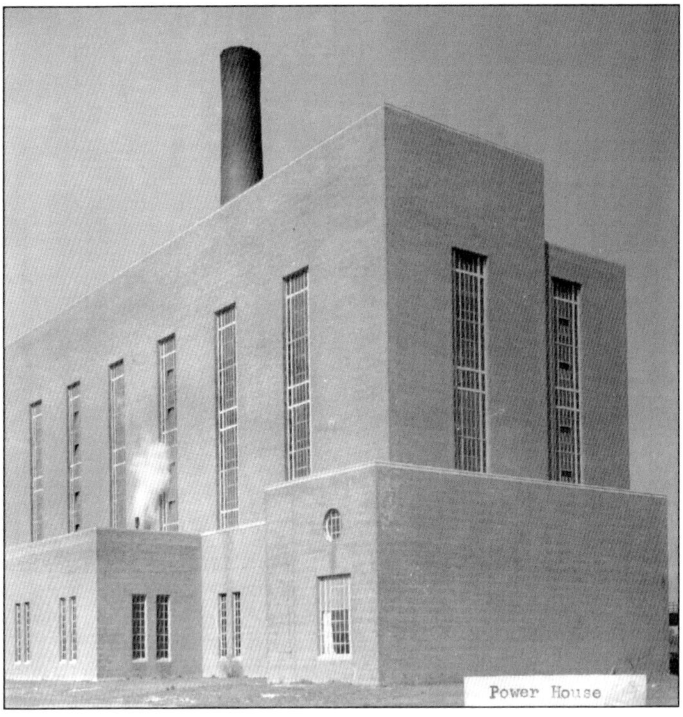

Building 135 was Edgewood State Hospital's powerhouse, complete with its own rail spur that received daily shipments of coal and visitors on the weekend. Although the main complex of buildings was on the Deer Park side of the property, the rail spur came through on the Brentwood side. (Courtesy of the Long Island Psychiatric Museum.)

Six

Suburban Paradise

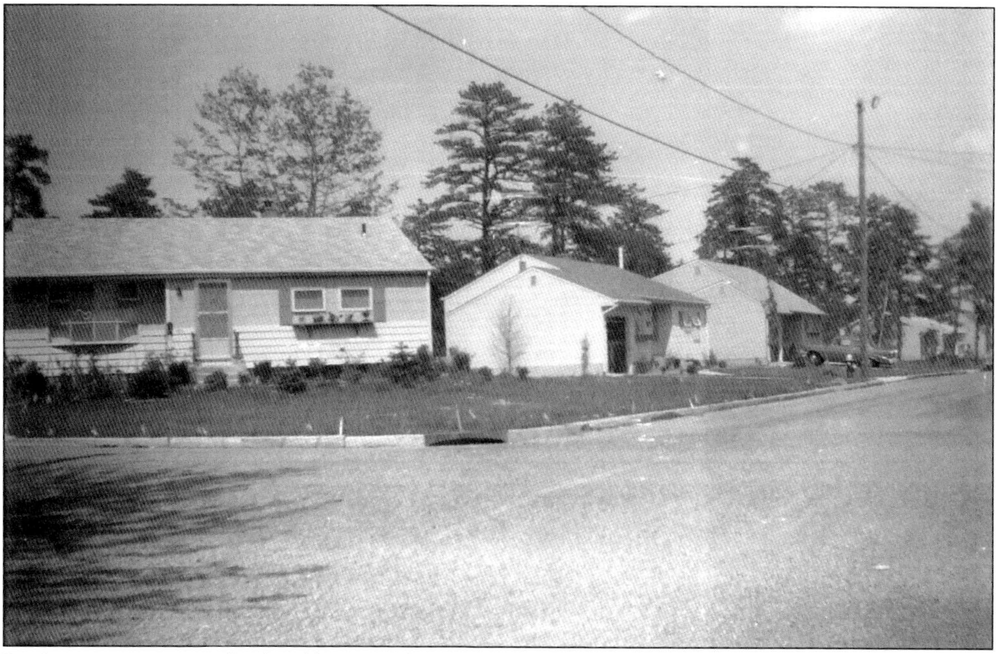

In the postwar era, suburbia blossomed on Long Island as millions left the city for the suburbs. In two decades, the majority of Long Island was transferred from rural hinterland to suburban bedroom communities. Cheap land brought contractors and developers to Brentwood, inspired by Abraham Levitt's standardized house plan for mass-produced communities. A Brentwood street in the 1950s reflects this new suburban standardized model. (Courtesy of the Brentwood Public Library.)

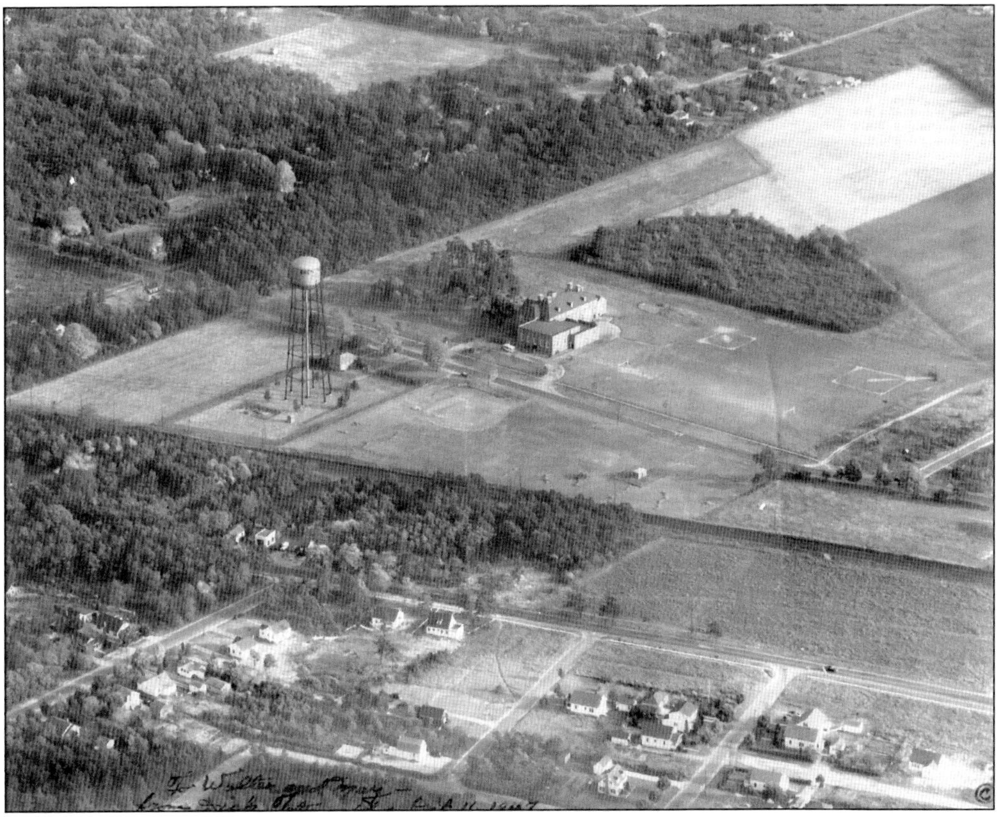

An aerial view of central Brentwood, taken on September 16, 1947, shows the Brentwood Village School and water tower. Note the high school has not been built yet; that land is still open farm fields. The scene eventually changed as housing developments arose and the population was driven up by the exodus of families from the city, the arrival of refugees from war torn Europe, and an influx of Puerto Ricans. (Courtesy of the Brentwood Public Library.)

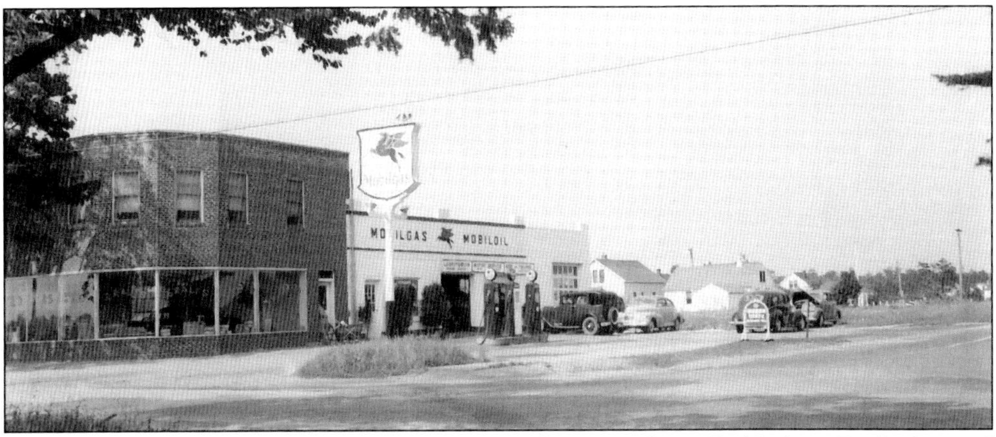

The corner of Fifth Avenue and Suffolk Avenue looking east shows Erali's Auto Dealership and Mobilgas station in the area of Brentwood known as Victory Farms in 1946. The gas station became a series of auto body shops, and the brick building was expanded and had a pointed roof added in the 1960s when it became Erale's Law Firm. Note the spelling of the last name; the family legally changed it when they created the law firm. (Courtesy of the Erale family.)

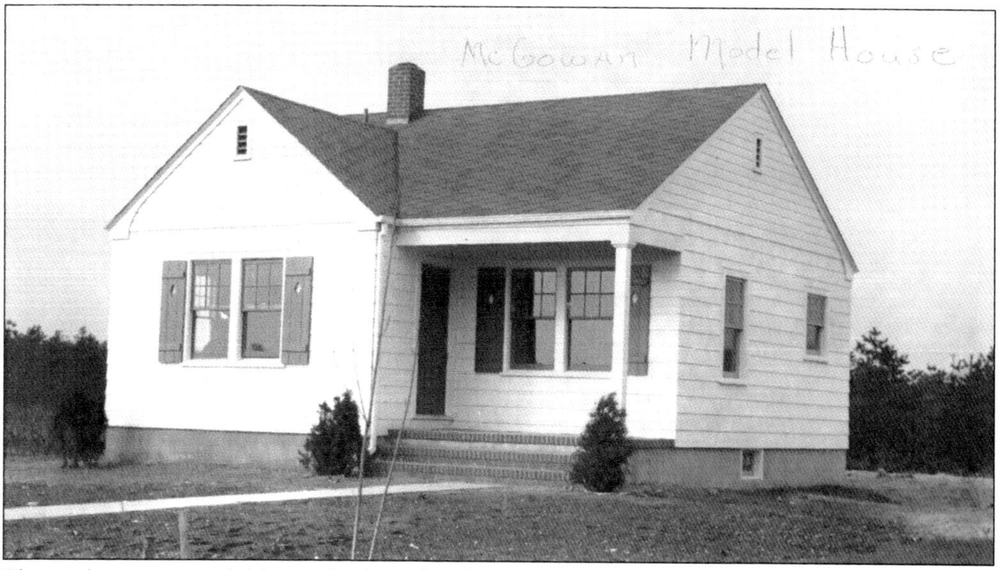

Shown here is a model home built by McGowan Reality and Developers to showcase their standardized economic homes. This photograph was taken by Brentwood historian Verne Dyson in the early 1950s. The McGowans built hundreds of these easy to produce, standardized houses across Deer Park, Brentwood, Bay Shore, and Central Islip. Most are still standing, and many having undergone renovations, expansions, and extensions in the decades after their construction. (Courtesy of the Sr. Anne Pulling Collection, Central Islip Public Library.)

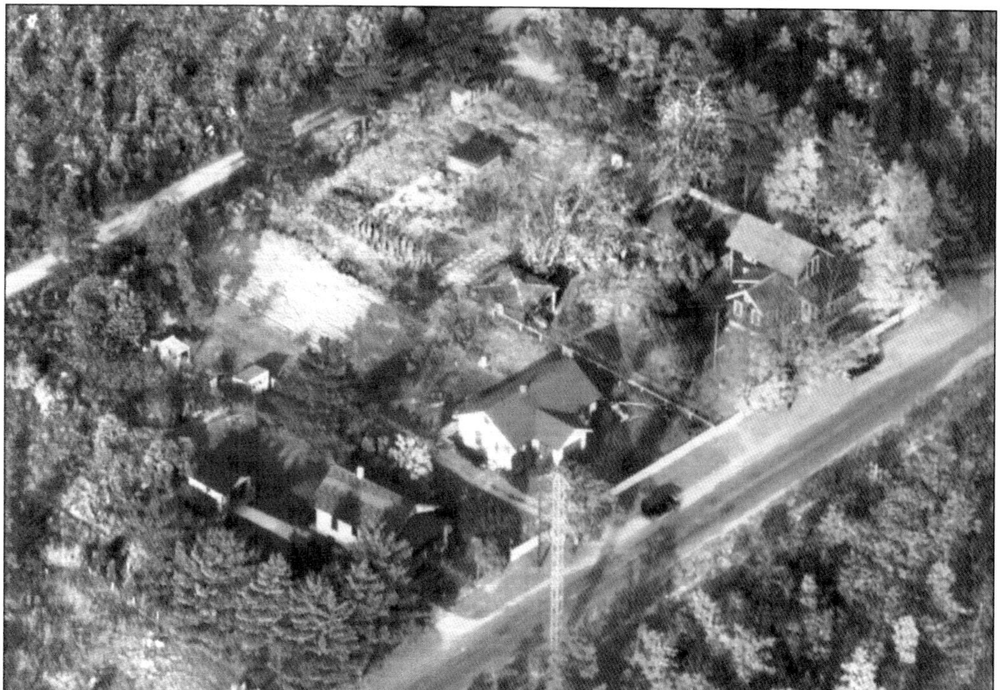

Clarke Street, looking north in 1955 just before it was developed with tract homes and suburban housing, was still heavily wooded with some small farms. (Courtesy of the Brentwood Public Library.)

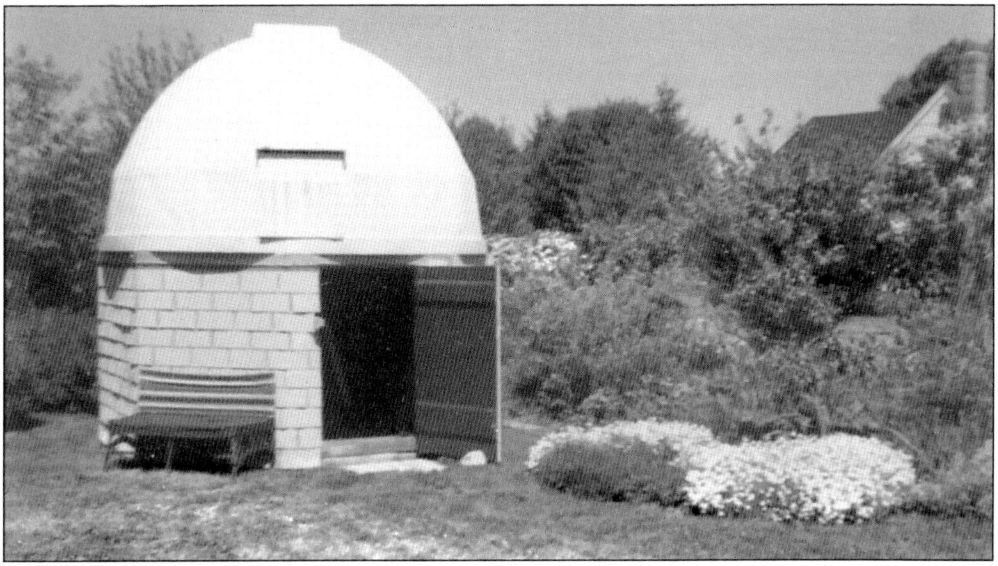

This observatory was built by amateur astronomer Walter Schad in the backyard of his home on Grant Avenue in 1956. From there, Walter made numerous surveillances and computations of the night sky, many of which were published in local papers. (Courtesy of Jeanne L. Taylor.)

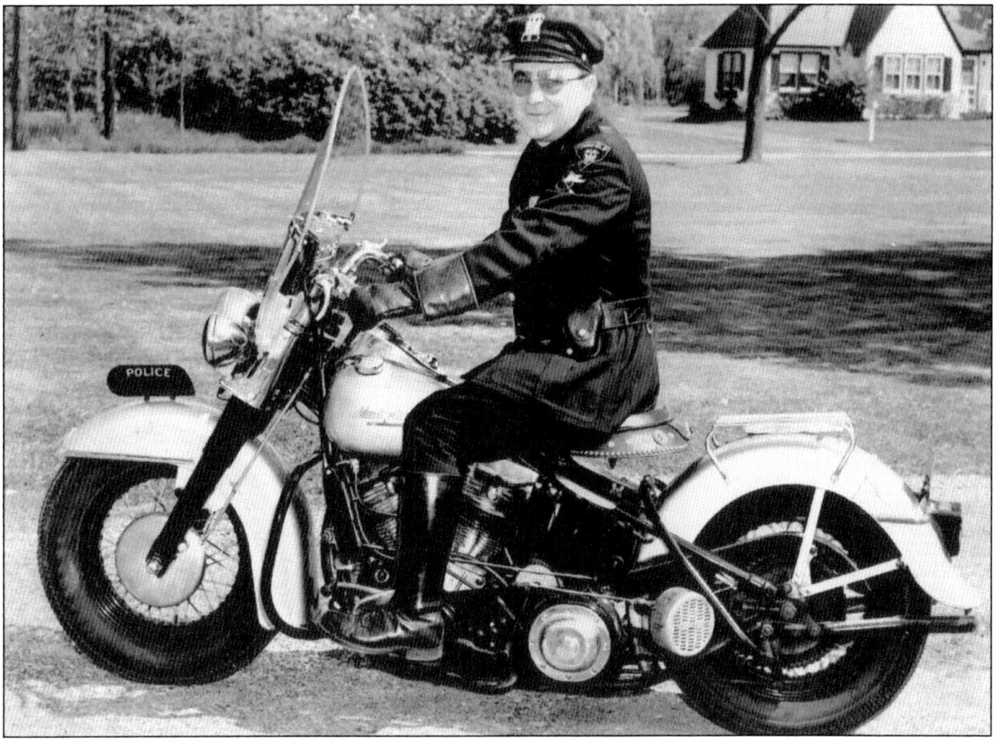

Town of Islip police officer Joseph Loeffler was a Brentwood resident whose family was very prominent in the community. He was named for his uncle, Brentwood's only World War I casualty. Serving in World War II before joining the police force, he served in the motorcycle unit and harbor patrol. Joe Loeffler eventually became the chief of police for Ocean Beach on Fire Island. He is buried in the Brentwood Cemetery. (Courtesy of the Suffolk County Police Museum.)

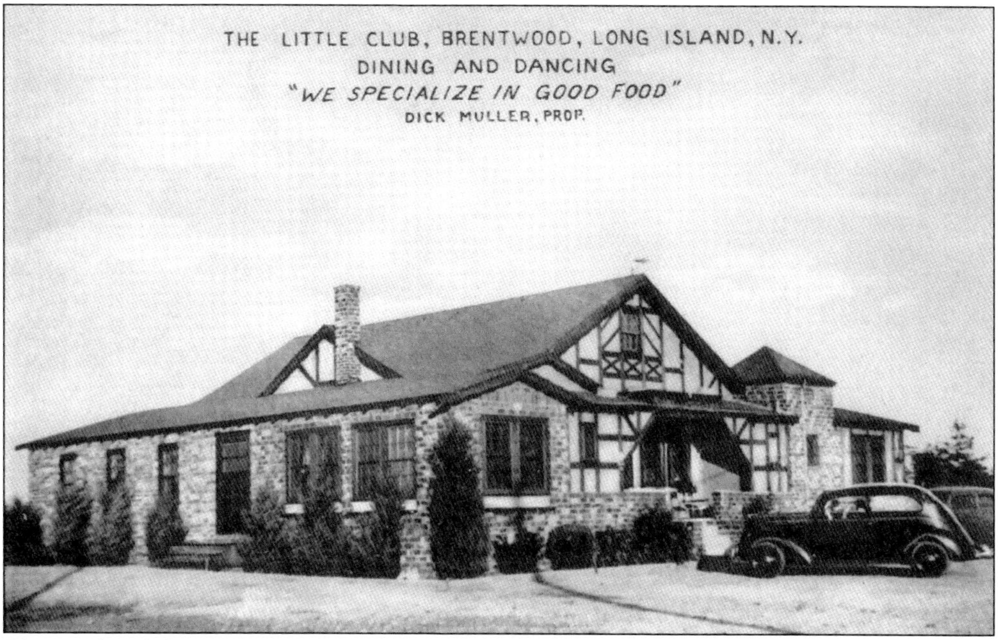

The Little Club Restaurant was located on Crooked Hill Road and was eventually bought and owned by Teresa Grant and Anna O'Boyle. The restaurant became one of many business establishments owned and operated by the Grant family across Brentwood and Central Islip. (Courtesy of the James Fordyce Collection.)

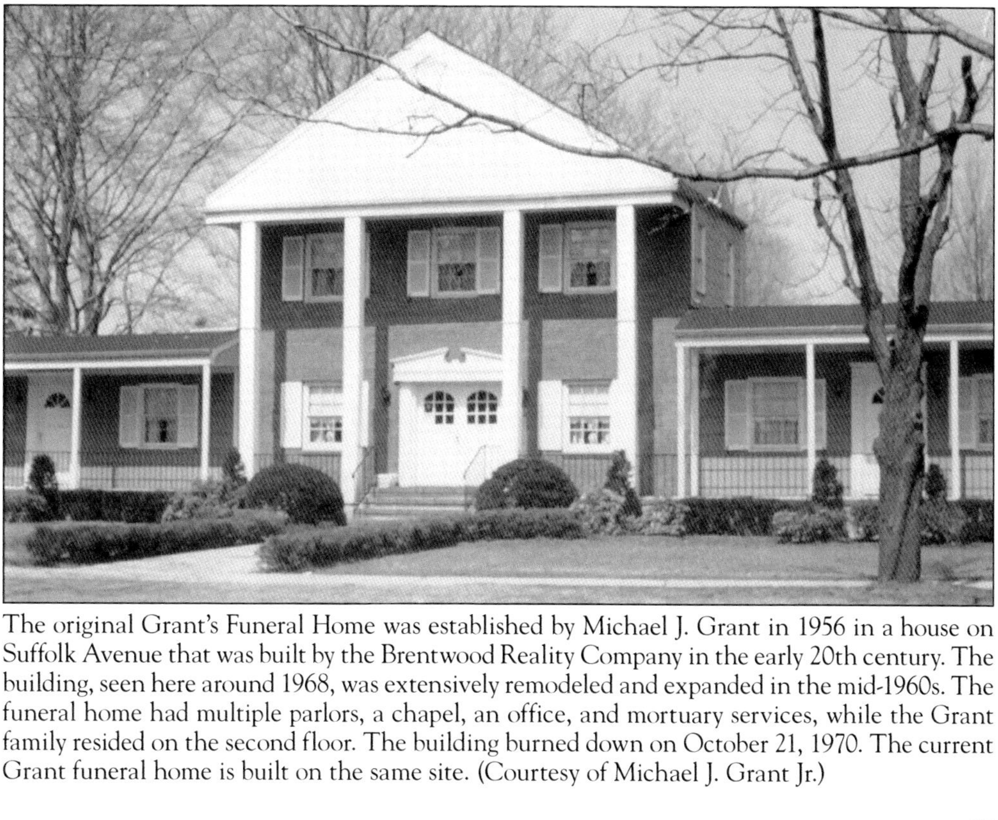

The original Grant's Funeral Home was established by Michael J. Grant in 1956 in a house on Suffolk Avenue that was built by the Brentwood Reality Company in the early 20th century. The building, seen here around 1968, was extensively remodeled and expanded in the mid-1960s. The funeral home had multiple parlors, a chapel, an office, and mortuary services, while the Grant family resided on the second floor. The building burned down on October 21, 1970. The current Grant funeral home is built on the same site. (Courtesy of Michael J. Grant Jr.)

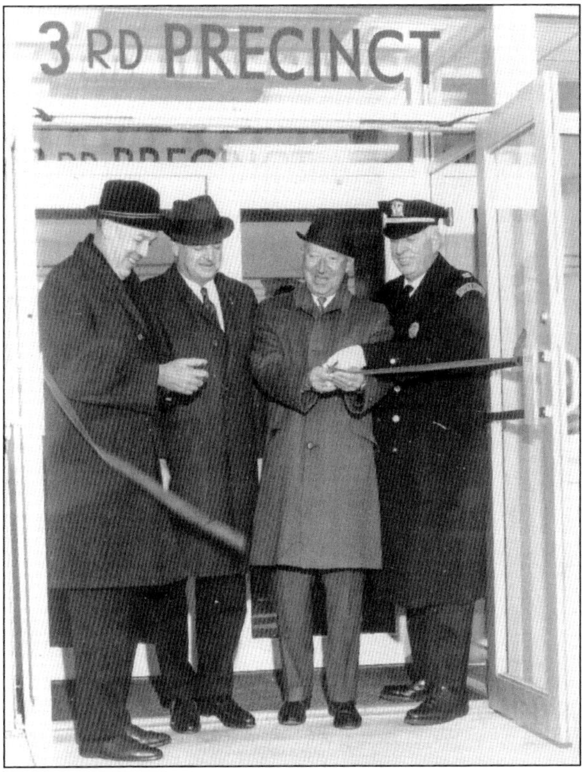

The Suffolk County Police Department was organized in the late 1950s. The original 3rd Precinct was located where the Bay Shore Library is today. Town of Islip supervisor Thomas J. Harwood, county executive H. Lee Dennison, Police Commissioner John L. Barry, and commanding officer Capt. A. Russell Richards are pictured, from left to right, at the ribbon-cutting ceremony of the new 3rd Precinct in the North Bay Shore section of Brentwood on December 16, 1964. (Courtesy of the Suffolk County Police Museum.)

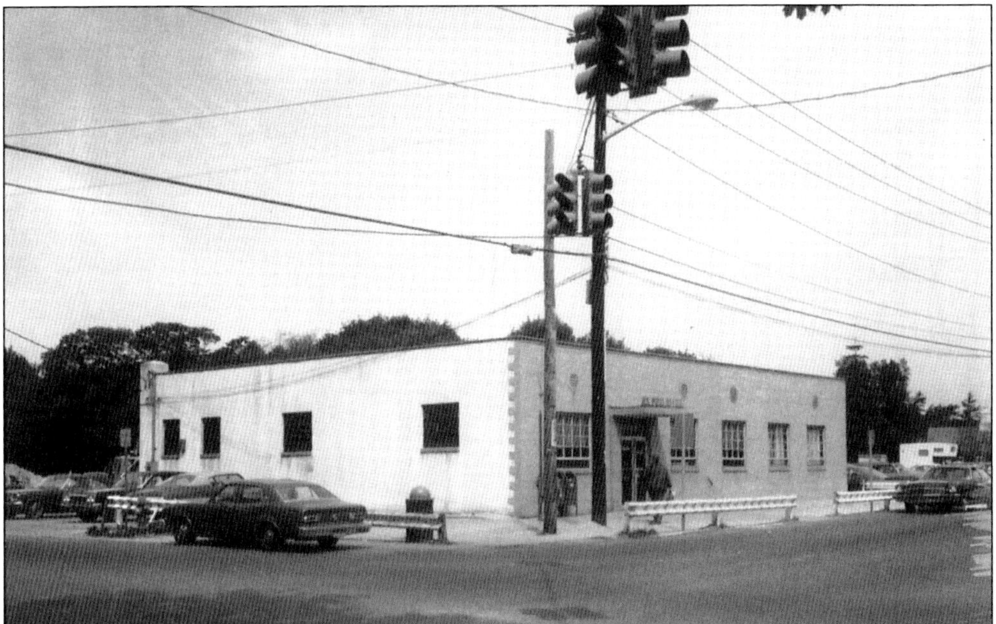

After seven decades, the Brentwood Post Office moved out of the Quanahassett Hotel and relocated a block away on Fourth Street in 1955. This post office operated until 1977, when a new modern post office was built on Second Avenue on the site of Dr. Edward Newberry's Modern Times home and dental office. (Courtesy of the Brentwood Public Library.)

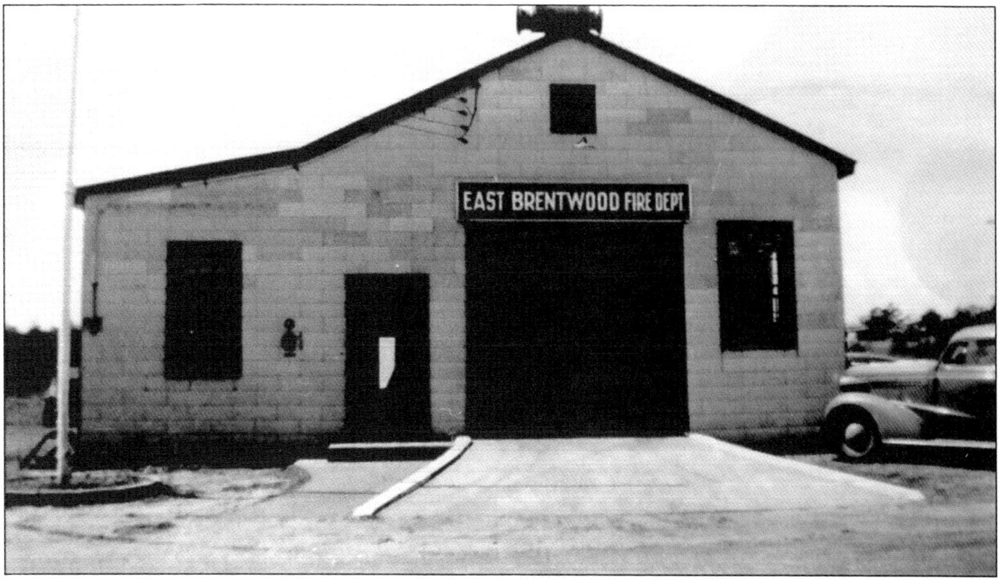

The East Brentwood Fire Department formed in 1938 for the emerging community of East Brentwood, which was intended to be its own separate village. As this section of the community grew, the department was expanded, and eventually a new department building was constructed on the spot of the original. East Brentwood was absorbed into the larger Brentwood community, and today, the fire district still serves this area and parts of Central Islip. (Courtesy of the Brentwood Public Library.)

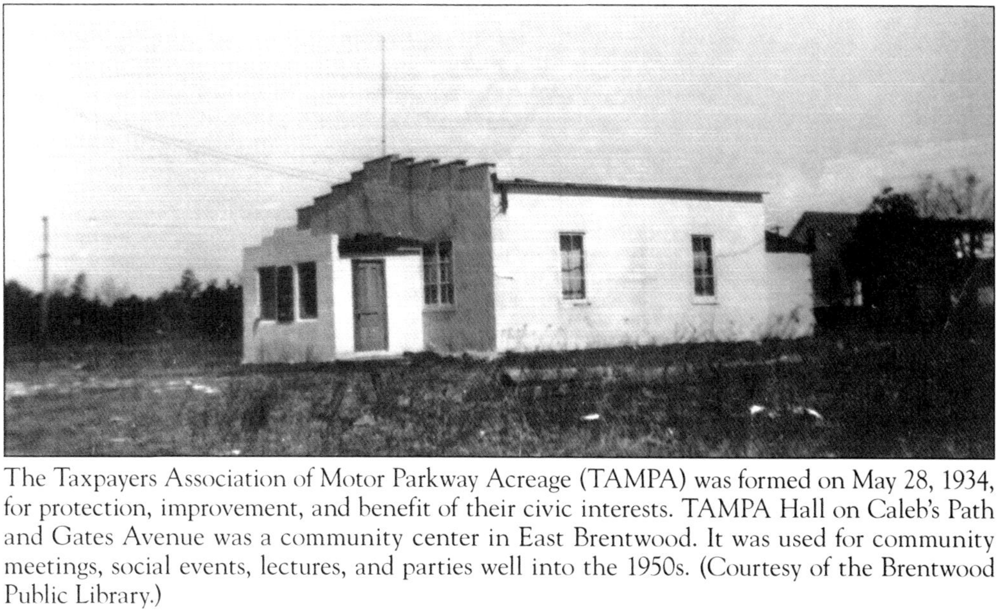

The Taxpayers Association of Motor Parkway Acreage (TAMPA) was formed on May 28, 1934, for protection, improvement, and benefit of their civic interests. TAMPA Hall on Caleb's Path and Gates Avenue was a community center in East Brentwood. It was used for community meetings, social events, lectures, and parties well into the 1950s. (Courtesy of the Brentwood Public Library.)

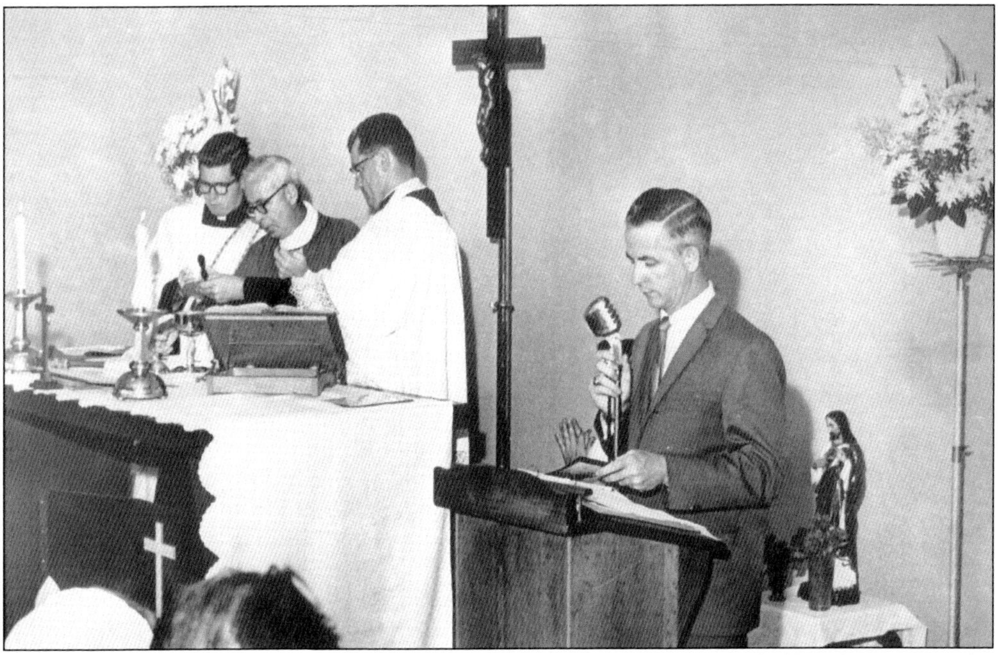

The newly established congregation of St. Luke's Roman Catholic Church held its first mass at the original Brentwood Fire Department building on First Avenue in June 1965. A church was built on Wicks Road soon after. Celebrating this first mass are, from left to right, Father Judge, Father Ryan, Deacon Bill, and Stephen Lyons (commentator). (Courtesy of Michael J. Grant Jr.)

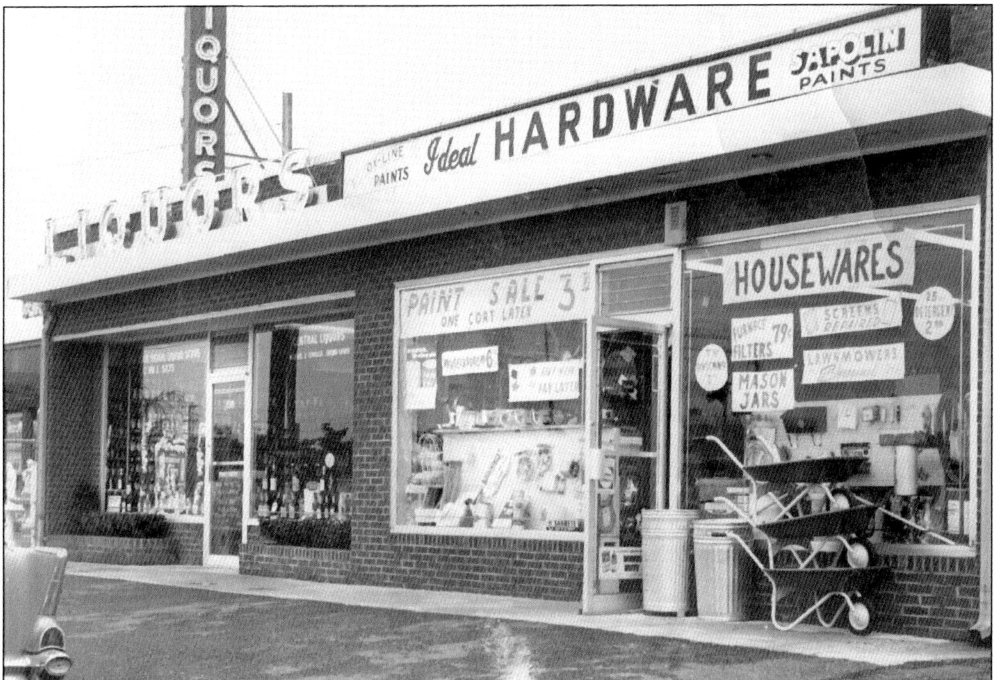

Ideal Hardware, located in a shopping center on Heyward Street, was owned by Al Gissi and operated from the 1950s well into the 1980s. (Courtesy of Michael J. Grant Jr.)

Daurice Snyder, a graduate of the American School of Ballet, appeared in shows with Milton Burrell, Jackie Gleason, and George Dewitt. Snyder taught at the Academy of St. Joseph and St. Anne's Parochial School after a leg injury ended her professional dancing career. A member of the Dance Masters of America, she even brought the Royal Academy of Dance from London to examine and award certificates to her students. (Courtesy of the Brentwood Public Library.)

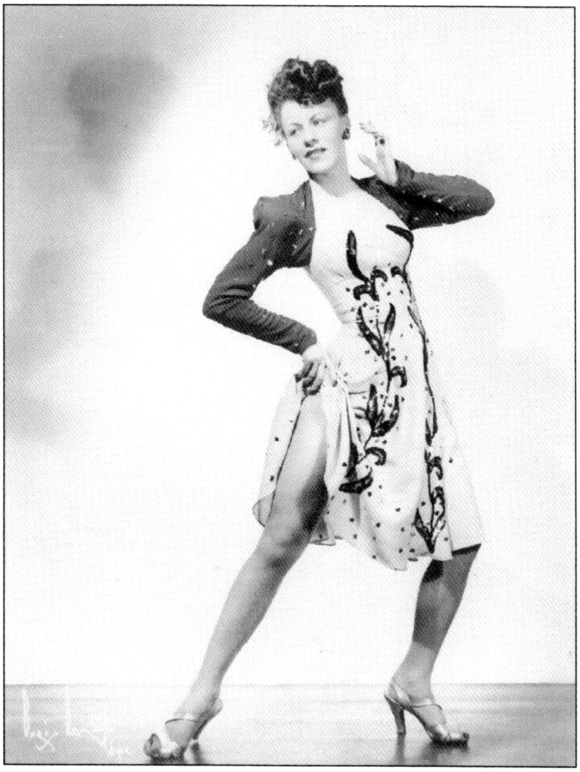

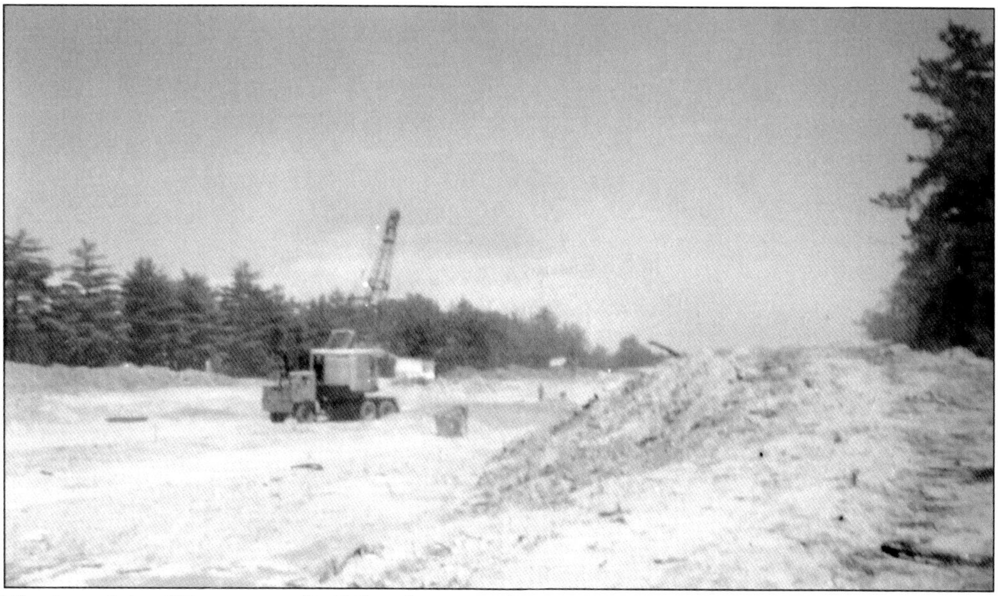

The Long Island Expressway (I-495) is shown under construction at Brentwood in October 1962. The LIE became the major arterial highway through central Long Island, enabling mass movement of commuters in all directions. Built in the northern section of Brentwood, it effectively severed the northernmost portion of the community around Vanderbilt Motor Parkway from the rest of Brentwood proper. The Brentwood sections north of the LIE became part of Hauppague. (Courtesy of the Brentwood Public Library.)

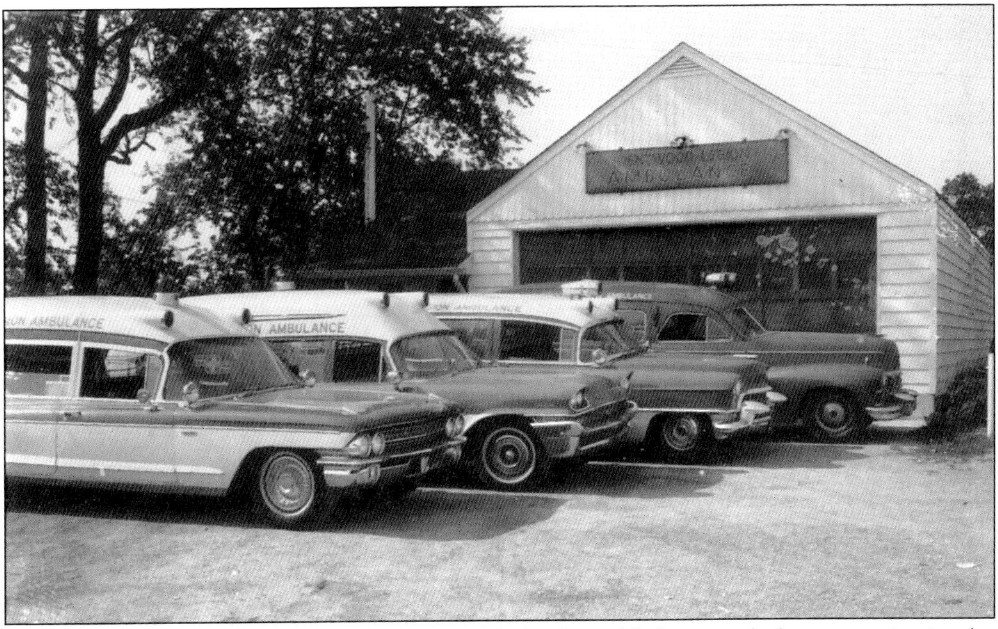

The Brentwood American Legion Post 1006 helped establish an ambulance service in the community in 1958. The Brentwood Legion Ambulance is seen here in 1963 at their new station on Third Avenue. Becoming one of the busiest EMS responders in the country, the station was expanded in the late 1960s with another garage before a new modern station was built on the same spot in the 1980s. (Courtesy of the Brentwood Legion Ambulance.)

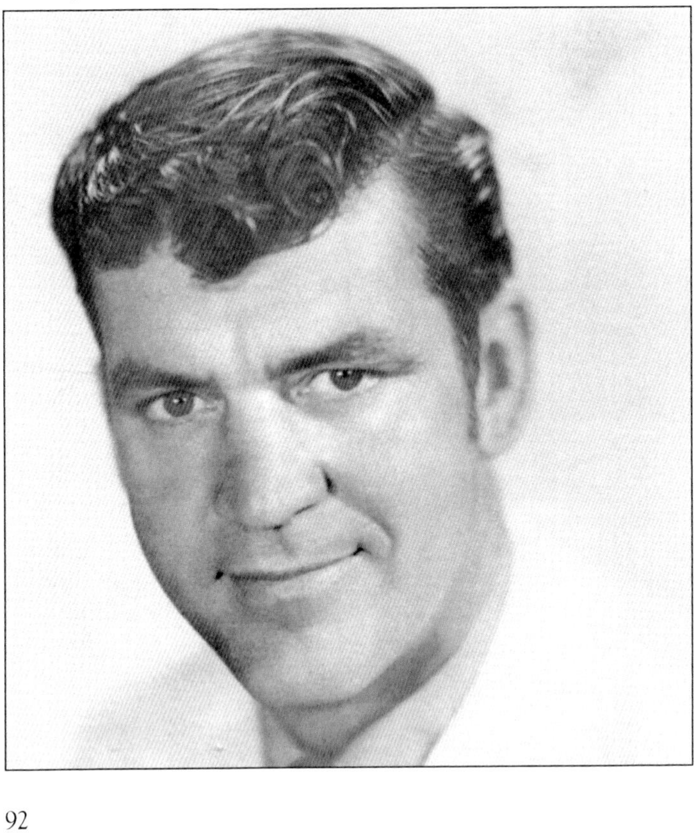

Legislator Michael J. Grant (R) (1932–1998) is photographed at left. A Korean War veteran and owner of Grant's Funeral Home in Brentwood, Grant was one of the great leaders of Brentwood though the second half of the 20th century. Known as the "Mayor of Brentwood," Grant's philanthropic efforts made him a heavily active member of the community, representing that town in matters of legislation as well as being a commissioner in the fire department. The Suffolk County Community College's western campus is named after him. (Courtesy of Michael J. Grant Jr.)

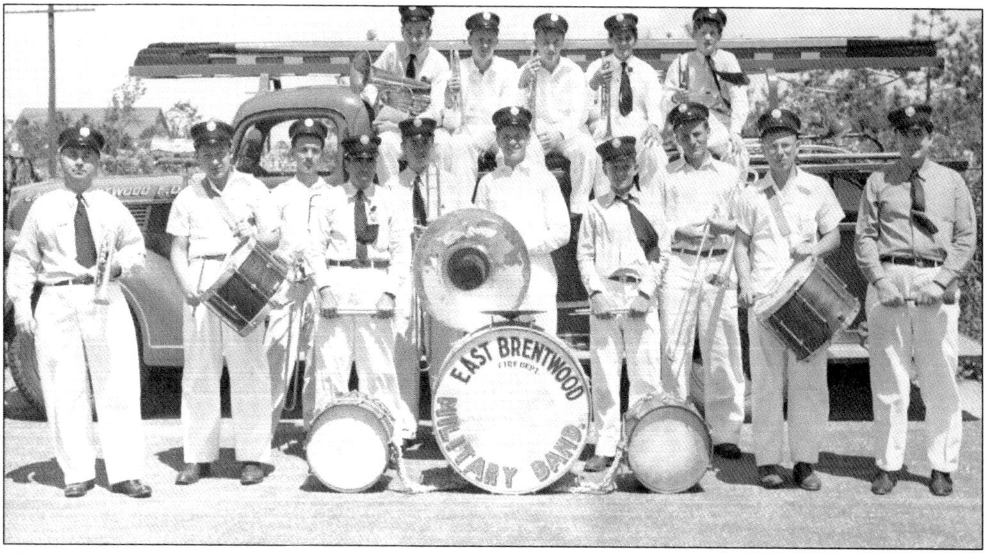

This c. 1950s photograph shows the East Brentwood Fire Department Band. The band marched in numerous Brentwood parades and played at many community events before it was folded. (Courtesy of the Brentwood Public Library.)

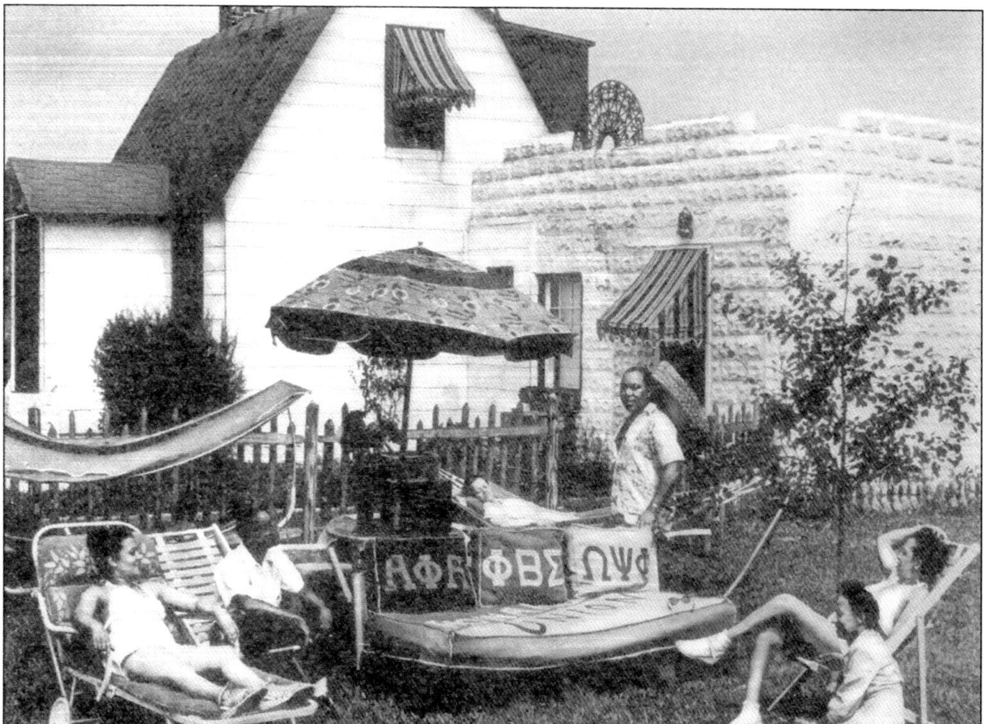

A Greek party at a house in the Edgewood section of West Brentwood was used as a postcard to promote the area in the early 1960s. (Courtesy of the James Fordyce Collection.)

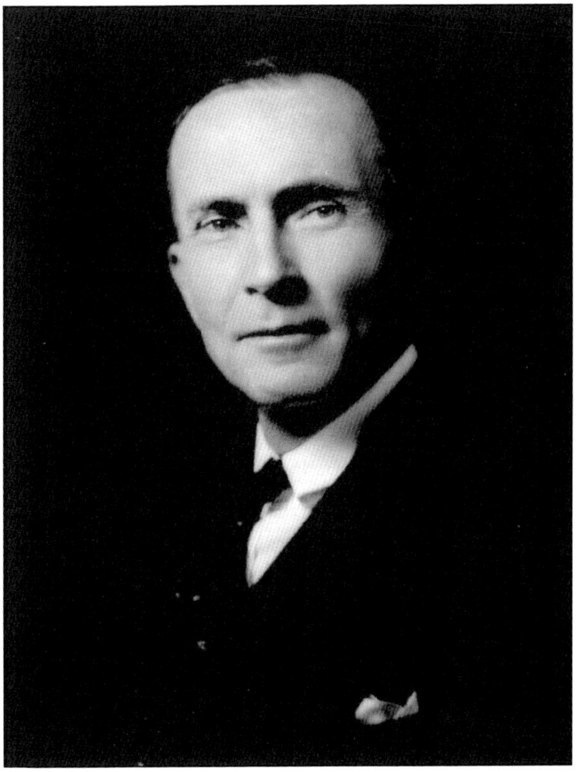

Verne Dyson (1879–1971) worked as a journalist in the Midwest and on the West Coast in the early 1900s before going to China as dean of Williams College. In 1921, Dyson was a professor of English and Chinese history at the University of the Philippines in Manila. He came to Brentwood in 1940, became the village historian, and was involved with the Brentwood centennial in 1952. Dyson was the founder of the *Brentwood Bulletin* and author of *A Century of Brentwood*. (Courtesy of the Brentwood Public Library.)

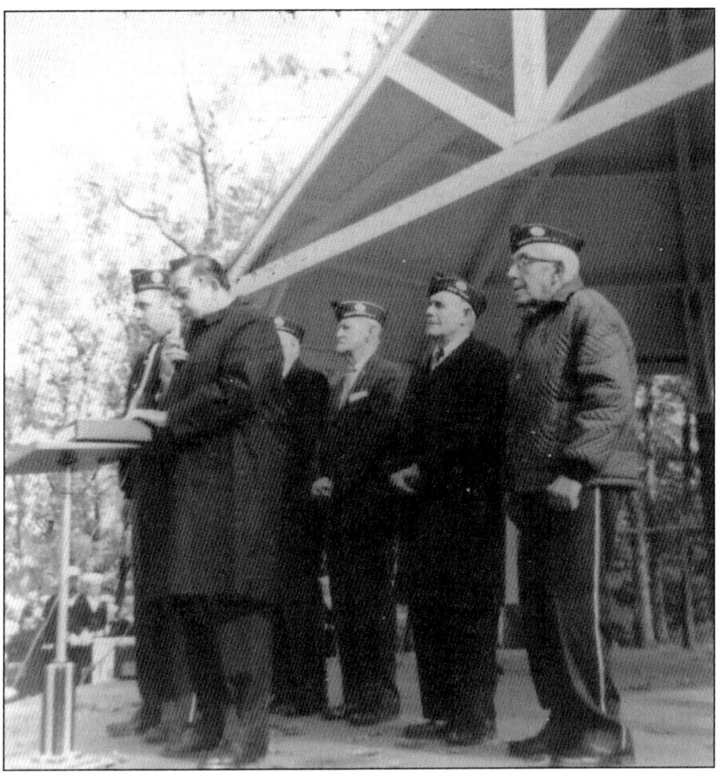

Sen. Caesar Trunzo (R) (1926–2013) was one of the leading political figures from Brentwood in the latter half of the 20th century. A former Islip Town councilman, he was a World War II veteran and a member of St. Anne's, the Brentwood Knights of Columbus, the Sons of Italy, and the Republican Club. Here, Senator Trunzo honors Brentwood's World War I veterans at Ross Park on Veterans Day in 1968. (Courtesy of American Legion Post 1006.)

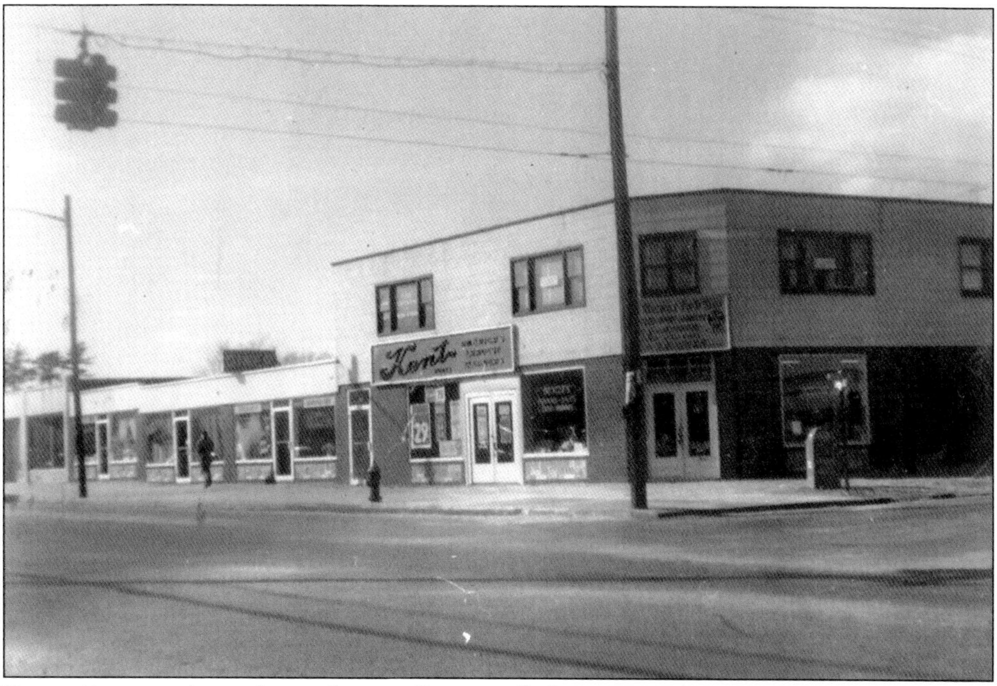

Pictured here is a chain of stores forming Brentwood's downtown. This is the corner of Washington and Suffolk Avenues in the late 1950s. (Courtesy of the Brentwood Public Library.)

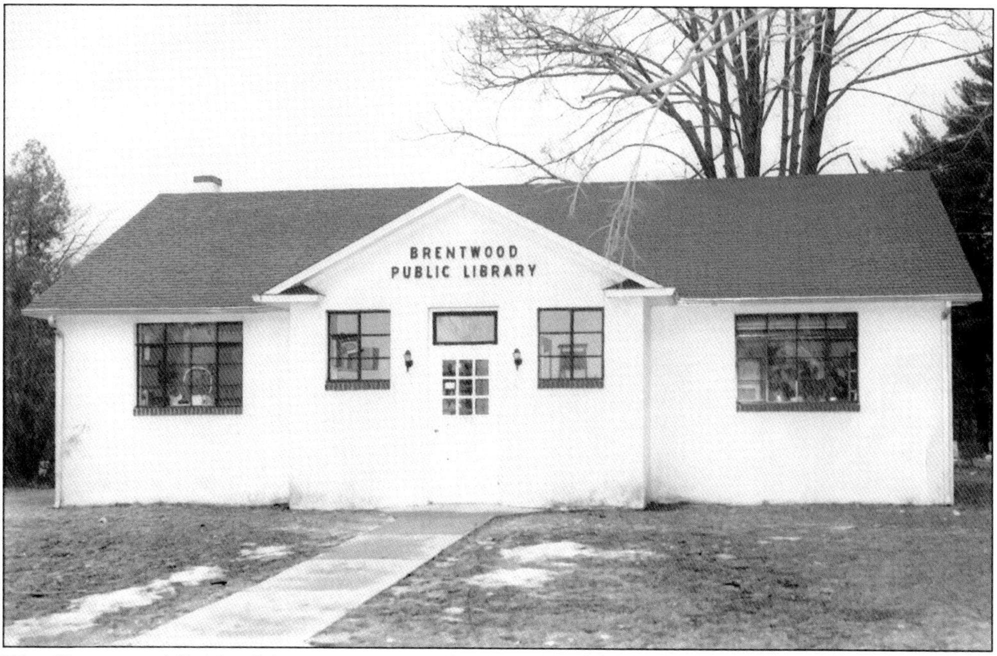

The Brentwood Public Library was started in 1937 and had several homes, including the fire department and the second schoolhouse. Throughout the 1950s, the Brentwood Public Library occupied this building on the southeast corner of Third Avenue and Fourth Street. There it remained until it moved across the street to its current location in 1961.(Courtesy of the Brentwood Public Library.)

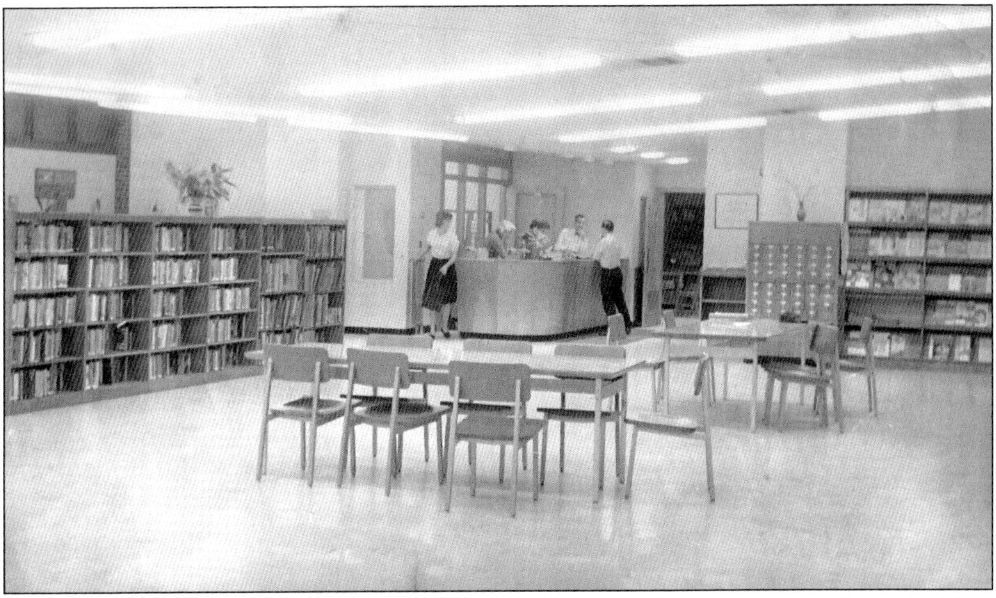

This c. 1960s photograph is an interior view of the Brentwood Public Library after it had just opened in its new permanent building on Second Avenue and Fourth Street. Extensions and alterations resulted in the Brentwood Public Library becoming one of the largest community libraries on Long Island. (Courtesy of the Brentwood Public Library.)

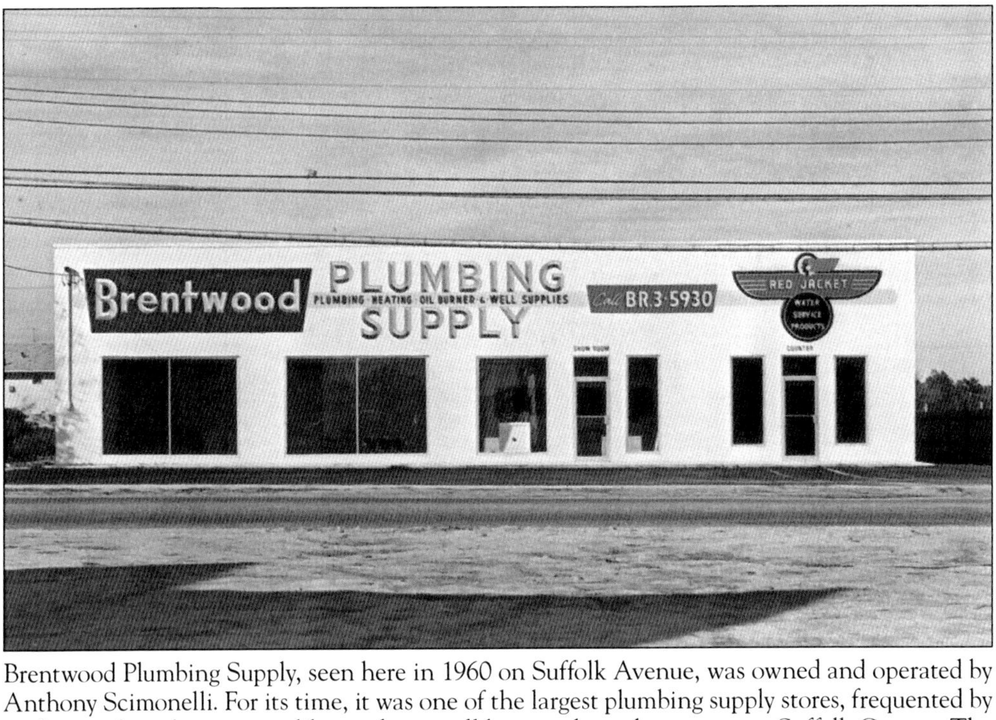

Brentwood Plumbing Supply, seen here in 1960 on Suffolk Avenue, was owned and operated by Anthony Scimonelli. For its time, it was one of the largest plumbing supply stores, frequented by professionals and amateurs alike, and was well known throughout western Suffolk County. The building eventually closed and was demolished. (Courtesy of the James Fordyce Collection.)

Seven

Brentwood Union Free School District

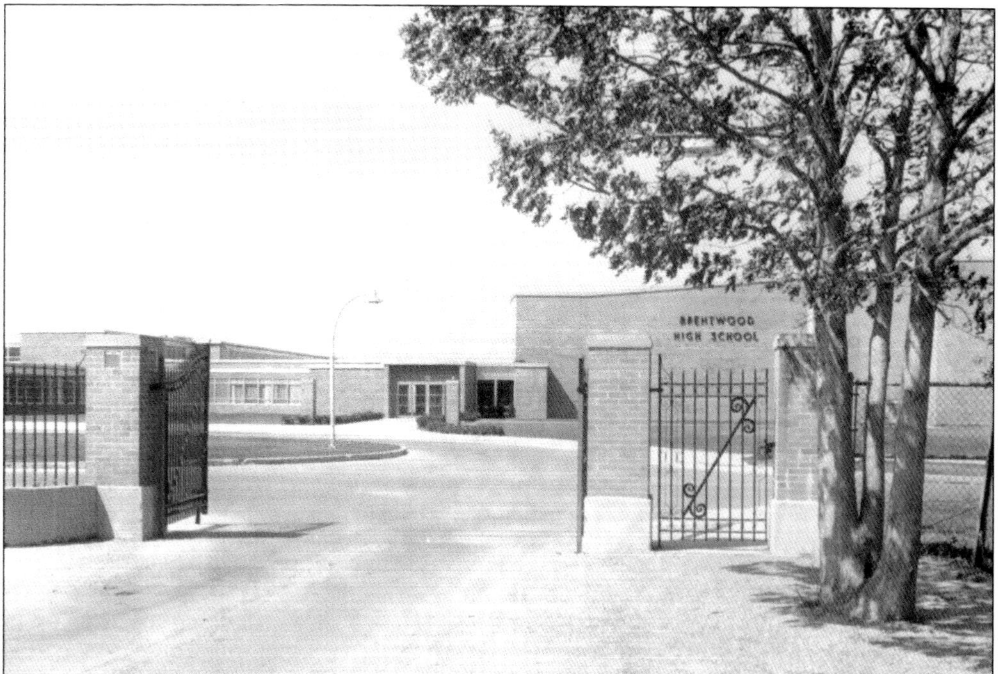

From humble beginnings in a one-room octagon schoolhouse to becoming one of the largest public school districts in the state of New York with over 20 buildings, the Brentwood School District has had millions of students pass through its hallways and thousands of teachers and educators. Pictured above is the Brentwood High School in 1957, later to be called Ross High School, then Brentwood High School, Ross Center. (Courtesy of the Brentwood Public Library.)

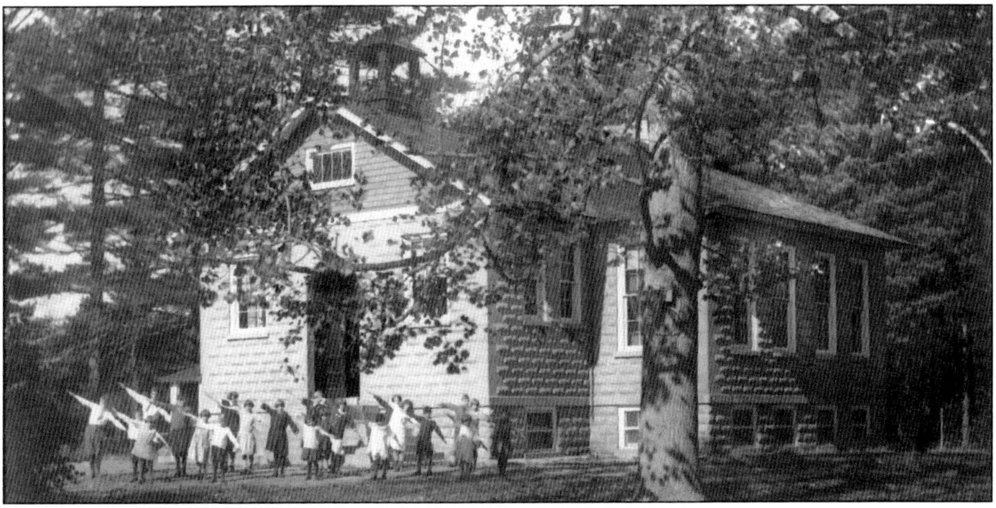

Brentwood's second schoolhouse, also referred to as Building No. 2, was a two-room school constructed in 1907 on the corner of Third Avenue and Fourth Street. The schools in Brentwood were organized into District No. 12 as far back as the 1860s. This photograph shows Building No. 2 with its original school bell on the roof and students performing calisthenics, an early form of gym class. (Courtesy of the Brentwood Public Library.)

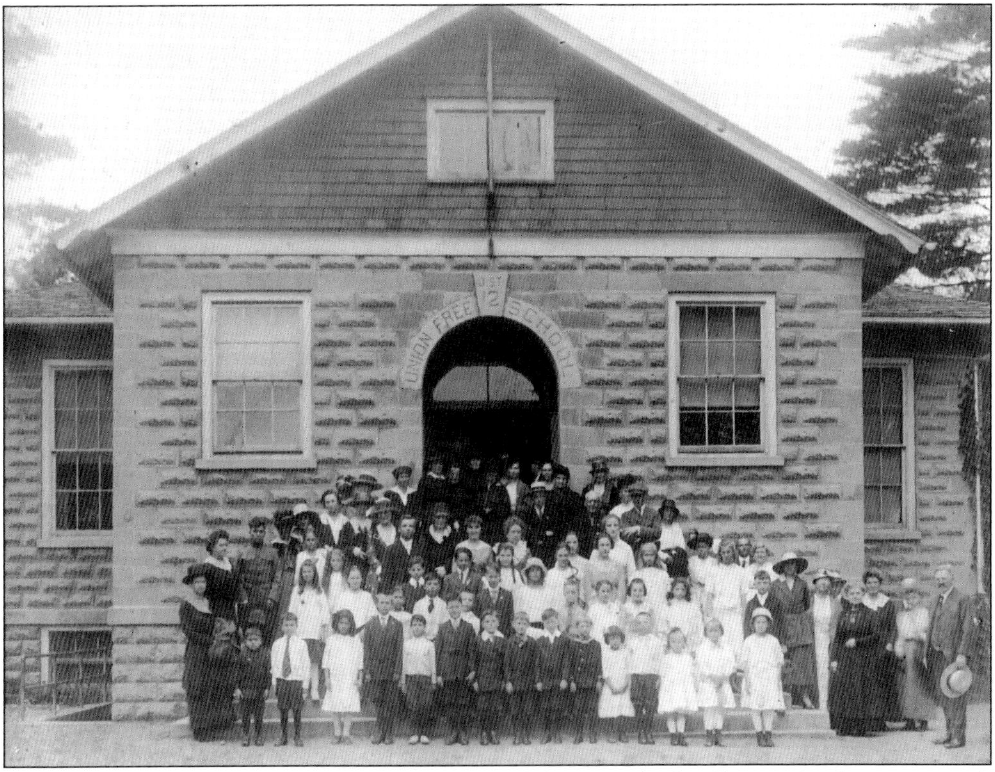

This c. 1915 class photograph was taken in front of the second schoolhouse. Students pose with parents and teachers, and the fashion denotes the approximate time period. A young man in an Army uniform stands on the steps on the left side, and Dr. William H. Ross, MD, is the last man standing on the extreme right. (Courtesy of the Brentwood Public Library.)

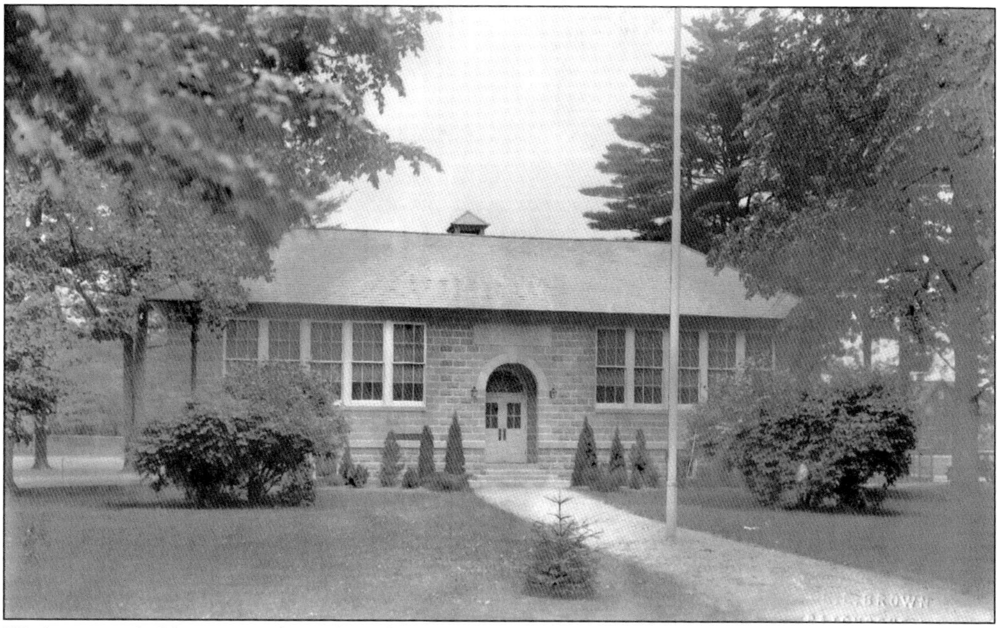

With more children attending the school district, Building No. 2 received an addition in 1932. This two-room extension brought the number of classrooms up to four. With the opening of the Village School in 1940, all elementary classes moved there. The second schoolhouse was then used as the administrative building for the Brentwood School District until 1985. (Courtesy of the Brentwood Public Library.)

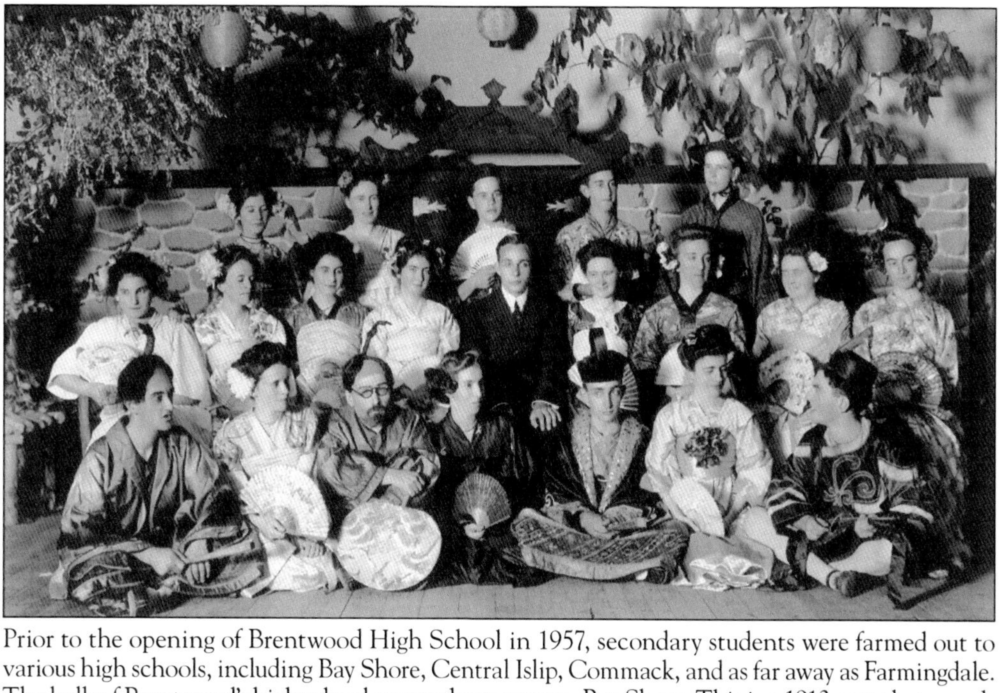

Prior to the opening of Brentwood High School in 1957, secondary students were farmed out to various high schools, including Bay Shore, Central Islip, Commack, and as far away as Farmingdale. The bulk of Brentwood's high school age students went to Bay Shore. This is a 1913 cast photograph of *The Mikado*, performed at Bay Shore High School by Brentwood students. (Courtesy of the Brentwood Public Library.)

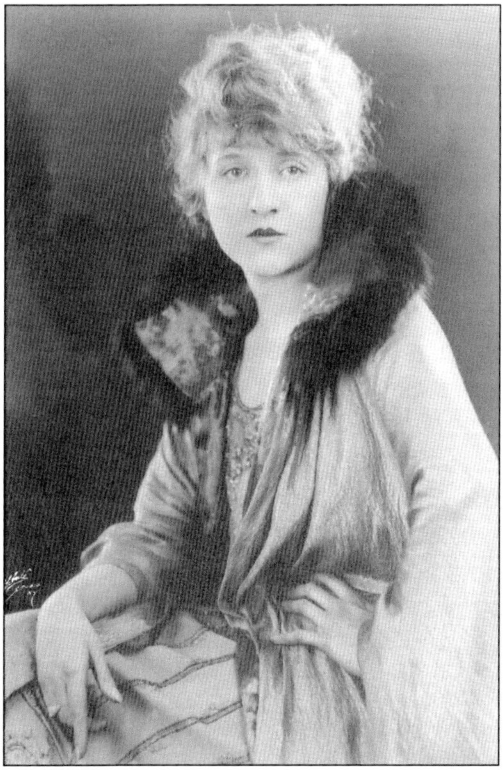

Eloise Mitchell (1900–1980) was hired by Principal Leigh P. Stuart as a teacher. She began her teaching career in Brentwood around 1920 in a rented store before moving to Building No. 2. She became a Brentwood resident and remained here the rest of her life, being heavily involved in the community. She would teach at the second school, the Village School, and eventually Southeast Elementary. (Courtesy of the Brentwood Public Library.)

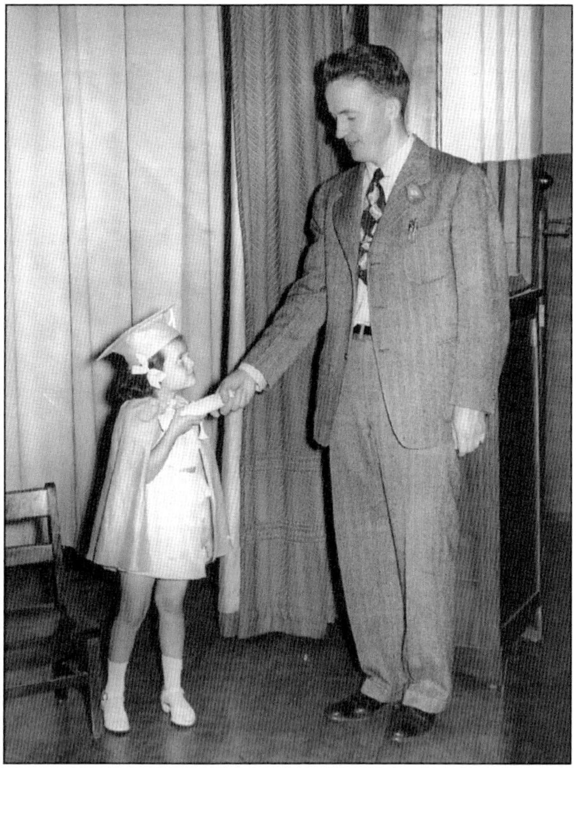

Leigh P. Stuart was appointed principal of Building No. 2 in 1938, and he later became principal of the Village School. Stuart served as district principal, a forerunner to the district superintendent, and was instrumental in helping the district expand to its current size, presiding over the first set of expansions. He worked closely with Dr. Ross, the president of the board of education, and retired in 1950. (Courtesy of the Brentwood Public Library.)

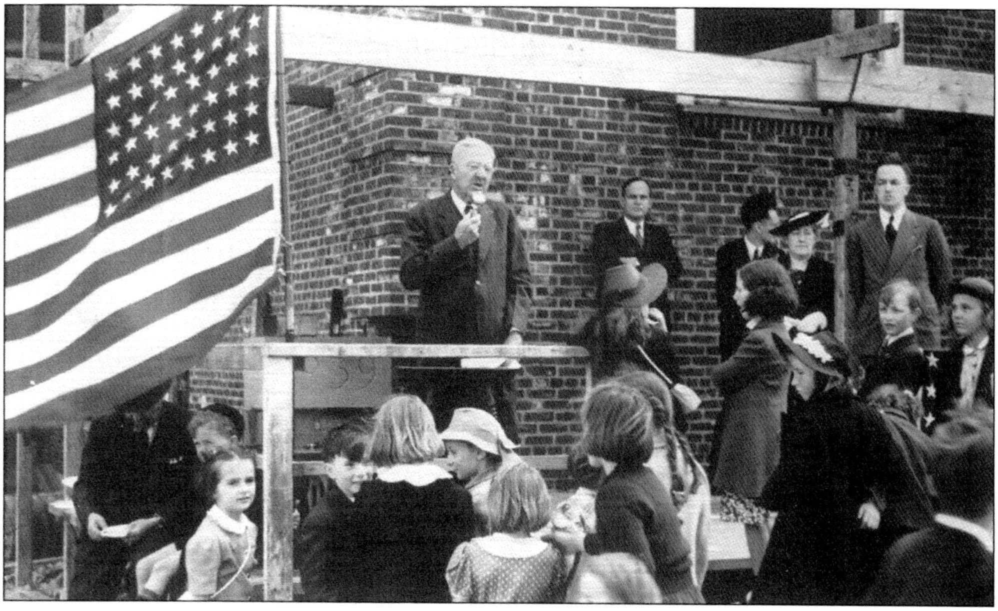

Dr. William H. Ross is photographed speaking at the dedication ceremony of the Village School while it was still under construction in 1939. The elementary school held its first class the following year, in 1940. (Courtesy of the Ray Welch Collection, Ruth Leboeuf Downer.)

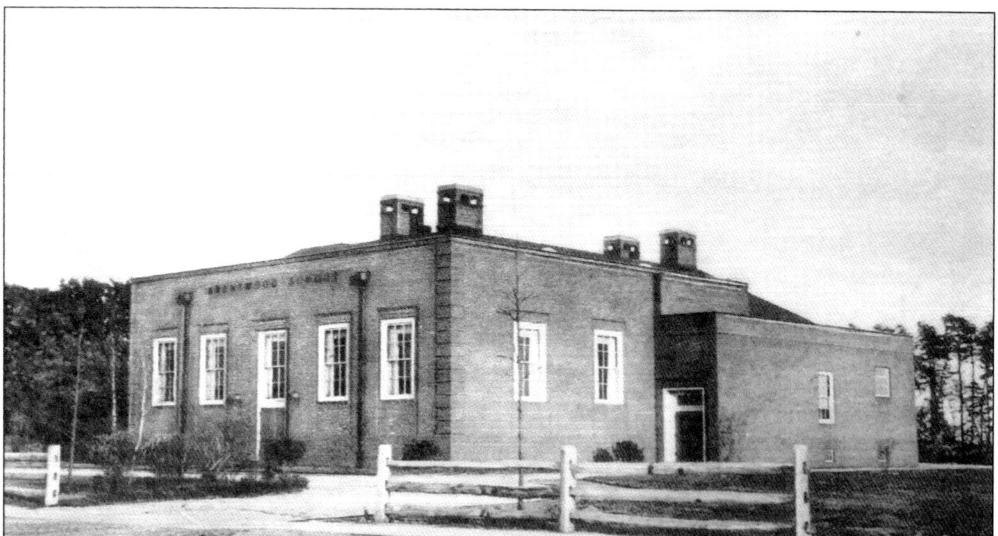

The Brentwood Village School is shown above as it appeared in 1940, looking east. The west wing extension and renovations took place in the 1950s. (Courtesy of the James Fordyce Collection.)

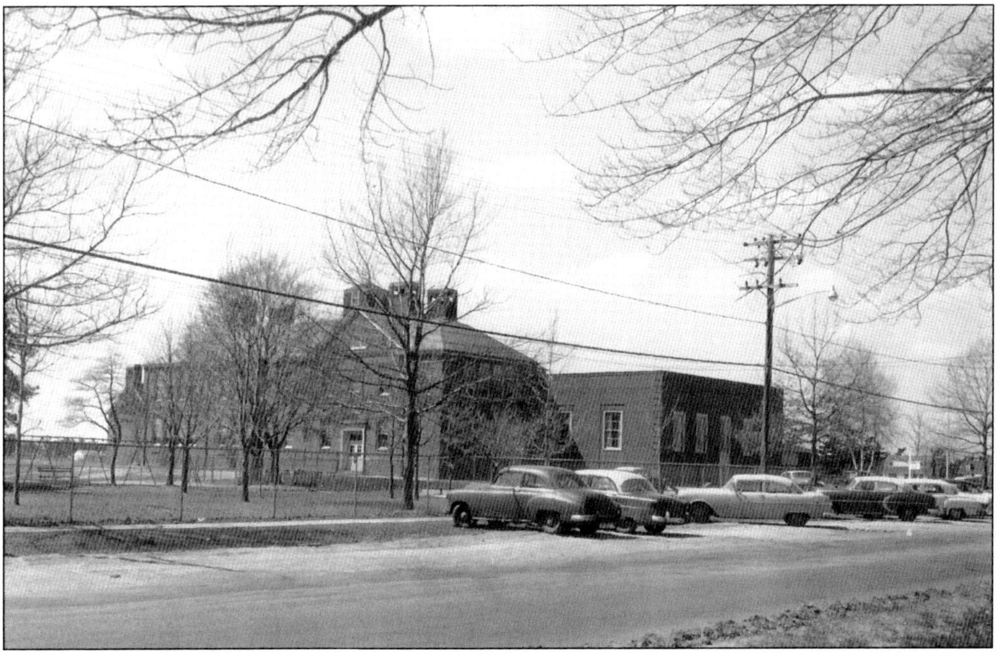

Looking west, this late-1940s photograph shows the Village School. Note the playground on the side of the building; today it is a parking lot. (Courtesy of the Brentwood Public Library.)

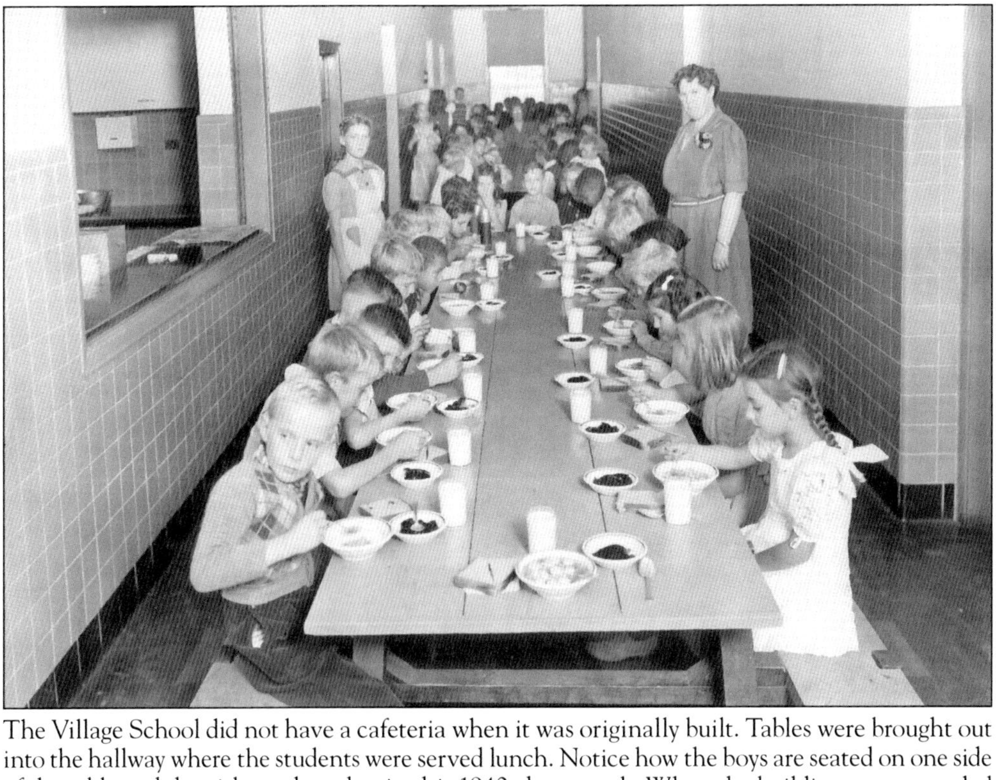

The Village School did not have a cafeteria when it was originally built. Tables were brought out into the hallway where the students were served lunch. Notice how the boys are seated on one side of the table and the girls on the other in this 1940 photograph. When the building was expanded in the 1950s, a proper cafeteria was installed. (Courtesy of the Brentwood Public Library.)

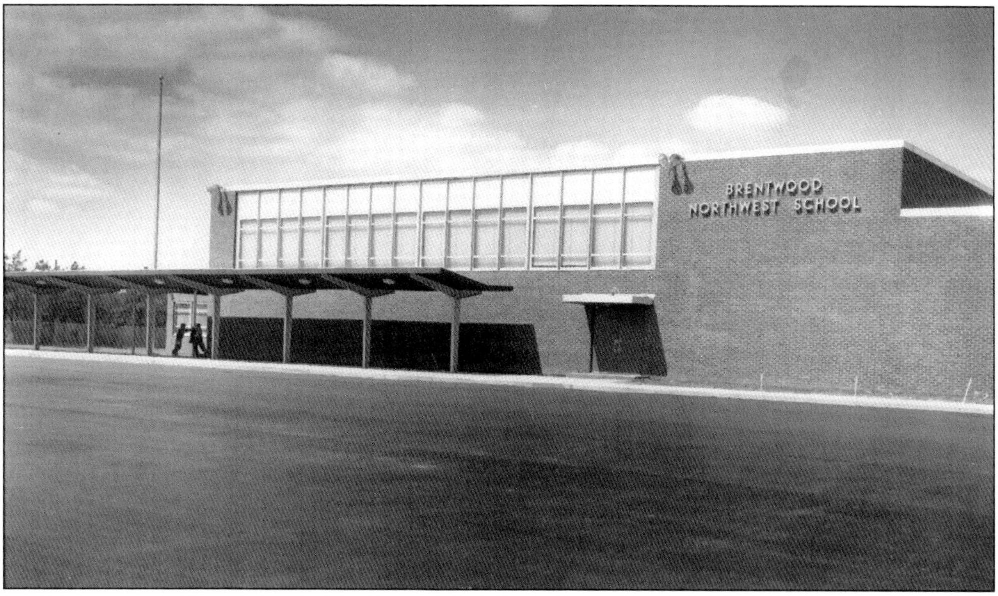

Brentwood Northwest Elementary School on Leahy Avenue was one of the first of the new elementary schools to be built throughout the district. Shifting enrollment numbers caused the school to be used for a variety of different purposes, including an elementary school in the 1950s, the 10th Grade Center in the 1960s, and the Brentwood Freshman Center from the 1980s onward. (Courtesy of the Brentwood Public Library.)

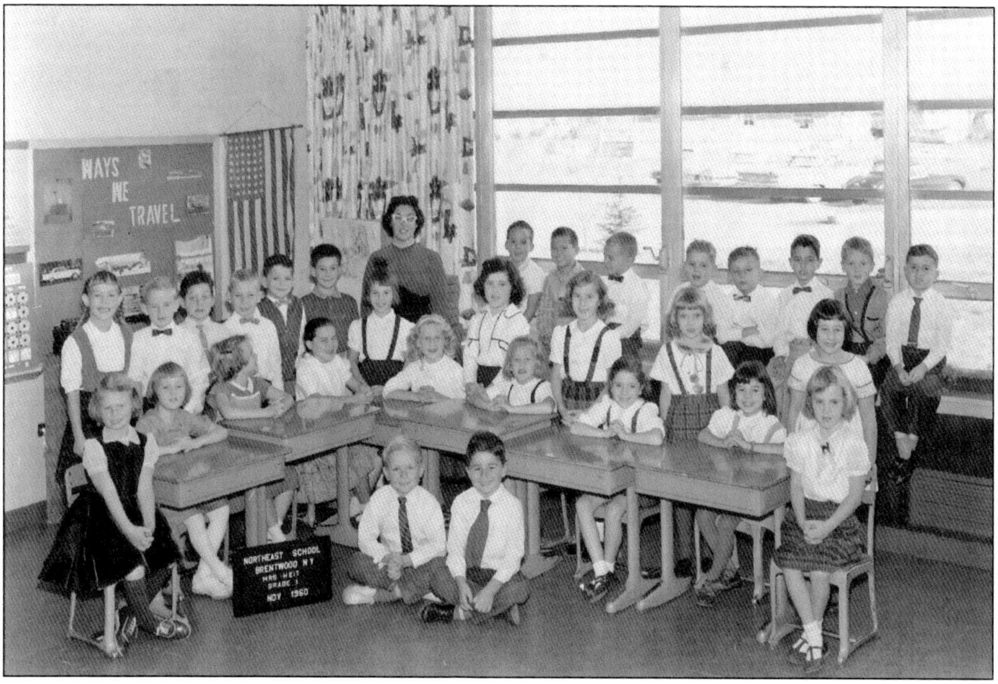

Mrs. Heit's class photograph from Brentwood Northeast Elementary School in 1960 illustrates the appearance of classrooms and the makeup of the student population in the Brentwood schools for that time period as well as showcasing the style of dress for children and teachers. (Courtesy of the Brentwood Public Library.)

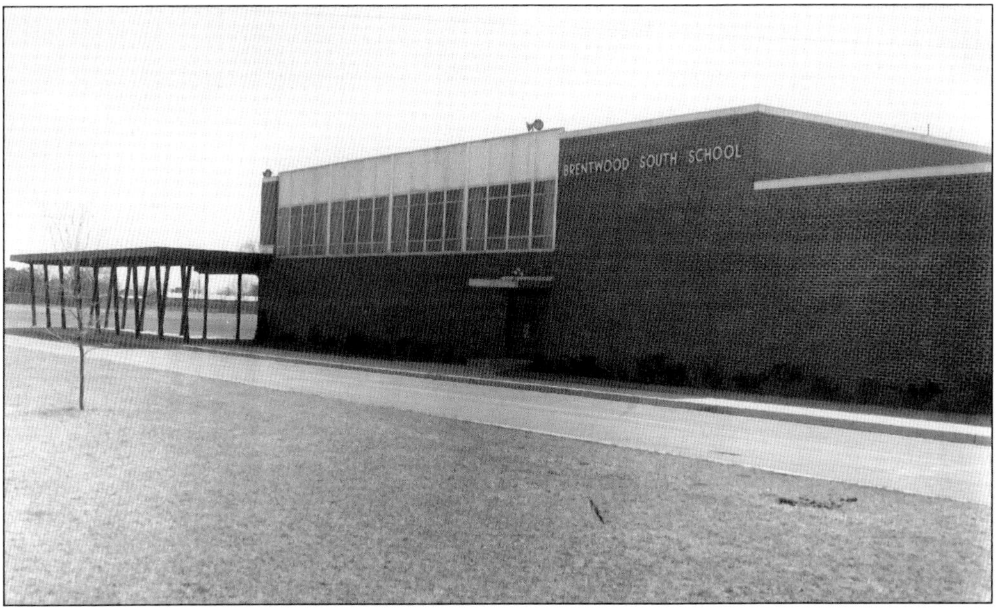

Brentwood South Elementary School on Paradise Lane, just off Fifth Avenue behind the Entenmann's bakery, was one of the first new elementary schools built by the district in the 1950s. National attention and local controversy came to this building when it was redeveloped as Maslow-Toffler School of Futuristic Education in 1974. Serving as an annex to the overcrowded high school it provided optional, alternative education to juniors and seniors who chose to attend here rather than remain in conventional classroom settings (Courtesy of the Brentwood Public Library.)

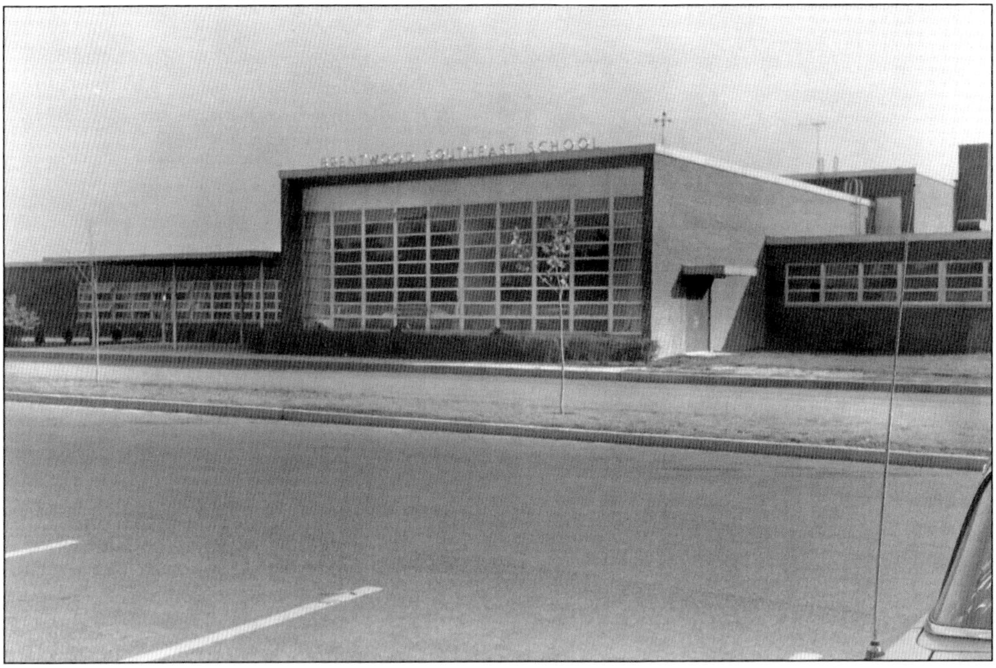

Brentwood Southeast Elementary School shows a change in architecture for the district's schools being constructed in the 1960s. These new schools would be larger than their older sister schools built a decade before. (Courtesy of the Brentwood Public Library.)

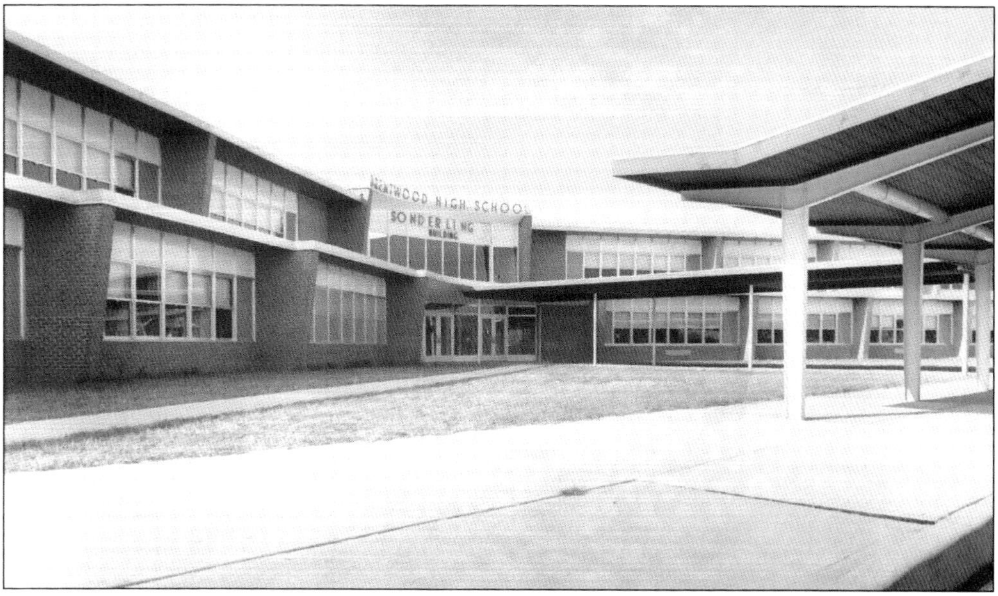

Originally built as Sonderling High School in 1962, it was the second high school in Brentwood and overcrowding necessitated its construction. Built next to Ross High School, enrollment was determined by what region of Brentwood the student resided in. Ross and Sonderling High Schools were finally united in the 1980s with the construction of the DiPietro Learning Center, joining the two buildings into one unified Brentwood High School. (Courtesy of the Brentwood Public Library.)

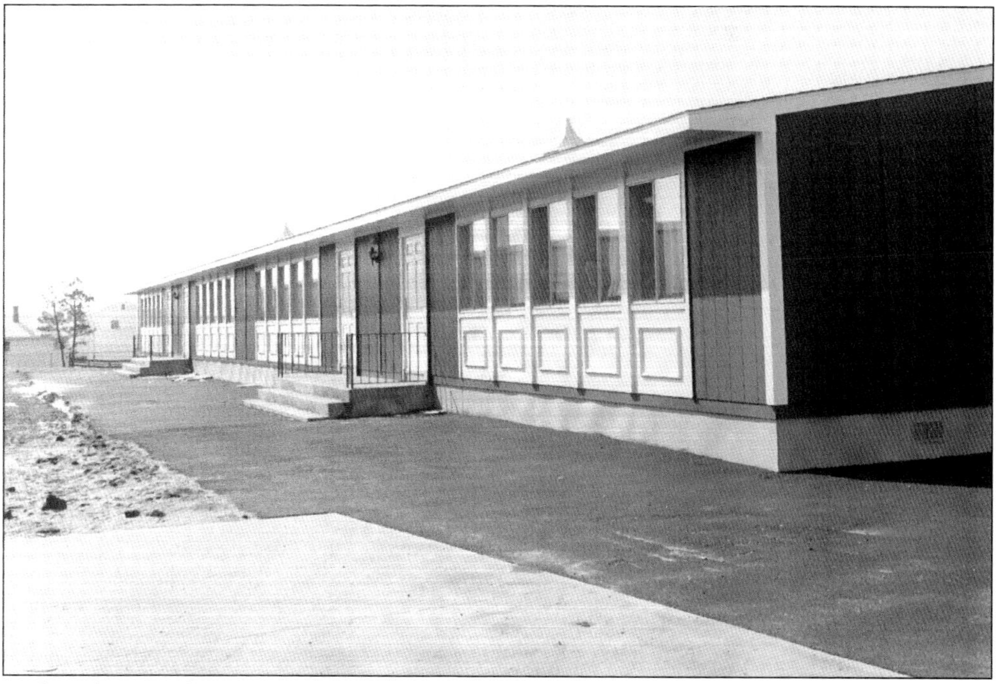

High student enrollment resulted in overcrowding in the Brentwood schools. To alleviate this strain on class size, wooden portable classrooms were built throughout the district. Here, portables are seen at Loretta Park Elementary School in March 1967. (Courtesy of the Brentwood Public Library.)

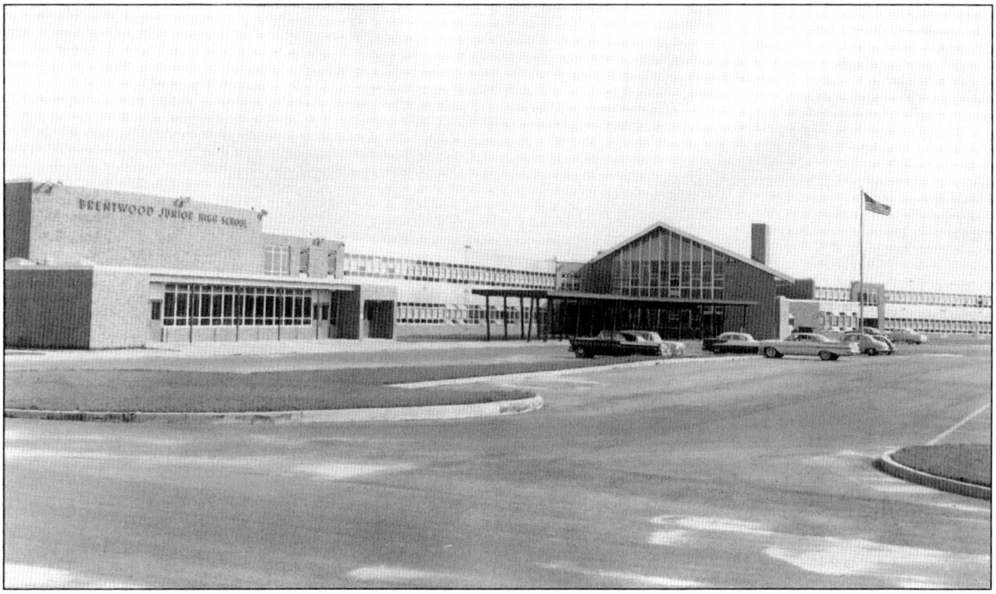

Brentwood Union Free School District built four junior high schools in the four different quadrants of the community—north, south, east, and west. The junior high school a student attended determined which high school they were sent to. The district changed from junior high schools, which had seventh to ninth grade students, to middle schools containing sixth to eighth grade students in the 1980s. Based on the flagpole's location, this is most likely South Junior High School/Middle School, the first junior high school built. (Courtesy of the Brentwood Public Library.)

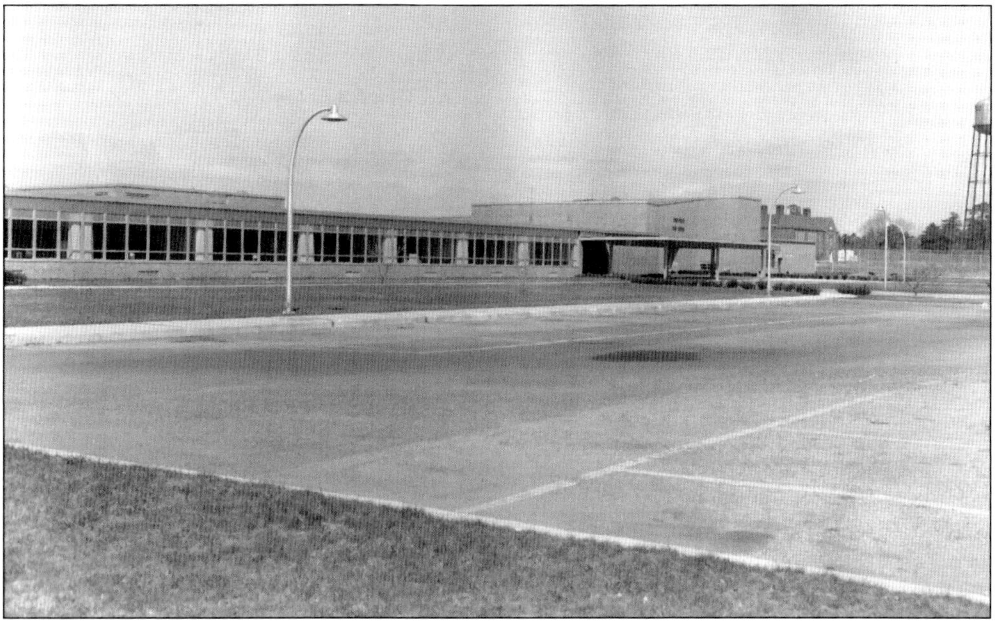

The Brentwood High School, Ross Center is seen in this early-1960s photograph. In the earliest existence of the two high schools, Ross High School was used for 11th graders before they went to Sonderling High School, which was the senior high school. This practice soon fell out of favor due to class size and the need for space. The Village School can be seen just behind the high school's auditorium. (Courtesy of the Brentwood Public Library.)

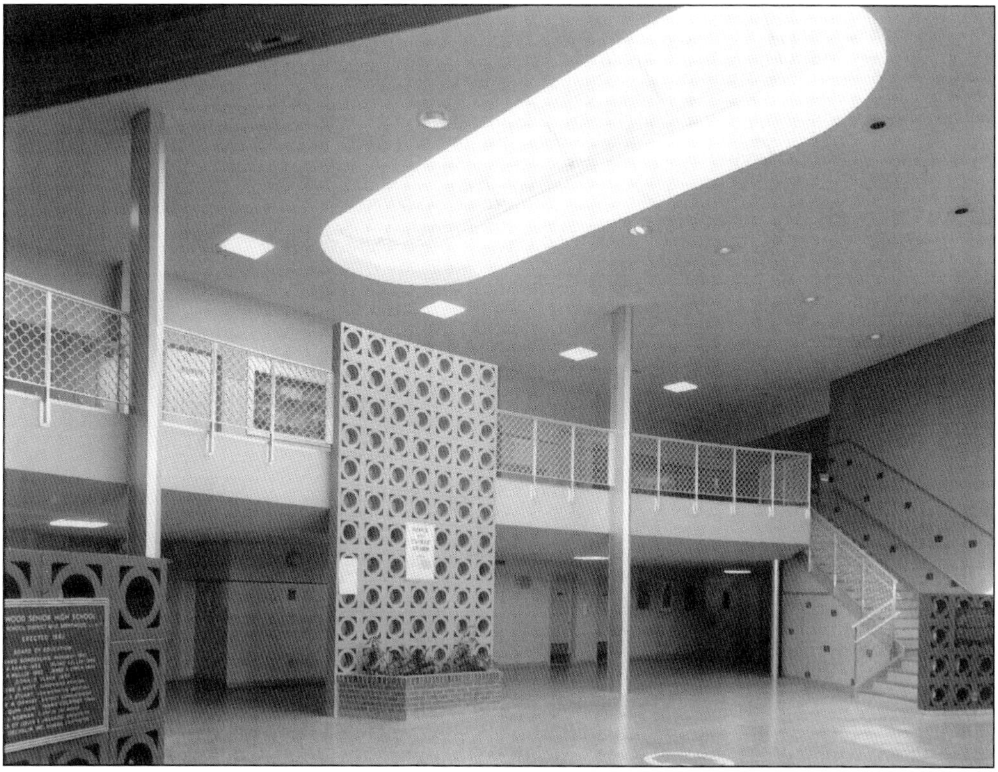

Shown is an interior view of Brentwood High School's Sonderling Center's main lobby just after the school opened in 1962. The main lobby has also been referred to at times as the Grand Salon or main foyer. (Courtesy of the Brentwood Public Library.)

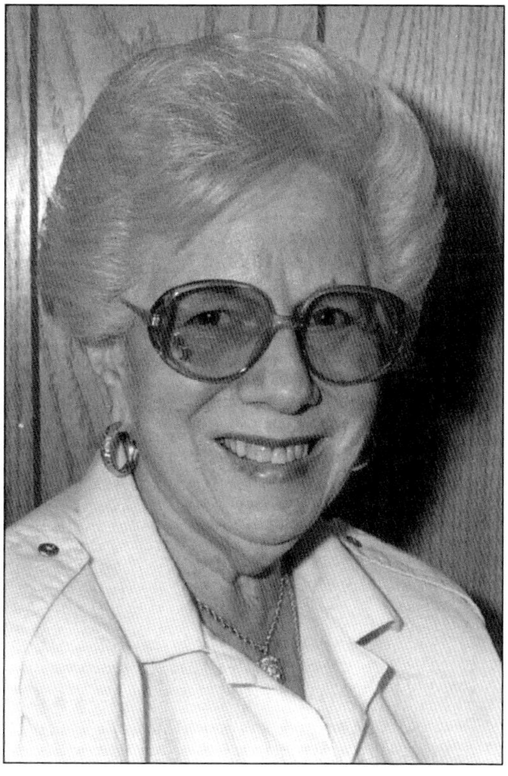

Ruth Rosenthal began her teaching career at Brentwood High School in 1957. In 1962, she was promoted to director of science, where she standardized the curriculum for the district and involved the district in national science programs. Rosenthal was an assistant principal at East Junior High in 1967 before becoming assistant principal at Sonderling High School in 1974. She was a longtime trustee of the Brentwood Public Library, a member of Brentwood's Temple Beth Am, and an adjunct professor at Hofstra University. (Courtesy of the Retirees of Brentwood Schools.)

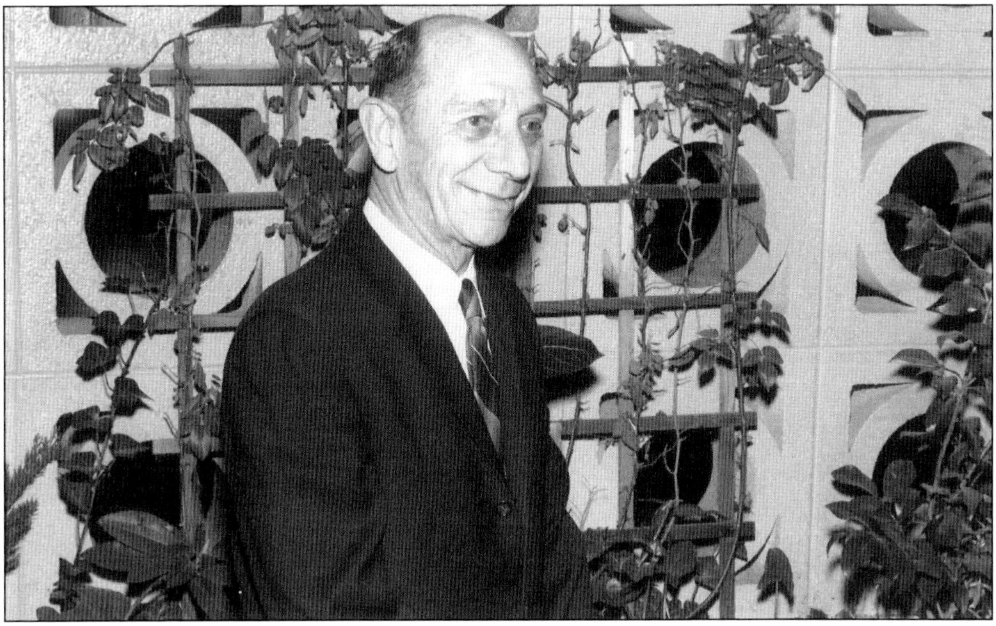

Edward Sonderling (1896–1978) became a resident of Brentwood in 1930. He served as the superintendent of the Brentwood Water District from 1935 until he retired in 1966. Sonderling was a member of the board of education for 27 years, with 15 of them as president. As president, he oversaw the widespread expansion of the district into what it is today. This 1965 photograph finds him in the lobby of the building that bears his name. (Courtesy of the Brentwood Public Library.)

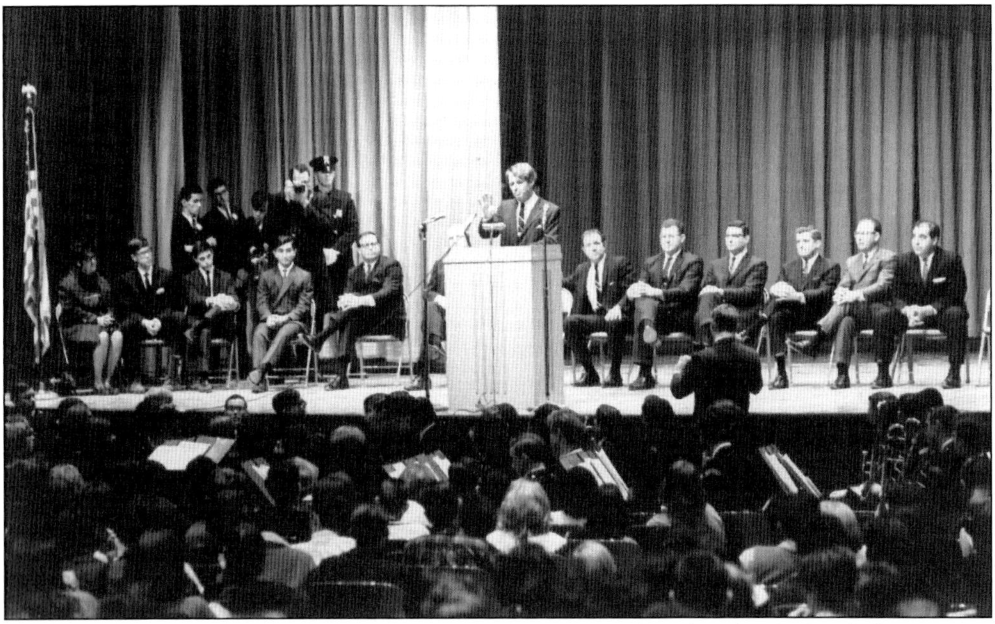

Sen. Robert F. Kennedy (D) (1925–1968) speaks at Brentwood High School's Sonderling Center on January 11, 1968, while on the campaign trail. The event drew a packed auditorium, and the Brentwood High School band can be seen in the pit below the stage. Kennedy arrived and left by a helicopter that landed on the school's football field. (Courtesy of the Retirees of Brentwood Schools.)

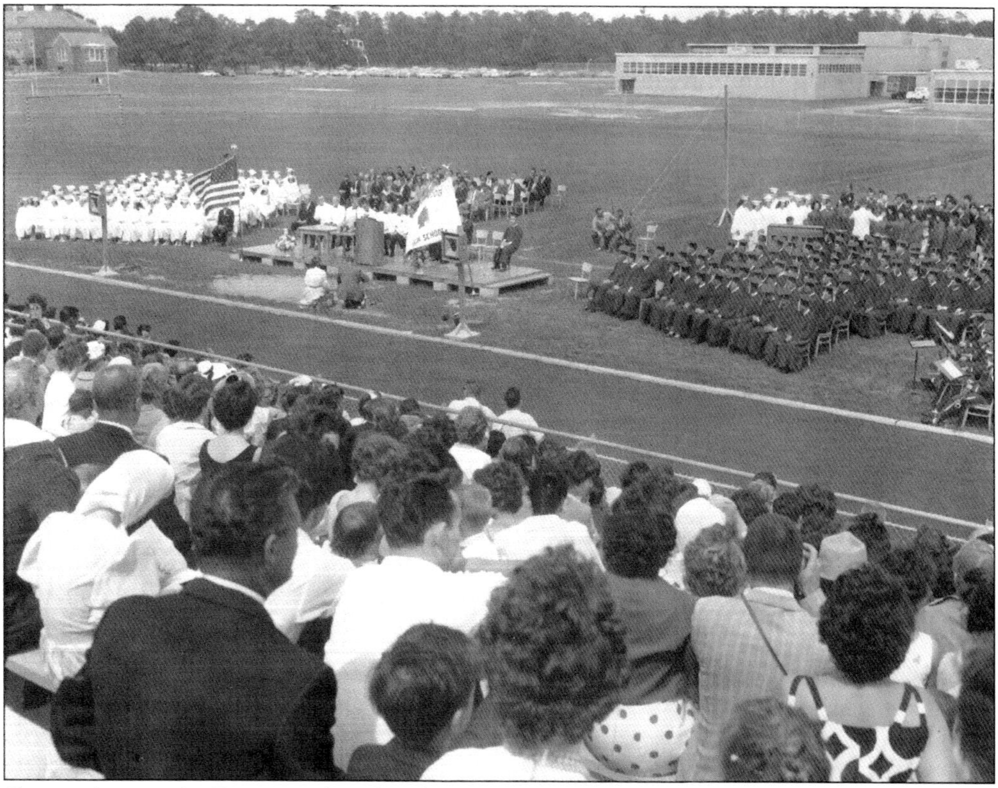

Shown above is the Brentwood High School commencement in June 1961. The first graduating class of Brentwood High School students arrived at the new school as freshmen when the school opened in the fall of 1957. Each year, the graduating class would grow increasing larger. Today's graduating class typically fills the field. (Courtesy of the Brentwood Public Library.)

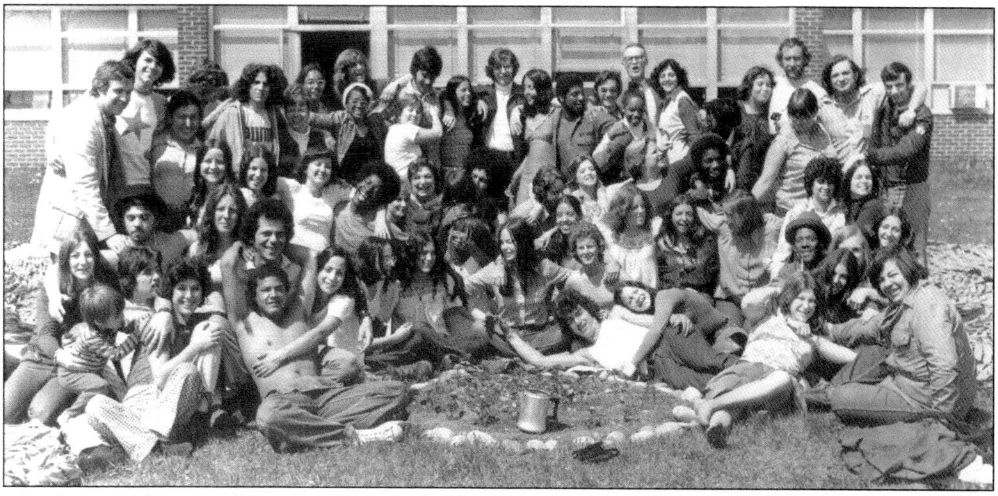

The first graduating class of the Maslow-Toffler School in 1975 is shown above. Students and staff gathered behind the school for a class photograph, marking the completion of the first successful experiential year. Although some students chose to participate at the high school's commencement, Maslow-Toffler maintained its own separate graduation ceremony. (Courtesy of Retirees of Brentwood Schools.)

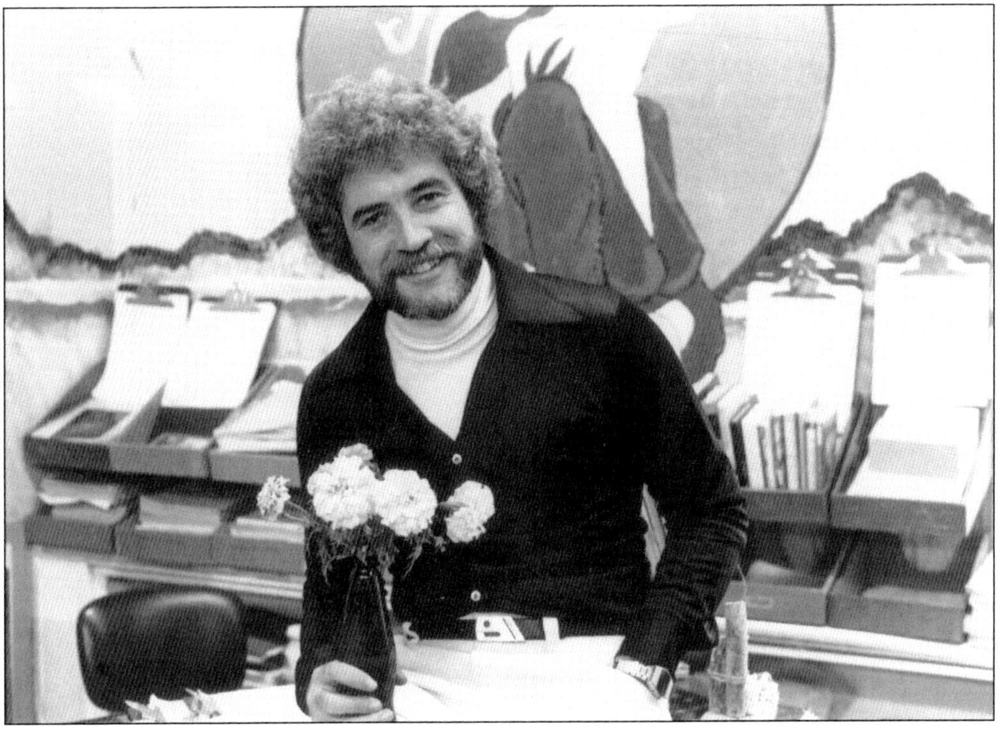

John Sherin, a teacher in the district, was moved by works of humanistic psychologist Abraham Maslow and futurists Alvin and Heidi Toffler. Receiving district support, he and Milton Siler became cofounders of the Maslow-Toffler School of Futuristic Education. In an era before personal computers, the school offered a different approach to education that was ahead of its time. Today, John Sherin is the official historian for the Retirees of Brentwood Schools. (Courtesy of the Retirees of Brentwood Schools.)

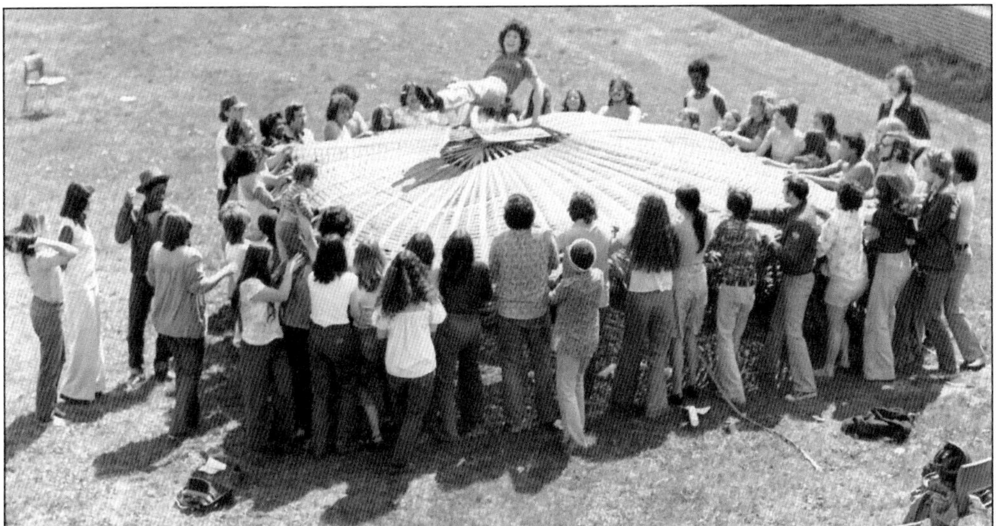

The parachute toss was one of many group processes used by the facilitators at Maslow-Toffler to engage and motivate students, some of whom are seen participating here in 1975. (Courtesy of the Retirees of Brentwood Schools.)

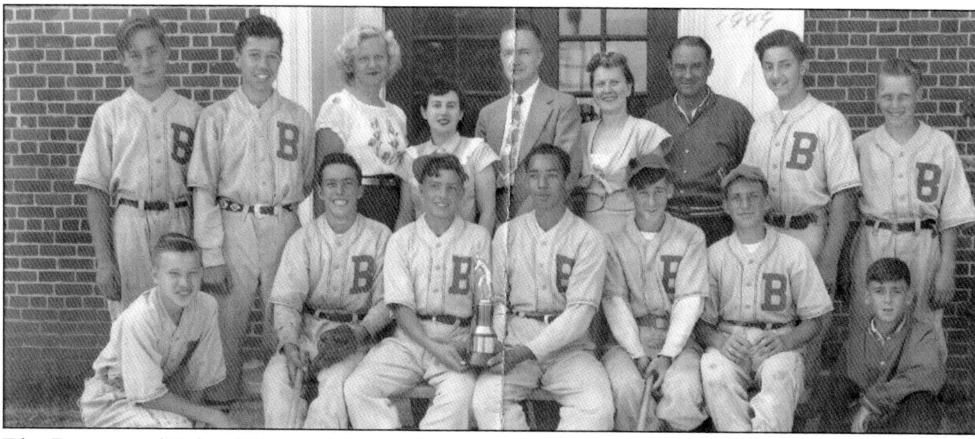

The Brentwood School District's baseball team is pictured here in 1949 after winning an award, with district principal Leigh P. Stuart, a Ms. Raeber, and Coach Walters also shown. (Courtesy of the Brentwood Public Library.)

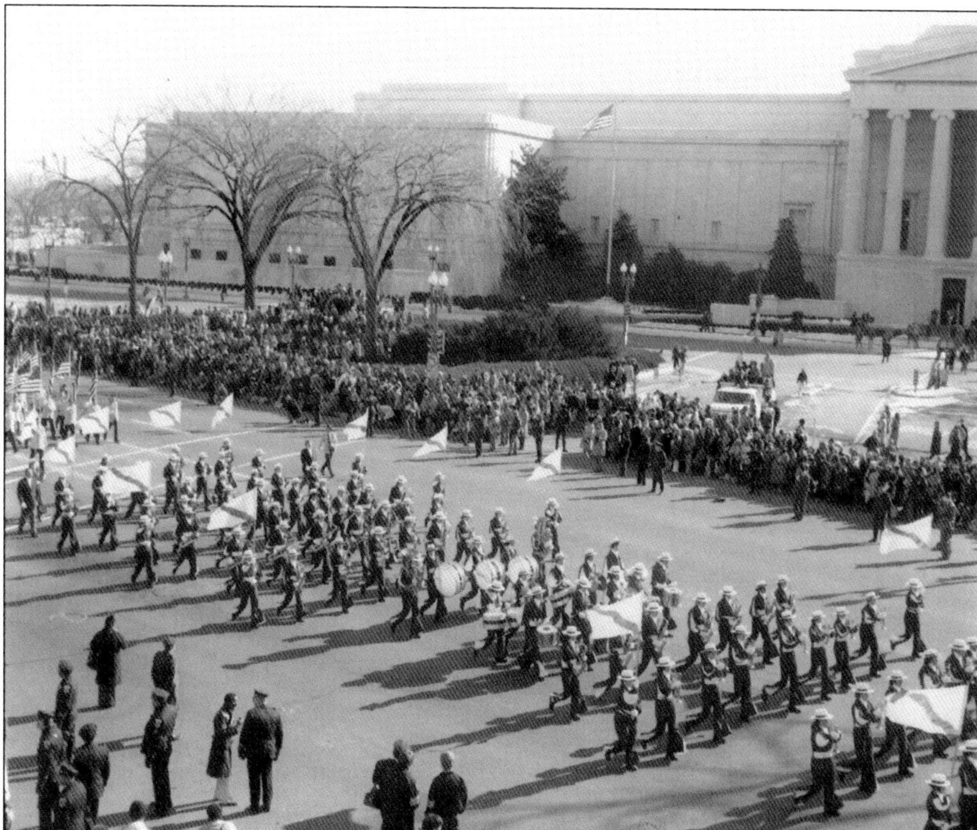

The Brentwood High School marching band, the "Green Machine," marches in Pres. Jimmy Carter's Inauguration Parade in Washington, DC, in 1976. The Green Machine is a nationally recognized marching band with numerous awards to its credit. The band has participated in many major parades and events throughout its history. (Courtesy of the Brentwood School District.)

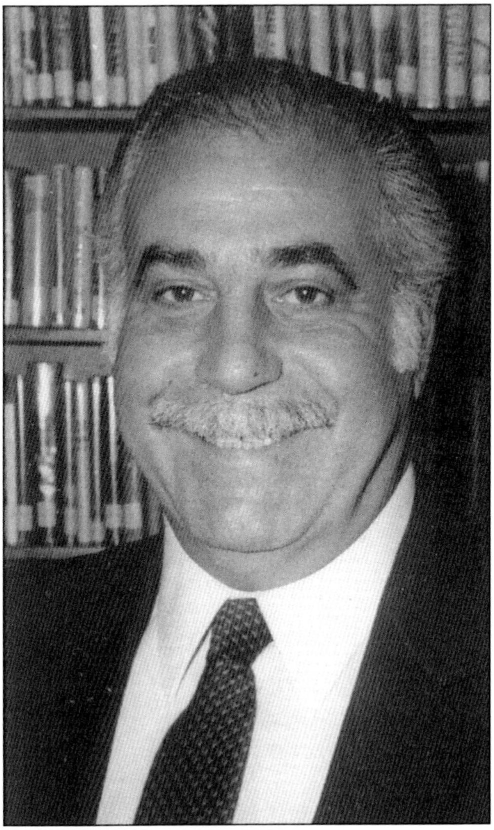

Anthony Felicio (1931–2003), a Korean War veteran, moved to Brentwood in 1957 and became instantly involved in the emerging suburban community. He lost his first election to the school board in 1963 but won in 1967 and began a career with the board of education that lasted until his death. His support of school functions and the multicultural nature of the community made the school district what it is today (Courtesy of the Brentwood School District.)

Dr. Joel Ratner, EDD, (1958–) became the district coordinator of music in 1996 and took an already good music program and built it into a nationally recognized one. Pushing music competitions, the department has received numerous awards, including top awards from NYSSMA, SCMEA, and the Grammy Signature Program. Ratner, a published composer, serves as the brass editor for the *School Music News Magazine*. (Courtesy of the Brentwood School District.)

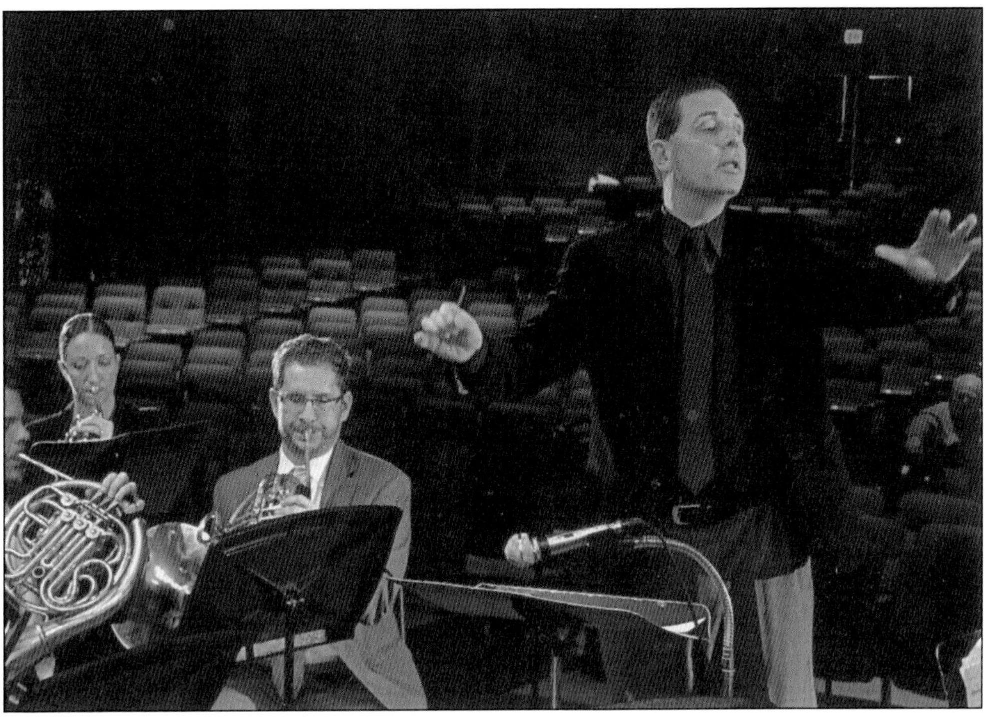

Eight

THE NEW PIONEERS

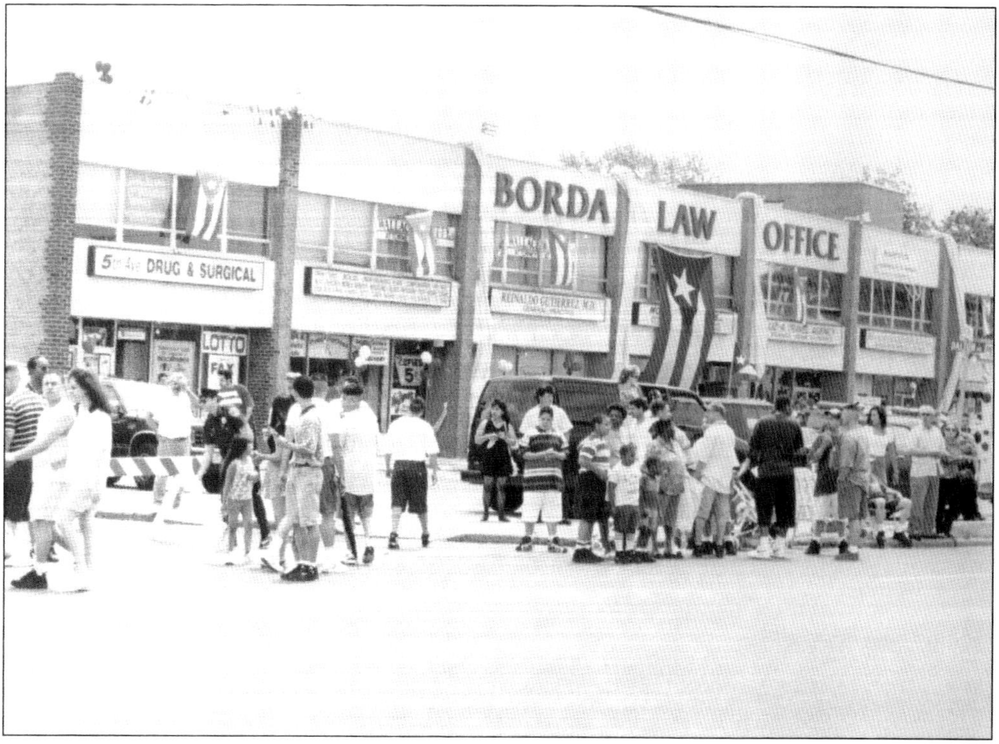

Brentwood today is internationally known as a Hispanic community. The first Puerto Rican families arrived in 1938. As the decades wore on, Hispanic immigration into the area skyrocketed. Brentwood's Adelante Day Parade is the largest Latin American parade outside the city of New York. Here, the Adelante Day Parade proceeds up Fifth Avenue in 1995.(Courtesy of Richard Borda.)

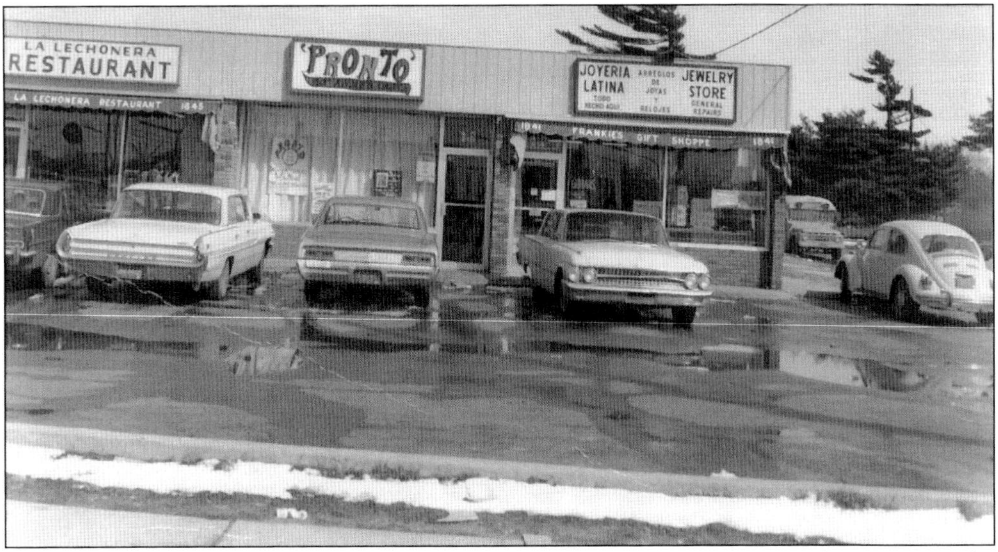

Pronto of Long Island's humble beginnings trace back to a storefront on Fifth Avenue in the 1960s. Begun as a church organization, Pronto had a food pantry and thrift store, and while these are still major aspects of Pronto, the organization also provides immigration aid, English lessons, and outreach. La Lechonera, one of the first Hispanic-owned restaurants in Brentwood, is next door. (Courtesy of Belinda Alvarez-Groneman.)

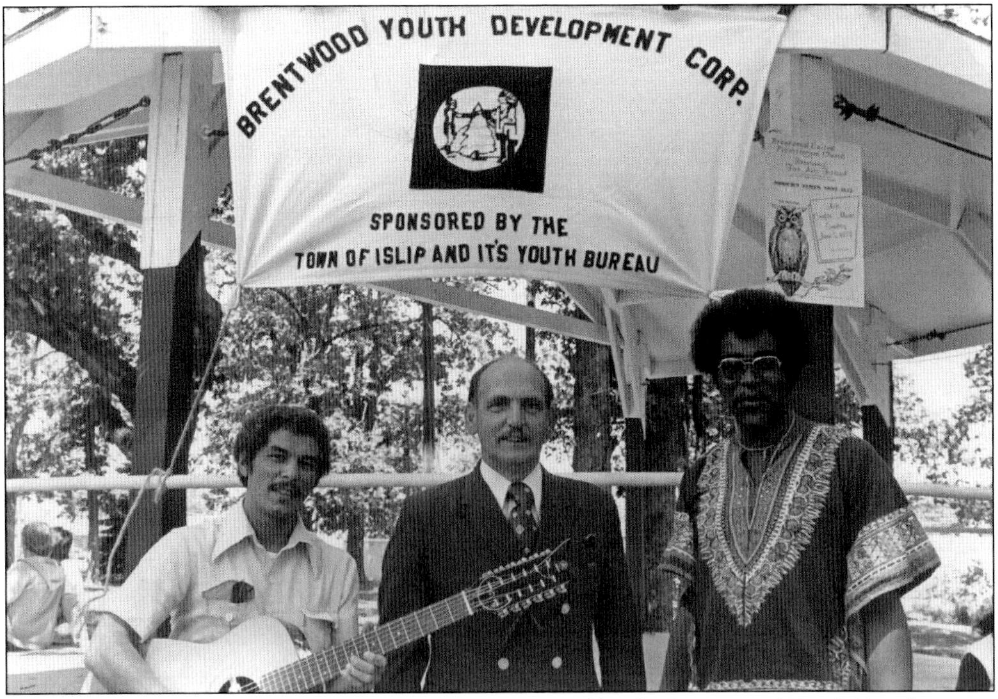

A music festival for the community's youth was sponsored by the Brentwood Youth Development Corporation and held at Ross Park's old grandstand in 1977. From left to right, Carlos Vidal, director of Brentwood Youth Development Corporation; Councilman Frank D. Boncore (R); and Vernon Dempsey, chairman of Brentwood Youth Development Corporation, are seen here. All three men were residents of Brentwood and leaders in the community. (Courtesy of the Vidal family.)

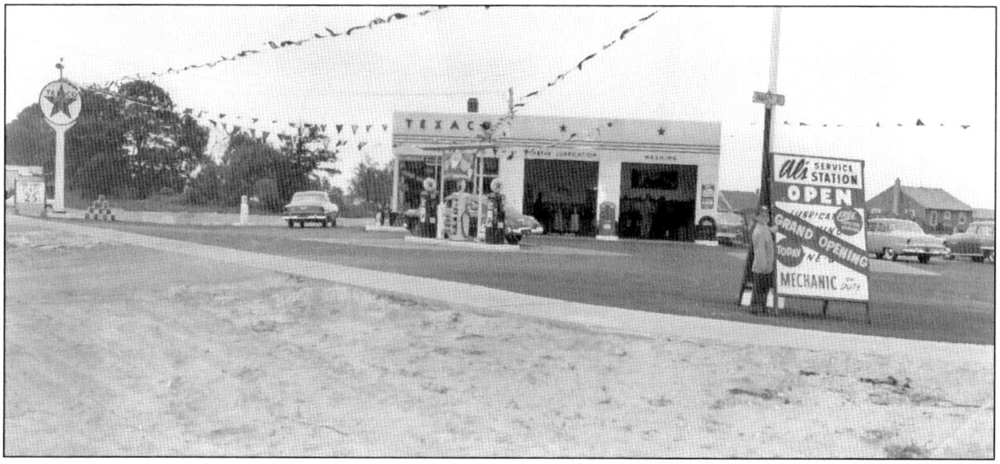

The Texaco gas station on the corner of Wicks Road and Bradley Street in 1957 is shown above; it was owned by Avelino Cancel. Cancel had previously owned and operated a Cities Service Station and grocery store from 1950 to 1956 directly across the street, where Pathmark is today, before opening the Texaco. The stations were some of the first Hispanic-owned businesses. (Courtesy of Roland Jimenez.)

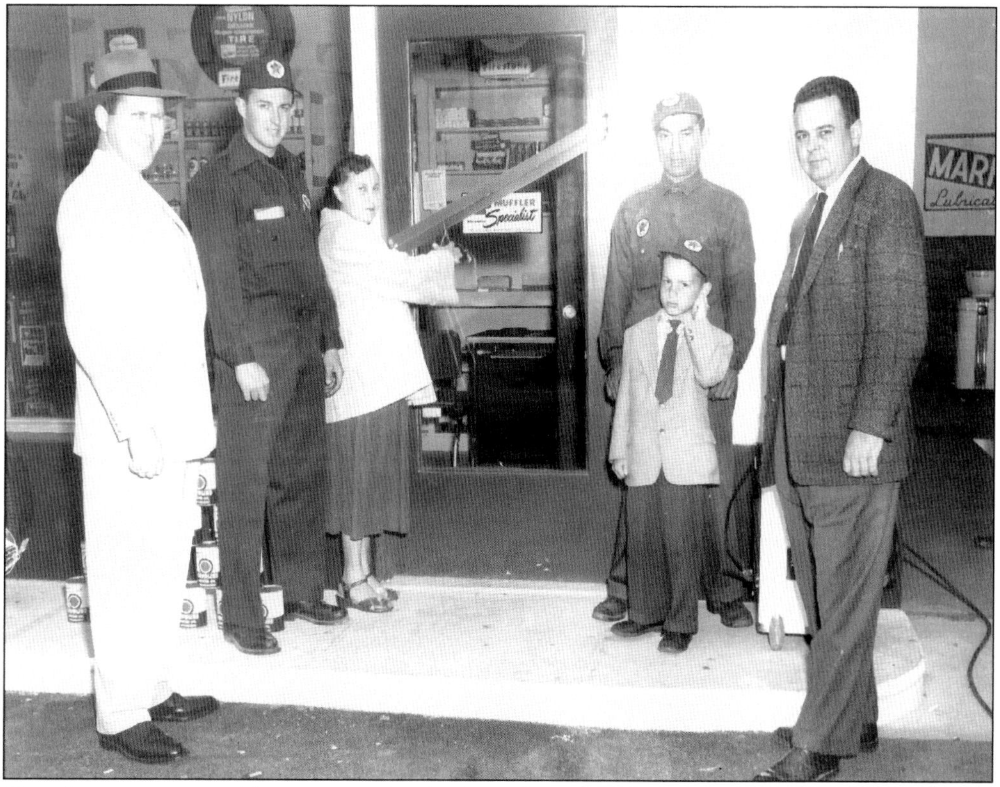

Grand opening and ribbon cutting for Avelino Cancel's Texaco gas station in 1957 is shown above. His wife, Margret, is cutting the ribbon. The area where the station stood is known as Regis Park, across the street the area was called Victory Farms and was the site of the first Hispanic settlements in Brentwood. Cancel's service stations became the first businesses one encountered in Brentwood when getting off the Northern State Parkway. (Courtesy of Roland Jimenez.)

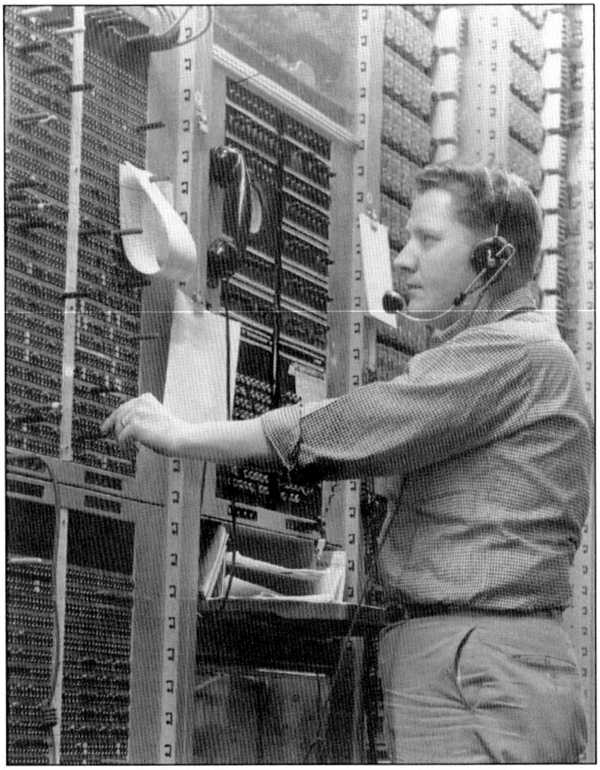

John James Kresse Sr. (1938–1992) worked in telephone repair in the city. In 1963, he married Milagros Cintron. Facing discrimination for marrying a Hispanic, he moved his family to the North Bay Shore section of West Brentwood in 1964. The house they bought was marked down because of the presence of another Hispanic family on the block. (Courtesy of Millie Kresse.)

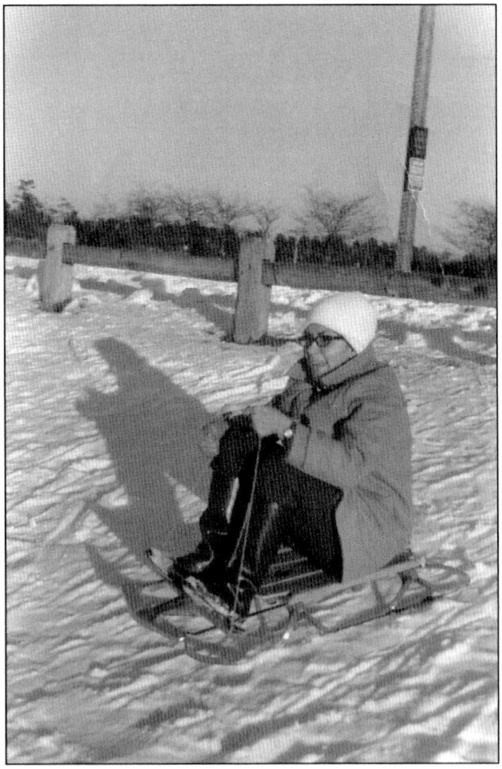

Milagros "Millie" Kresse is shown sledding on the overpass hill where Manatuck Boulevard crosses the Southern State Parkway near her home in 1969. This area was a local hot spot for the youth of the area to sled and play in the winter snow. (Courtesy of Millie Kresse.)

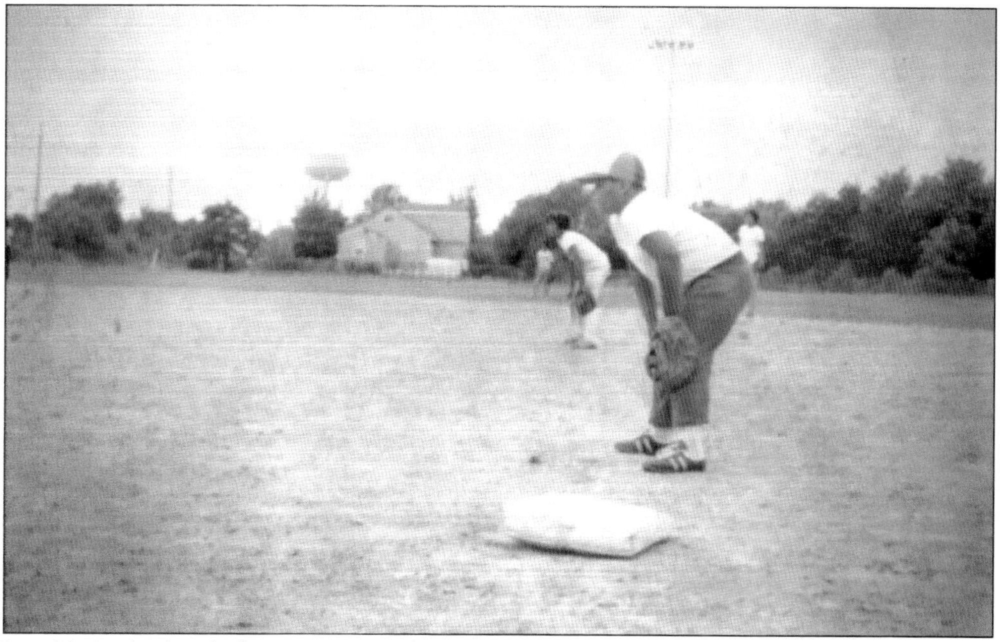

Local kids play baseball in Vazquez Park on MacArthur Avenue in Regis Park sometime in the 1970s. The park, previously called MacArthur Park, was renamed in honor of Jose A. Vazquez (1945–1966), a Brentwood resident and high school graduate who was killed in Vietnam. The park was eventually developed over. (Courtesy of the Vidal family.)

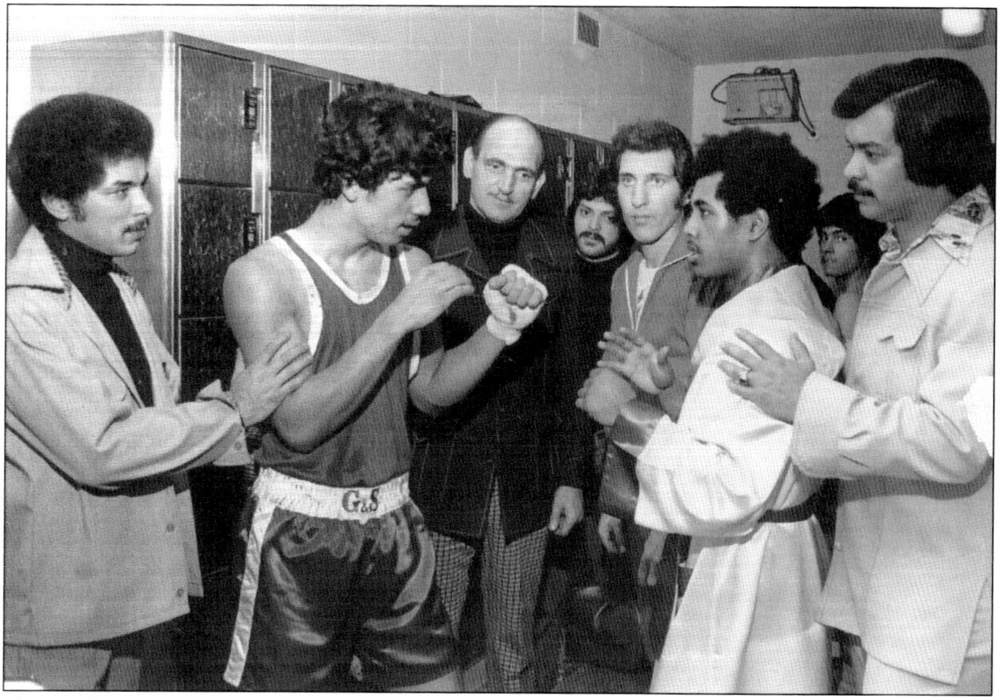

Shown above is a promotional shot for the Golden Gloves Tournament in 1977, a youth community event held at the Brentwood Recreation Center. Carlos Vidal, Councilman Frank Boncore (R), and Tony Fortunado, a boxing promoter, helped organize the event. (Courtesy of the Vidal family.)

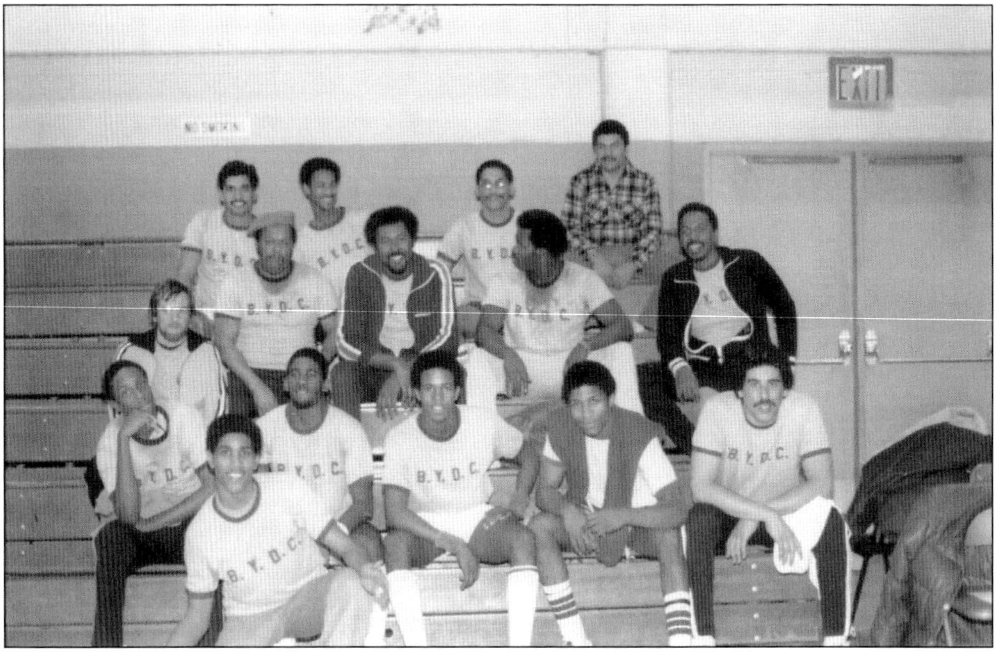

The Brentwood Youth Development Corporation basketball team is shown above at Brentwood Recreation Center in 1978. The boy in the plaid shirt in the upper right corner is Phil Ramos, a future New York state assemblyman, and in the lower right corner is Phil Barerro, who would become a Suffolk County human rights commissioner. (Courtesy of the Vidal family.)

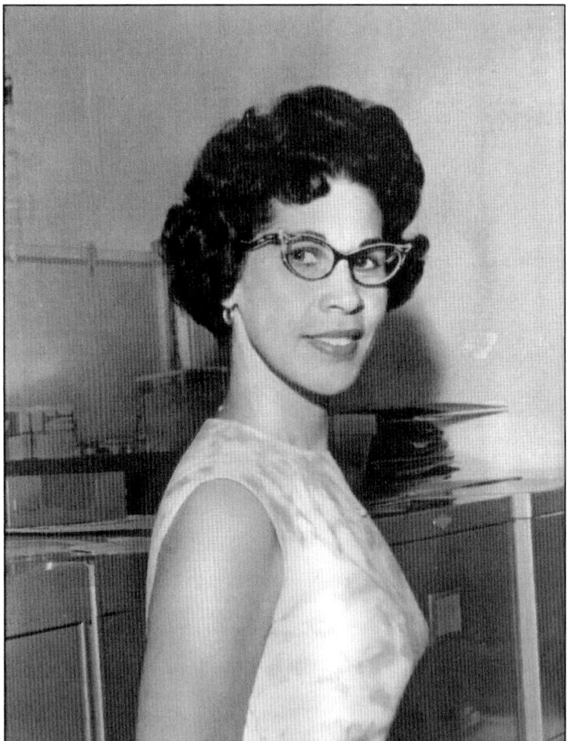

Carmen Hines (1919–) was born Carmen Torres and moved to Brentwood in the early 1950s. Working for *Newsday*, she was heavily involved in Puerto Rican and later Pan-Hispanic civic affairs. Carmen was a principle founding member of Adelante of Suffolk County and Pronto of Long Island. She was involved with the Pan American Civic Center, organizer of Latin American parades in Brentwood, and helped establish the Suffolk County Community College campus in Brentwood. (Courtesy of Carmen Hines, Jeanne L Taylor.)

In 2004, Gov. George Pataki (R) visited Brentwood and met with Hispanic community leaders. He met with Santiago Reyes, a leader in the El Salvadorian community, at his restaurant, Comolapa, on Timberline Drive in East Brentwood. (Courtesy of Santiago Reyes.)

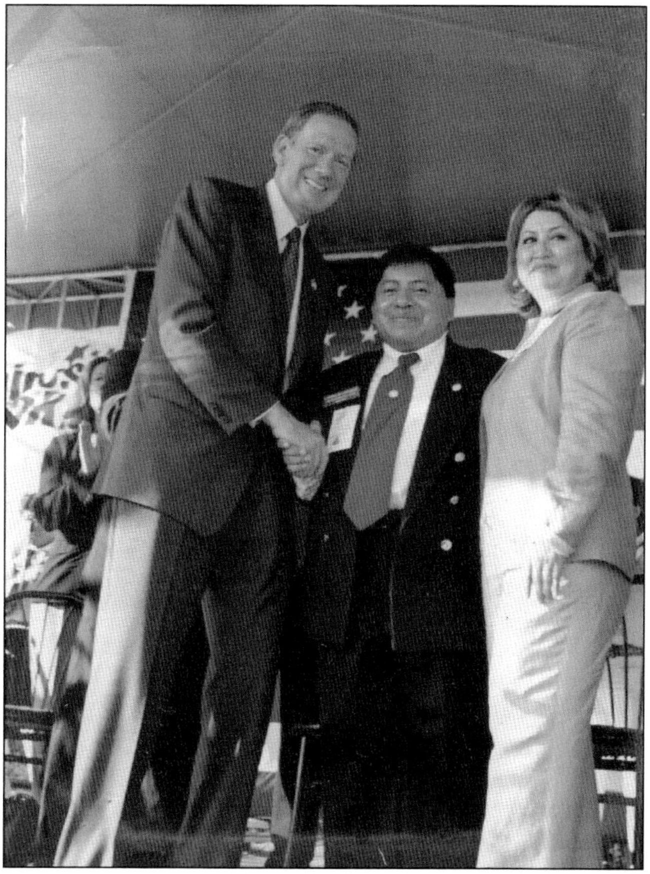

Richard Borda, Esq., (1933–) may not have been the first Hispanic lawyer in Brentwood, but he has become the most prolific. Of Columbian decent, Borda came to Brentwood in 1970 and opened a private practice on Fifth Avenue. Active in civic and cultural affairs, he has become a leader in both the Anglo and Hispanic communities. (Courtesy of Richard Borda.)

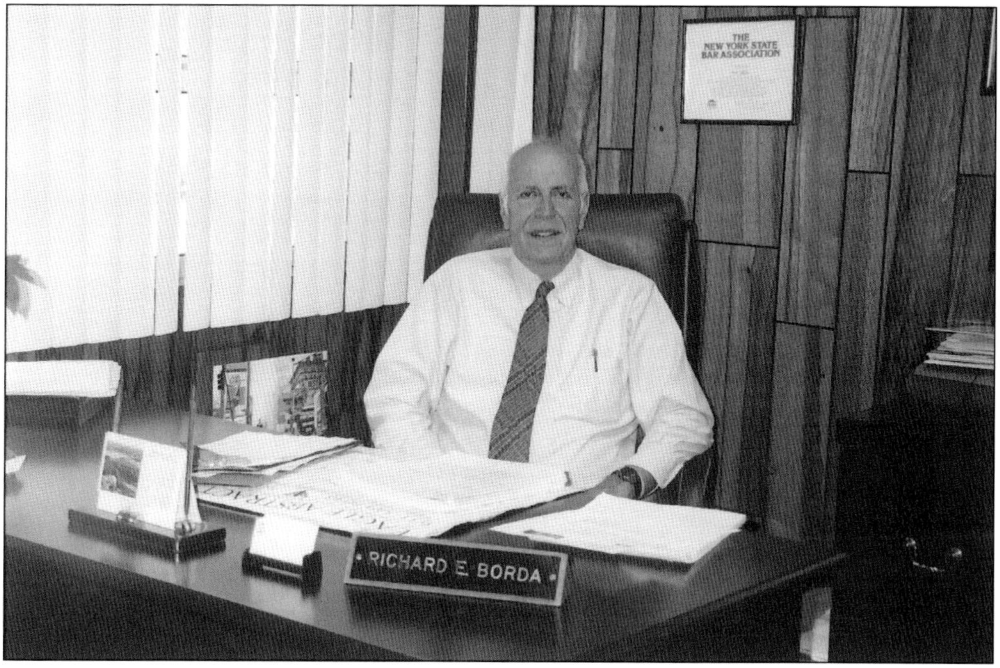

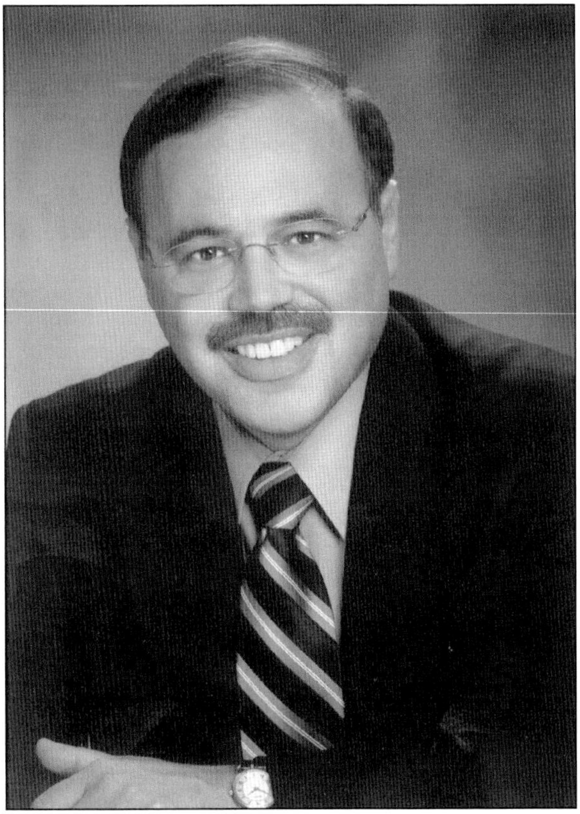

Legislator Ricardo Montano (D) (1950–), a Brentwood High School graduate, had a successful career as an attorney before returning to Brentwood. In 2003, Rick was elected to the Suffolk County Legislature where he represents Brentwood and neighboring communities. Since then, he has worked tirelessly for the betterment of the community and is involved with numerous organizations. (Courtesy of Ricardo Montano.)

Assemblyman Phil Ramos (D) (1956–), a Brentwood High School graduate, recognizes leaders of the Latin American Chamber of Commerce, which provides networking opportunities for Hispanic-owned businesses. With the assemblyman (at left) are, from left to right, founder Santiago Reyes, Max Rodriguez, and the consul general for El Salvador, Luis Motes Brito. (Courtesy of Santiago Reyes.)

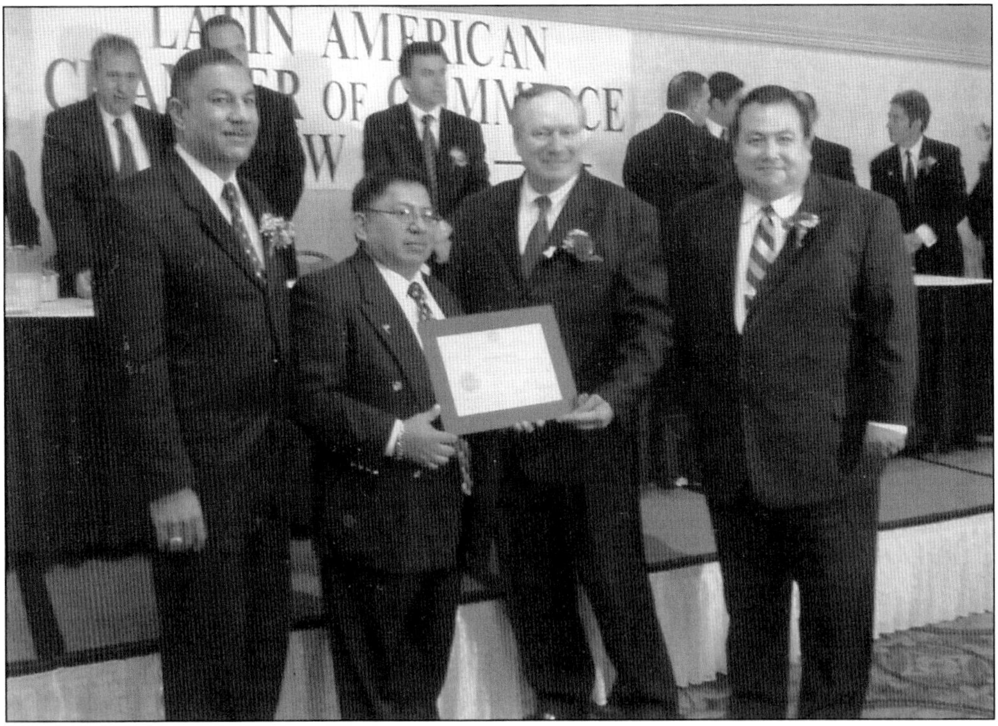

Nine

Bedroom Community of the World

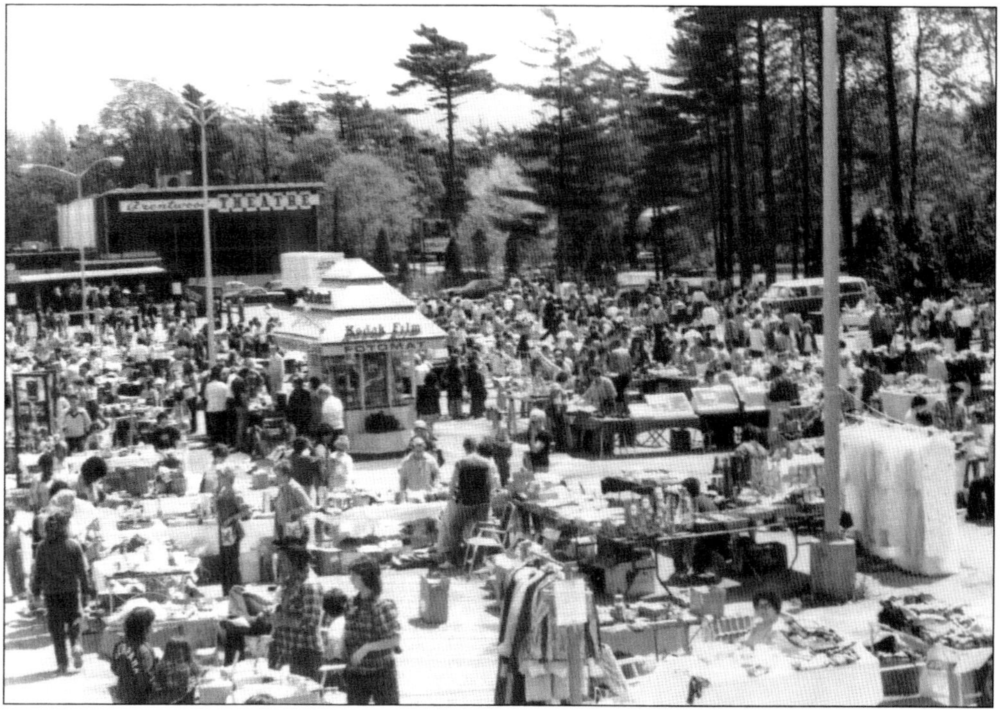

In the 1970s, Brentwood became its most ethnically diverse. The community was now solidly at suburban, blue-collar town, becoming a bastion of Hispanic life outside of New York City; those of Indian, Pakistani, Arab, and Asian descent would also find their way to the diverse community. While many lived in Brentwood, they commuted to work elsewhere. Pictured here is a street fair in the Brent-City Shopping Center in 1982. The Brentwood movie theater is in the background. (Courtesy of the Brentwood Legion Ambulance.)

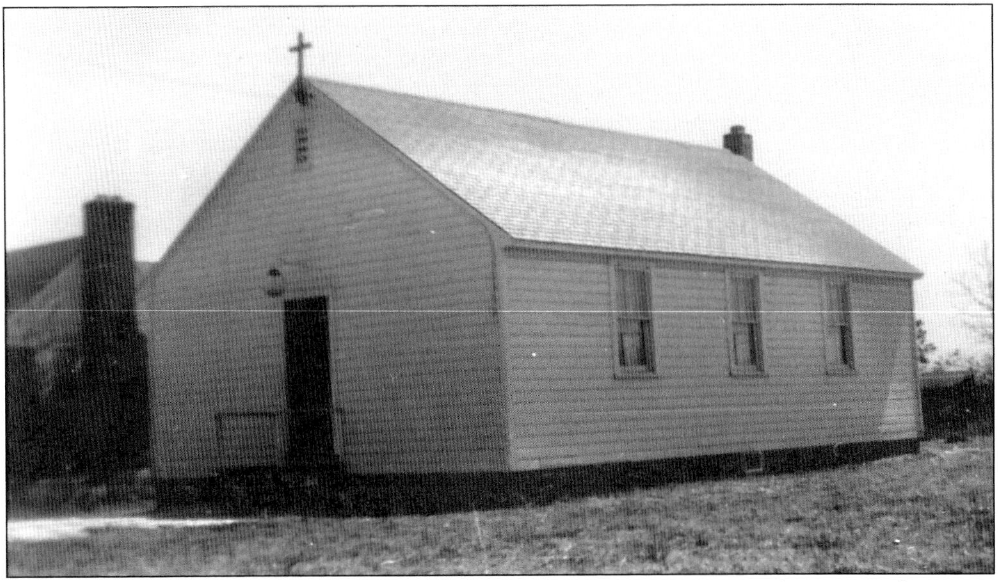

Grace Lutheran Church was the first Lutheran congregation in Bentwood. Organized in 1943, they met at TAMPA Hall until a church was built on Caleb's Path in 1944. The congregation grew, and eventually the church was relocated to a larger building in Central Islip, where it still meets today. (Courtesy of the Brentwood Public Library.)

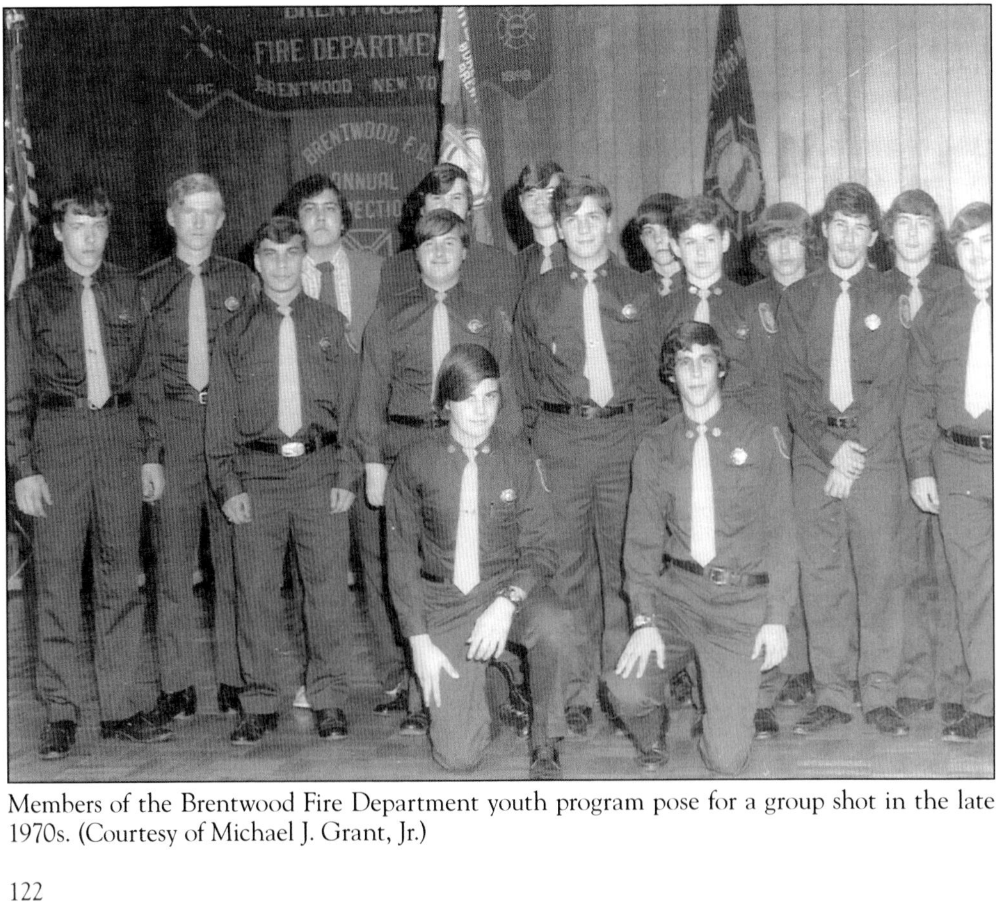

Members of the Brentwood Fire Department youth program pose for a group shot in the late 1970s. (Courtesy of Michael J. Grant, Jr.)

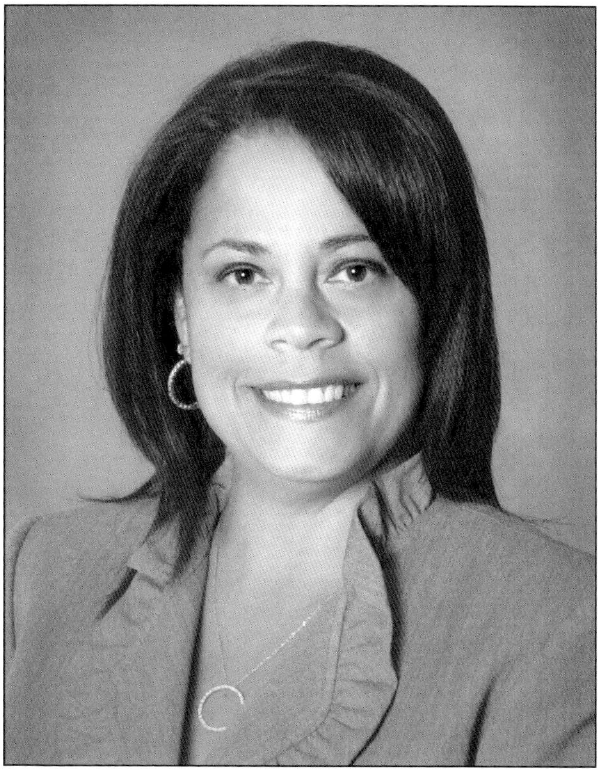

Belinda Alvarez-Groneman has been a key figure in Suffolk County, and Brentwood specifically, for a number of years. She started her career with the Suffolk County Police Department and after retiring has spent her time giving back to her community. She is on the board for the Brentwood campus of Suffolk County Community College, Adelante, Pronto, and the Suffolk County Hispanic Advisory Board as well as being a member of the Bentwood Lions Club. (Courtesy of Belinda Alvarez-Groneman.)

Inspired by Brentwood's legacy of octagonal structures, Mario Ciriscione built his own octagonal home out of cement on Walbridge Avenue in the 1970s. (Courtesy of the Brentwood Public Library.)

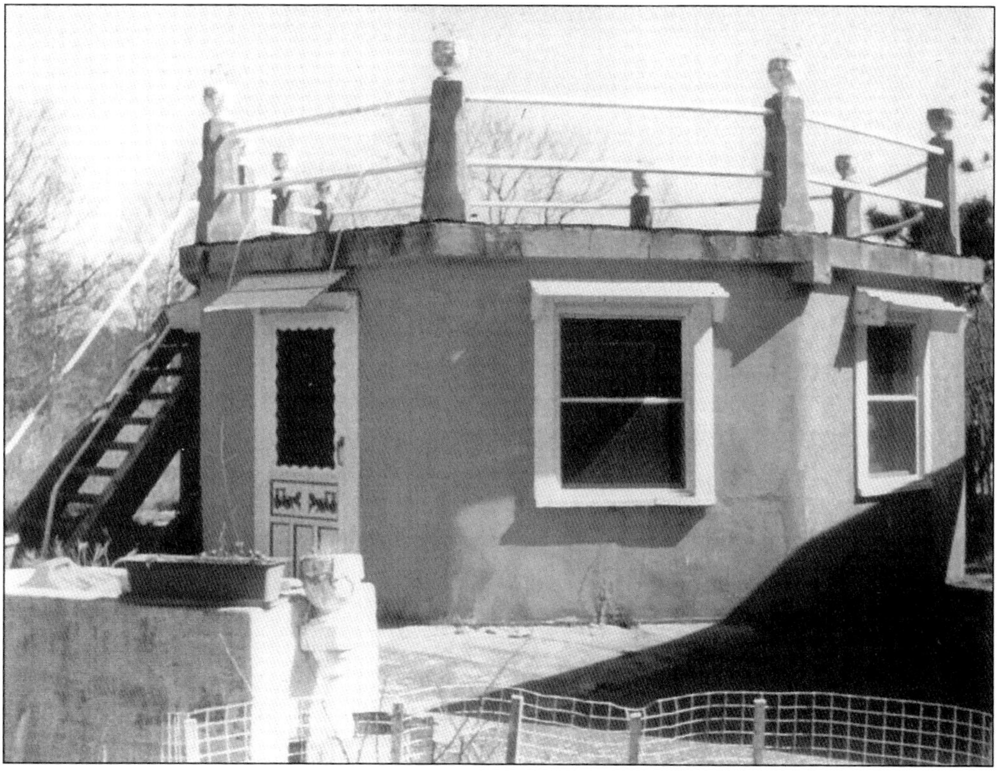

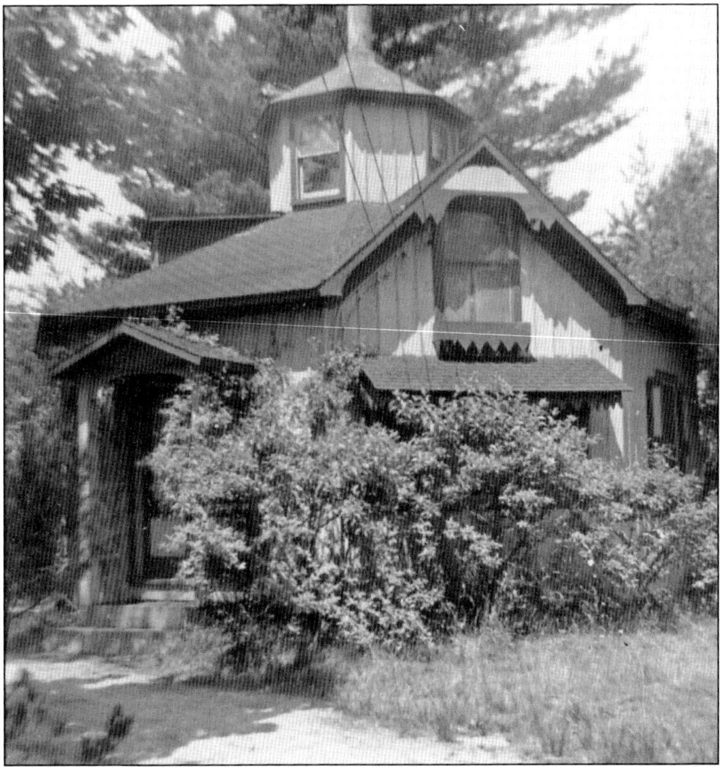

Brentwood's original one-room schoolhouse, seen here, spent the last years of its life as a private residence. In the 1970s, the building was abandoned and quickly began to decay. The Brentwood School District acquired the structure and has moved it near the administration building with the goal to renovate and restore the historic ruin. (Courtesy of the Brentwood Public Library.)

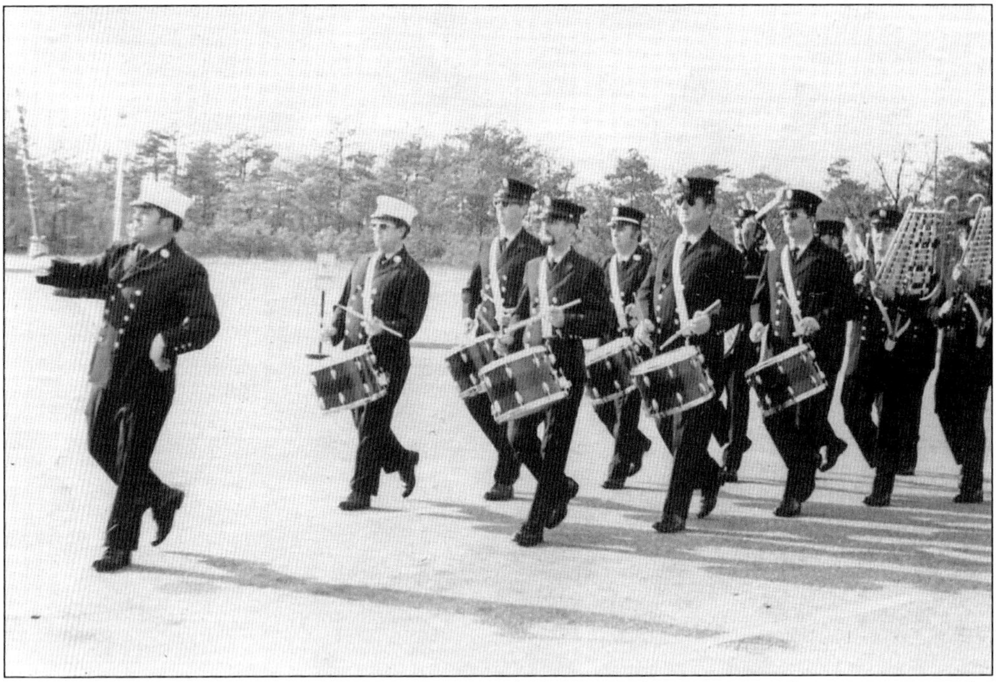

The Brentwood Fire Department's marching band, the "Wanderers," is seen here in 1973, in the parking lot of St. Luke's Roman Catholic Church as it prepares for the St. Patrick's Day parade. (Courtesy of the Brentwood Public Library.)

Lt. Col. Msgr. Thomas E. Molloy, JCD (1944–), has been the leader of Brentwood's Catholic population for almost half a century. Serving as associate pastor, executive pastor, and pastor emeritus of St. Luke's, he was instrumental in starting Spanish masses at the church. He has also served as a chaplain at Pilgrim State Hospital, St. Joseph's Convent, and the Northport VA Hospital. Having studied at the Vatican, Monsignor Molloy holds a doctorate in Canon Law and has worked as a lawyer and judge for the Diocese of Rockville Centre. He has also served as a chaplain in the US Army and taken part in the global war on terrorism, including Operation Enduring Freedom and Operation Iraqi Freedom. Monsignor Molloy is fluent in Spanish, Italian, and Latin and is proficient in French, Arabic, and Greek.

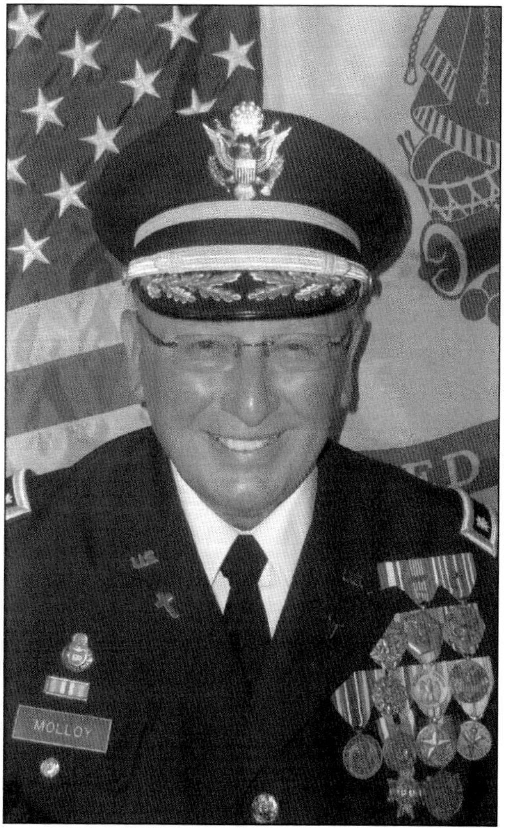

The Brentwood High School kick line performs at a street fair fundraiser for the Brentwood Legion Ambulance in the Brent-City Shopping Center in 1982. They performed in front of the Brentwood Theatre. (Courtesy of Brentwood Legion Ambulance.)

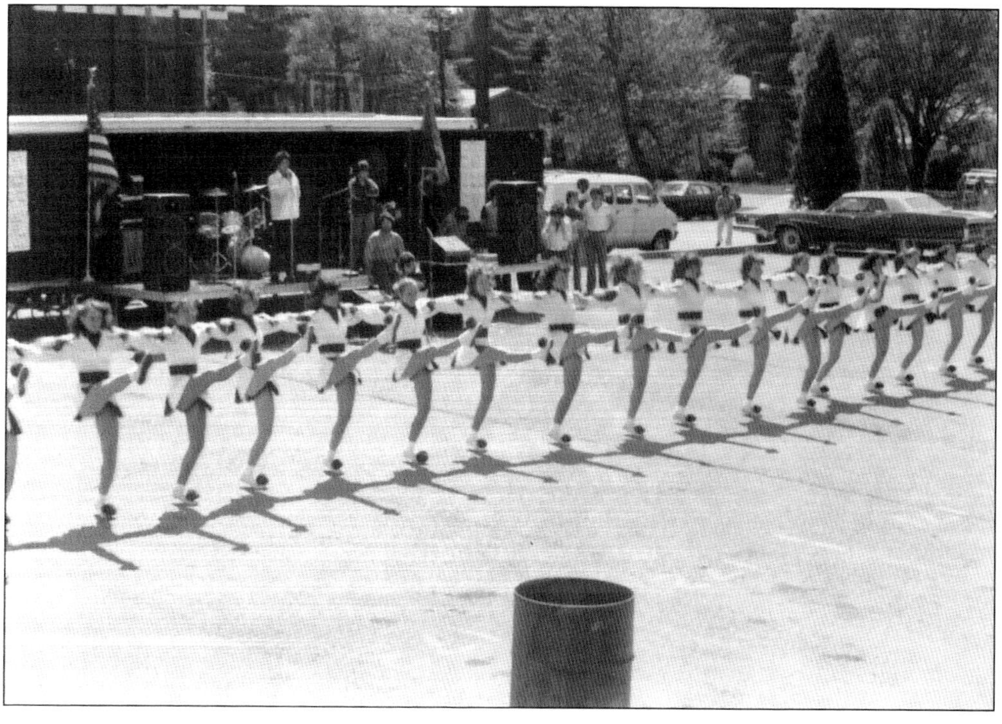

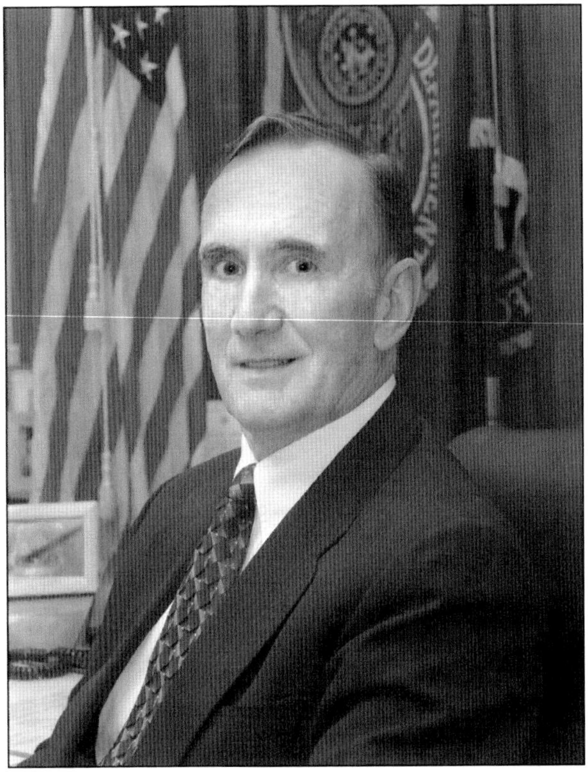

Suffolk County police commissioner Edward Webber began his life in Brentwood and graduated from Brentwood High School in 1964. He is a certified public accountant and a Vietnam War veteran, in addition to his 40 years as a police officer. He rose from the bottom to leadership positions quickly, and after serving in numerous roles, he was named police commissioner in 2012. (Courtesy of Commissioner Webber.)

Taking after his father, Michael J. Grant Jr. has been a vital and active part of the Brentwood community for a number of years. He currently serves on the Brentwood Chamber of Commerce, Brentwood Parade Committee, and the Brentwood Republican Club. He is also a member of the Brentwood Knights of Columbus. (Courtesy of Michael J. Grant Jr.)

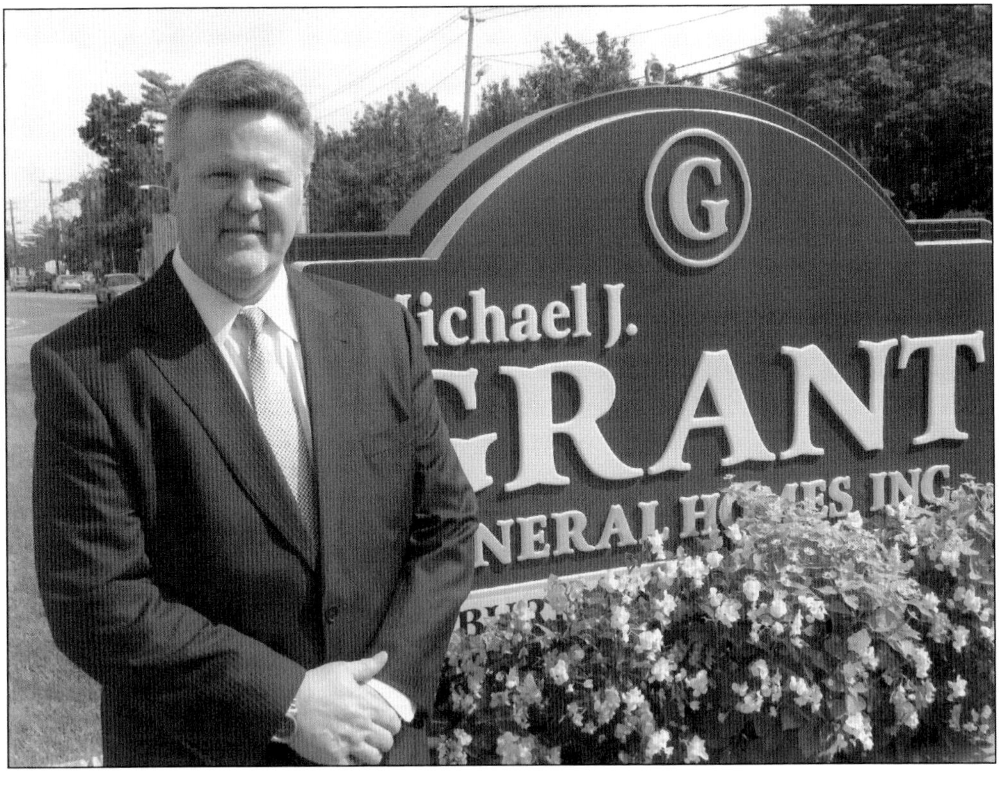

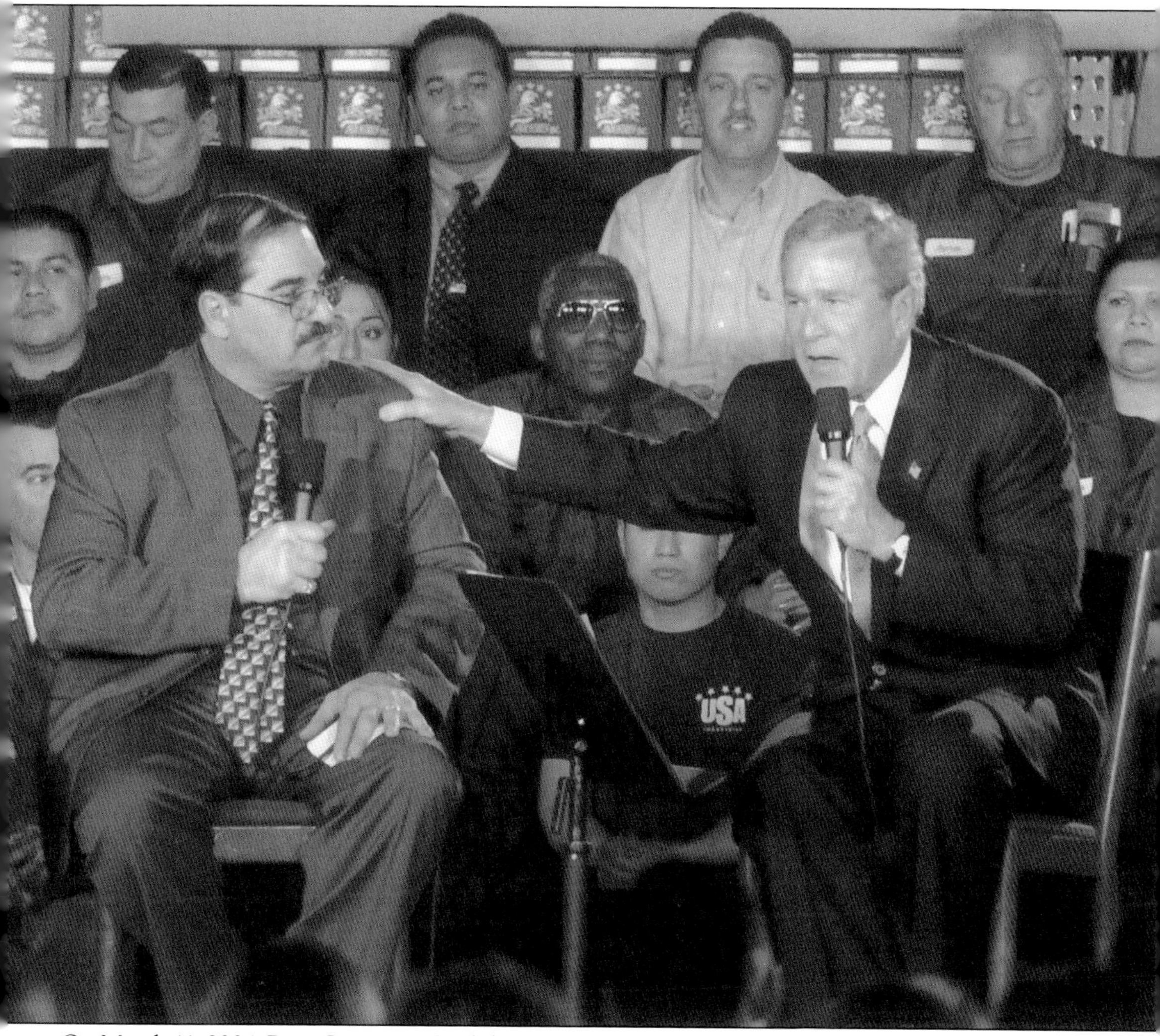

On March 11, 2004, Pres. George W. Bush became the first sitting president to come to Brentwood when he toured USA Industries' RD Electrical Manufacturing Facility on Candlewood Road in the North Bay Shore section of the community. After touring the facility where automotive parts such as alternators, starters, CV drive axles, and brake calibers were manufactured and remanufactured, President Bush held a town hall–style meeting. Vincent Trapani, founder, president, and CEO of USA Industries, hosted the president at his business; the tour was part of President Bush's reelection campaign and the president was promoting small business and the results of his tax incentives. This picture of Vincent Trapani, President Bush, and USA Industries employees sums up the collective image and experience that is Brentwood. Men, women, white, black, Hispanic, wealthy, poor, businessmen, and employees, all in one space coming together, building towards something better. That is the legacy of the Brentwood community. (Courtesy of Vince Trapani, USA Industries, Inc.)